CONTENTS

PREFACE

FIRST YEAR Study Guides are a new series targeted specifically at the needs of:

- first year students taking business studies degrees;
- students taking business-related modules of other degrees;
- HND students;
- others requiring business information at this level.

This *Information Technology* Study Guide has been written with two key goals in mind.

- To present a substantial and useful body of knowledge on information technology degree level. This is not just a set of revision notes - it explains the subject in detail and does not assume prior knowledge.

- To make learning and revision as easy as possible. Each chapter:

    o starts with clear objectives;
    o contains numerous exercises;
    o includes a chapter roundup summarising the points made; and
    o ends with a quick quiz.

The philosophy of the series is thus to combine techniques which actively promote learning with a no-nonsense, systematic approach to the necessary factual content of the course.

BPP Publishing have for many years been the leading providers of targeted texts for students of professional qualifications. We know that our customers need to study effectively in order to pass their exams, and that they cannot afford to waste time. They expect clear, concise and highly-focused study material. We expect first year degree and HND students to be equally demanding. And we have addressed the specific requirements of degree courses: each title has been developed in consultation with university lecturers.

We believe that the resulting material will prove to be the most helpful - and cost-effective - resource available to today's business students.

BPP Publishing
September 1993

If you would like to send in your comments on this Study Guide, please turn to the review form on page 267.

HOW TO USE THIS BOOK

This Study Guide can simply be read straight through from beginning to end, but you will get far more out of it if you keep a pen and paper to hand. The most effective form of learning is *active learning*, and we have therefore filled the text with exercises for you to try as you go along. We have also provided objectives, a chapter roundup and a quick quiz for each chapter. Here is a suggested approach to enable you to get the most out of this book.

(a)   Select a chapter to study, and read the objectives in the box at the start of the chapter.

(b)   Next read the chapter roundup at the end of the chapter (before the quick quiz and the solutions to exercises). Do not expect this brief summary to mean too much at this stage, but see whether you can relate some of the points made in it to some of the objectives.

(c)   Next read the chapter itself. Do attempt each exercise as you come to it. You will derive the greatest benefit from the exercises if you write down your solutions before checking them against the solutions at the end of the chapter.

(d)   As you read, make use of the 'notes' column to add your own comments, references to other material and so on. Do try to formulate your own views. In business, many things are matters of interpretation and there is often scope for alternative views. The more you engage in a dialogue with the book, the more you will get out of your study.

(e)   When you reach the end of the chapter, read the chapter roundup again. Then go back to the objectives at the start of the chapter, and ask yourself whether you have achieved them.

(f)   Finally, consolidate your knowledge by writing down your answers to the quick quiz. You can check your answers by going back to the text. The very act of going back and searching the text for relevant details will further improve your grasp of the subject.

Further reading

While we are confident that the FIRST YEAR Study Guides offer excellent range and depth of subject coverage, we are aware that you will be encouraged to follow up particular points in books other than your main textbook, in order to get alternative points of view and more detail on key topics. We recommend the following books as a starting point for your further reading on *Information Technology*.

Anderson, *Information Systems in Development and Operation*, 1989, Pitman

Cashmore, *Business Information: Systems and Strategies*, 1991, Prentice Hall

Corbitt, *Information Technology and its Applications*, 1990, Longman

1 COMPUTERS

Your objectives

After completing this chapter you should:

(a) know the components of a computer's hardware;
(b) be able to explain the distinction between hardware and software;
(c) know the main types of computer;
(d) understand the functions of a processor;
(e) know the different types of computer memory;
(f) know what factors determine the power of a computer.

1 Hardware, software and processing

A computer is an electronic machine for handling information (which may be words or figures). Thus when talking about computers, people refer to *information technology* (ways of handling information) and to *data processing*. Data is the input to a computer, such as a list of employees to be paid.

We can make the following initial points about computers.

(a) The machines themselves, that is the physical components of a computer system, such as processor, screen, keyboard and printer, are referred to as the computer *hardware*.

(b) A computer processes data. The elements of data processing are input, processing, storage and output.

(c) A computer's operations are performed under the control of a *program*. Programs are needed to make the computer's hardware process data. A program is a set of *instructions* which tells the computer what to do. The general term used to describe programs is *software*.

(d) Almost all business computers (and most scientific computers) are *digital computers*. This means that they operate by performing arithmetical operations on exact numbers, such as amounts of money. They do not measure continuously variable quantities, such as electrical voltages. *Analogue computers* measure rather than count.

The basic components of a computer's *hardware* consist of the following.

(a) *Input devices* accept input data for processing.

(b) *Storage devices* hold data and programs on file until they are needed for processing and also hold the results after processing.

BPP Publishing

(c) *Output devices* accept output from the data processing device and convert it into a usable form. The most common output devices are printers (which print the output on paper) and screens (which display the output).

(d) *A processor* performs the data processing by taking in data from input devices and storage devices, processing it, and then transferring the processed information to an output device or storage device. The processor has its own memory to hold instructions, data and results while it is working.

Exercise 1

A small computer is used to process the payroll for a large organisation, but it cannot hold the data for all the employees in memory at once. Which hardware component would solve this problem?

Input devices, storage devices and output devices are often referred to collectively as *peripherals*. The term 'computer system' refers to the processor together with its associated peripheral equipment. An *interface* is the term used to describe, amongst other things, the connection between two devices. The links between all the devices can be shown diagrammatically, as follows.

2   Types of computer

Computers can be classified according to size, although the differences between these categories can be quite vague.

Supercomputers

A *supercomputer* is used to process very large amounts of data very quickly. They are particularly useful for occasions where many calculations need to be performed, for example in weather forecasting.

Mainframes

A *mainframe computer* is a large computer in terms of price, power and speed. Well-known manufacturers include IBM and ICL. A mainframe will probably:

(a)   cost over £1,000,000;
(b)   have a wider variety of peripheral devices than are found with smaller computers;
(c)   require an airconditioned room, or even water cooling;
(d)   support several hundred users.

Many organisations do not need mainframe computers for their data processing, because they would be too big and expensive to justify the volume of processing that is needed.

Minicomputers

A *minicomputer* is a computer whose size, speed and capabilities are less than those of a mainframe. A major manufacturer of minicomputers is Digital Equipment Corporation. However, the advent of more powerful processors means that some 'superminis' can run more powerfully than small mainframes. With the growing power of PCs (see below) and with mainframes now being physically smaller than in the past, the definition of a minicomputer has become rather vague.

PCs or personal computers

An independent 'free-standing' *PC* (also called a *personal computer* or a *microcomputer*) consists of three major components.

(a)   The *basic module* contains the processing device, one or two floppy disk drives and an integrated hard disk unit. (These are storage devices, which store data and programs on magnetic disks. Details are given in the next chapter.) The processing device is on a chip (a piece of silicon containing complex electronic circuitry) and the type of chip (such as 386 or 486) is often incorporated into the PC's name. The basic module can also act as a pedestal for the visual display unit.

(b)   The *keyboard* is connected to the basic module by a cable. A *mouse*, a device used to draw diagrams and sometimes as an alternative to using the keyboard to input instructions, is attachable either to the basic module via another socket or to the keyboard.

BPP Publishing

(c) The *visual display unit* displays input or output items, as letters and numbers or in graphical or picture form. It may display in colour or in black and white, and, like a television set, has contrast and brightness controls. The screen is usually adjustable in all directions so that it can be placed where the user can see it without eye or neck strain.

Exercise 2

A major bank processes all cheques written by its customers on one computer. What sort of computer is it likely to use?

Portable computers

Miniaturisation is the key technological development governing usage. Some computers are now portable, being laptop computers (bigger than this book), notebook computers (about the same size as this book) or pocket computers (even smaller).

A typical laptop or notebook computer:

(a) may be powered with a rechargeable battery, but might be able to use the mains;
(b) uses $3\frac{1}{2}$" floppy disks;
(c) sometimes has a hard disk;
(d) uses a liquid crystal or gas plasma screen;
(e) sometimes has communications facilities, so that the user can transmit data over the telephone and/or transfer data to other computers when back in the office.

Pocket computers range from machines which are little more than electronic diaries and address books to relatively powerful computers.

Exercise 3

Give three examples of businesses where it would be especially useful for staff to have portable computers.

3 The processor

The processor is the 'brain' of the computer. It is a collection of electronic circuitry and registers that carries out the processing. The processor is divided into three areas, the control unit, the arithmetic and logic unit, and memory. The set of operations that the processor performs is known as the *instruction set,* or repertoire, and this determines in part the speed at which processing can be performed. Processors for PCs are located on single *chips* (very small pieces of silicon or some other substance, containing complex electronic circuits).

The control unit

This supervises the execution of program instructions and accesses peripheral (input and output) devices. The control unit sends out *control signals*, co-ordinated by a clock: the number of pulses (cycles) produced per second is an indication of processing speed, and is usually measured in megahertz (MHz). One MHz is one million pulses (cycles) per second.

The arithmetic and logic unit (ALU)

This is the part of the processor where the arithmetical, logical and other operations are carried out. These include arithmetic (such as add, subtract, multiply and divide), comparison (such as 'does selling price exceed cost?'), branch operations (which change the order of program instructions) and the movement of data.

Memory

This is circuitry which is used to store data within the processor whilst the computer is operating. The memory will hold the following.

(a) *Programs.* The processor's control unit acts on (executes) program instructions that are held in the memory. However, a computer's memory is limited in its size. A program can be too big for some computers, because the computer's memory might be too small to hold it.

(b) *Input data.* Part of the memory is needed to hold the data that will be processed next, for example (in a payroll program) data on the next few employees.

(c) A *working area.* The computer will need some memory to hold data that is currently being processed or is used for processing other data, for example wage rates to be used in conjunction with hours worked to find gross pay.

BPP Publishing

(d) *Some output data*. A small area of store is needed to hold temporarily the data or information that is ready to send to an output device, for example the figures ready to be printed on payslips.

Data representation in memory

A digital computer holds data in its memory, and *characters* (letters, numbers and other symbols) are represented in binary digits or *bits*. A group of eight bits is known as a *byte*. A computer's operations depend on simple circuits which can be switched ON or OFF. These two states can be conveniently expressed by the numbers 1 and 0 respectively. Any piece of data or instruction must be *coded* in these symbols before processing can commence. Thus in one commonly used code (ASCII) the capital letter A is coded as 1000001. (ASCII uses only seven bits in each byte.)

Types of memory

(a) Random access memory (RAM) is memory that is directly available to the processor. Data can be written on to or read from random access memory. RAM can be defined as 'memory with the ability to access any location in the memory in any order with the same speed'. Random access is essential for the main memory of a computer.

RAM in PCs is 'volatile' which means that the contents of the memory are erased when the computer's power is switched off.

(b) *Read only memory* (ROM) is memory into which fixed data is written permanently at the time of its manufacture. New data cannot be written into the memory. The data in ROM will usually be commonly-used sets of instructions.

ROM is 'non-volatile' memory because its contents do not disappear when the computer's power source is switched off. A computer's start-up program, known as a 'bootstrap' program, is always held in a form of a ROM.

(c) PROM is *programmable ROM*. ROMs are supplied by the manufacturer already programmed. With a PROM, the memory is provided for the *user* to program. Special equipment is needed, and the contents are not normally alterable.

(d) *Erasable programmable* ROM (EPROM) differs from PROM in that the contents of the memory can be erased and new contents written (with special equipment). In an EAROM (electronically alterable ROM) the old contents do not have to be erased first.

Exercise 4

An electronic diary stores all its software on a chip. It includes a program to work out the days of the week for dates up to the year 2100. In what sort of memory should that program be stored?

Many PCs offer the user the option to increase the size of RAM, so that larger programs can be run. Memory can be increased in the following ways.

(a) An *expansion slot* allows a chip providing extra RAM to be plugged into the PC, so as to become a part of the computer's main memory.

(b) An *extension card* or board fulfils the same function, but fits inside the PC box itself. A PC may have space inside it to accept extra printed circuit boards, to enhance its memory or its processing capabilities.

Memory size is calculated in kilobytes (1 kilobyte = 1 kB = 1K = 1,024 bytes), megabytes (1 megabyte = 1 MB = 1,024 kB) and gigabytes (1 gigabyte = 1 GB = 1,024 MB). So a computer described as having a 4 MB RAM memory has, in addition to ROM, a random access memory of 4 × 1,024 × 1,024 bytes = 4,194,304 bytes.

Buses

Data is transferred within the processor or between the processor and peripherals by means of *buses*. A bus carries a number of bits (depending on its size) along a number of tracks. A bus with eight tracks therefore carries one byte at a time.

4 The power of a computer

The factors that determine the power of a computer (how much it can do, and how fast) are as follows.

(a) The speed of handling program instructions, which for a mainframe is measured in millions of instructions per second *(MIPS)*. Smaller mainframes only manage 11 MIPS, whereas the largest IBM mainframe can handle 80 MIPS. Alternatively, speed and power can be measured in *megaflops* (millions of floating point instructions per second).

(b) The MHz (Megahertz) rate of the internal clock (the rate at which timing pulses are emitted from the control unit). 1 MHz = 1,000,000 pulses a second. The higher the rate, the faster the computer can work.

(c) The efficiency of the *instruction set*. Some computers combine a fairly small set of instructions in clever ways to increase efficiency.

(d) The size of the processor's memory.

(e) The number of tracks on the computer's buses.

Exercise 5

Computer A has a 33 MHz chip and 4 MB of RAM. Computer B has a 25 MHz chip and 8 MB of RAM. Which computer could run the larger programs, and which one could run small programs faster?

Chapter roundup

(a) A computer comprises input devices, external storage devices, output devices and a processor.

(b) A computer operates under the command of stored programs. These programs are software, as distinct from the physical components which are hardware.

(c) Computers may be supercomputers, mainframe computers, minicomputers or PCs. Different sizes of computer are suitable for different applications.

(d) A PC's components are a basic module, a keyboard and a VDU. In some small computers, such as laptop and pocket computers, these components are combined in a single unit.

(e) The processor processes input to produce the desired output. It includes a control unit which is in overall charge, an arithmetic and logic unit to do the computations and a memory in which to hold data about to be worked on and put output ready to be worked on further or sent to an output device.

(f) Types of memory include RAM, ROM, PROM and EPROM. Memory is measured in bytes, kB, MB and GB.

(g) Several factors affect the power of a computer.

Quick quiz

1   What is an interface in a computer system?

2   For what sorts of application are supercomputers suitable?

3   What is the smallest type of computer in common use?

4   What, in a computer, is measured in MHz?

5   When a computer is executing an instruction in a program, where will that instruction be held?

6   How is data represented in memory?

7   How may a computer's memory be enlarged?

8   What does MIPS stand for?

Solutions to exercises

1   Storage devices

2   A mainframe computer

3   Architects: computers could be taken to building sites.
Accountants: computers could be taken to clients' offices.
Insurance loss adjusters: computers could be taken to the sites of damage.

4   ROM

5   Computer B could run the larger programs, but computer A could run small programs faster

2 STORAGE

Your objectives

After completing this chapter you should:

(a) understand the function of storage devices;
(b) know the different types of magnetic disk;
(c) know how data is stored on magnetic disks;
(d) know how data is stored on magnetic tape;
(e) know the capabilities of optical storage devices;
(f) understand the hierarchy of files, records, fields and characters;
(g) be able to distinguish between transaction files, master files and reference files;
(h) understand the different methods of file organisation and file access;
(i) know which methods of access can be used with disks, and which can be used with tape;
(j) know the steps in updating disk and tape master files.

1 Storage devices

A processor has a certain amount of memory, but business computer files are required to hold far more data than any memory can handle, and so there has to be a method of holding data on file when it is not required inside the CPU. The function of *storage devices* is to hold data until it is needed for further processing. Storage devices must therefore be input/output devices, capable of use for both input and output of data.

The principal media used for storage are magnetic disks, magnetic tape and optical disks.

2 Magnetic disks

The most commonly used storage medium with computers is magnetic disks. A magnetic disk consists of a flat circular disk covered on both sides with a magnetic material. Data is held on a number of circular, concentric tracks on the surfaces of the disk and is read or written by rotating the disk past read/write heads, which can write data from memory on to disk, or can read data from it for input to memory. So as to make it easier to locate data, each circular track is divided into several sectors. Data can then be found by its track number and its sector number. The mechanism that causes the disk to rotate is called a *disk drive*.

Exchangeable disk packs

An exchangeable disk pack is a pack of hard magnetic disks, arranged one on top of another on a spindle. It is commonly used in larger computer systems.

Read-write heads go in between the disks to read the data from the disk surfaces. Thus there is simultaneous access to several corresponding tracks of data, one on each surface. The set of corresponding tracks is known as a *cylinder* (or sometimes, the *seek area*).

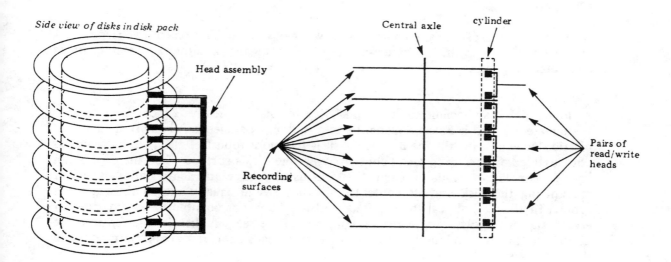

Access time is the time taken to locate the data on the disk and to read it into memory. This requires moving the head assembly to the correct cylinder, selecting the appropriate read/write head, and waiting until the appropriate part of the track is reached.

Smaller hard disks

To enhance the appeal of minicomputers and PCs, and to provide storage facilities in addition to the generally-used floppy disks (of relatively low capacity), smaller *hard disks* have been developed. These give a good recording density at a low cost, and are also quite small in physical size. 5¼" hard disks have a storage capacity of 40–500 Megabytes. They are used in computer operations that need files of such a large size that floppy disks would be inefficient and large exchangeable disk packs too big.

To protect the disks physically, they must be kept free of airborne particles, and so each disk is encased in a sealed container. Hard disks with a microcomputer might be:

(a) *external*, sitting alongside the computer in an extra box with its own power supply;
(b) *internal*, incorporated inside the PC itself.

It is common to dump (that is, copy) the contents of a hard disk onto *magnetic tape cartridge,* using a *tape streamer* (a device which copies the data onto tape very quickly) because this is quicker than dumping on to floppy disks.

Exercise 1

Why is it sensible to make an extra copy of the data on a hard disk?

Floppy disks

Although PCs will often have a hard disk drive, they will also have one or two floppy disk drives too. The *floppy disk* provides a cost-effective means of storage for small business computer systems.

A floppy disk is an exchangeable circular, flexible disk (typically 5¼ inches or 3½ inches in diameter) which is held permanently in a square paper sleeve (5¼ inch) or in a hard plastic sleeve (3½ inch). The 3½ inch disk is the more robust of the two; its casing is not flexible and a sliding metal shutter covers the disk's surface when the disk is not in use. The sleeve cover on each disk will usually have an identification label for recognising the disk and its contents. A disk's sleeve usually incorporates a write protect facility: a hole can be exposed, and it is then not possible to add to, alter or erase data on the disk, although the data can still be read. A disk is inserted into the disk drive (the mechanism which rotates the disk, reads data from it and writes data on it) in its sleeve.

The disk has a coating of a magnetic material which is used to store data (on one or two sides), and may offer *double density storage* or *high density storage* (which is higher than double density). Modern 3½ inch floppy disks can take 1.44 MB of data. Access times are longer than with hard disks.

The disks must be compatible with the floppy disk drive that is used. Disk drives might be for single-sided, double-sided or high density disks, and for 3½ inch or 5¼ inch disks.

Floppy disks do not require special storage conditions, and indeed, they are often stored in open trays. However, data on them can easily be corrupted. In particular, they are subject to physical wear, because the read/write head actually comes into contact with the disk surface during operation. This is not the case with other types of disk. Because they can be left lying around an office, they are also prone to physical damage, such as having tea spilled over them.

Directories

Many files that PC users keep are quite small, and so it is common for the same physical disk, especially a hard disk, to hold a large number of files.

In order to organise these many files on the disk in such a way that they can be found easily and quickly when they are wanted, files are grouped into directories and sub-directories. There is a 'root' directory, from which sub-directories and files then branch out. For example, a computer user might organise his or her files so that the root directory includes a sub-directory for word processing (as well as a sub-directory for, say, a database). The word processing sub-directory might include several files, such as a file for the word processing program itself and several data files, each for a particular document. The sub-directory might also include a sub-sub-directory for documents of a particular type, such as purchase orders. The purchase order sub-sub-directory might then include several data files, each for a different type of purchase order.

Exercise 2

A PC user wants to store about 5 MB of data, and to be able to pass the data to another user without setting up a direct physical link between their two computers. What storage medium would be appropriate, and why?

---

3   Magnetic tape

Magnetic tape consists of a strip of plastic tape coated with a magnetic material deposited in grains, each of which may be magnetised in one of two possible directions. To each of the directions, the significance 0 or 1 is attached so that data can be written onto, stored on and read from tape. As with domestic audio tape, a recording can be erased and the tape re-used. As data is read from a tape or written onto a tape, the tape moves past a read/write head, from one reel onto another, again like audio tape.

Data is held along the length of a tape in blocks. A block may consist of just one data record (for example the data on one customer), but it might consist of several records. Blocks can be read from tape into memory, and written from memory on to tape, one at a time. After one block of data has been written, the tape stops (so as not to waste space) until the *write* instruction for the next block is given. This stop-start process involves slowing down the tape until it comes to rest, and then accelerating again to full speed. Data can only be read or recorded when the tape is moving at full speed and consequently there are blank stretches of tape between blocks. The existence of inter-block gaps means that the practical storage capacity of magnetic tape is usually less than two thirds of the maximum possible storage capacity.

Because the processor will only deal with one record at a time, the rest of the block will be held in a *buffer* area in memory. This is called *buffering*.

Magnetic tape cartridge and cassette

The development of PCs has led to the use of magnetic tape in cartridge form as a storage medium. Cartridges are similar to but larger in size than normal audio cassettes. They have a capacity of up to 60 MB, depending on size and format. Cartridges are being used increasingly to provide a back-up copy of data held on hard disks. Fast tape recording devices which can be used to create back-up files very quickly are known as *tape streamers*.

Exercise 3

The proportion of a reel of tape taken up by inter-block gaps could be reduced if more records were put into each block. Why might putting too many records into each block create a problem for the processor?

---

4 Optical storage

Optical disks are now being used for data storage. Optical technology is similar in principle to the compact disc (CD) used for audio recording. There are three basic types of optical disk: CD-ROM, WORM and magneto-optical.

CD-ROM is a read-only technology. This means that all data is implanted at manufacture, in the same way as music is recorded on a CD. Users can only retrieve information; they cannot write their own data. CD-ROM is used primarily as a medium for publishing large amounts of data. Microsoft, for example, advertise the *Microsoft Bookshelf* (with such titles as *Roget's II: Electronic Thesaurus, The US Zip Code Directory, Houghton Mifflin Spell Checker and Usage Alert, American Heritage Dictionary*), and *Microsoft Small Business Consultant* containing tax, accountancy and legal information. In the UK data available on CD-ROM includes British Telecom's directory listings and company information published by Extel.

Write once read many times (WORM) devices are more advanced than CD-ROM in that users can enter their own data. However this data can never be erased. A WORM device is an alloy disk, covered on both sides by plastic. A laser burns holes in the plastic, and these burnt pits represent the data. To read the data, a low powered laser is passed over the disk and the reflected light is detected. WORM devices have the following features.

(a) Most WORM devices are written in *sequence*. Rather than arrange data in concentric tracks, data on many WORM devices is written into one long continuous *spiral*.

(b) It is not possible to erase data on a WORM device. Instead, if it is used to contain data which changes (such as records of goods in stock), new versions of the file are added to the disk. Some manufacturers make a virtue out of this necessity by advertising a *history facility* (the ability to look up old versions of a file on disk).

(c)   The more a disk is used, the slower access speeds will be, as more old data is retained.

(d)   WORM devices are ideal for archiving very large amounts of data (for example where permanent records are required by legal or taxation authorities).

Recently, *magneto-optical disks* have been developed. These comprise a magnetised recording medium sandwiched between two plastic disks. The contents of the disk can be altered magnetically at high temperatures. The area to be altered is heated by a laser, and then its magnetic charge is reversed, a state in which it remains when cooled down. Bits are therefore represented by changed magnetic orientations in the disk. With these disks, old data need not build up but can be erased.

The main advantage of optical disks over other storage media is that very large volumes of data can be stored on one disk. One writer has indicated that the cost per megabyte is only 1% of that of magnetic disk storage. However, before purchase, an organisation has to make sure that its data storage requirements are vast enough to warrant the use of optical disks.

Exercise 4

Give three examples of businesses where a history facility might be particularly useful.

---

5   Files, records, fields and characters

We will now look at how disks and tapes are actually used in the storage and processing of data.

A *file* is a collection of data records with similar characteristics. Every file has a name to distinguish it from other files. A file name is included as data on a file, as a 'header label'. Examples of files are:

(a)   stock records;
(b)   a price list;
(c)   letters and memos relating to one matter;
(d)   data in a spreadsheet model (a spreadsheet file);
(e)   a word processed letter (a document file).

A *record* consists of data relating to one logically definable unit of information. A collection of similar records makes up a file. For example, a price list consists of records for the items available for sale.

Records consist of *fields* of information. A field of information is an item of data relating to a record. For example, a record on the price list file will include the following fields.

(a) Name of item
(b) Method of sale (by weight, by packets or by individual units)
(c) Price
(d) Details of discounts for bulk purchases
(e) Rate of VAT chargeable

A field consists of *characters* (letters and numbers) which themselves are composed of bits (see Chapter 1).

Exercise 5

A company which is not organised into separate departments has a file of payroll data. What entity would each record represent? Give examples of the fields you would expect to find in each record.

---

6 Files in more detail

Transaction files, master files and reference files

In some systems files can be classified into transaction files, master files and reference files.

A *transaction file* is a file containing records that relate to individual transactions that occur from day to day. The transaction records must all be processed. Thus in a system to record sales of goods, each sale must be recorded and processed.

A *master file* is a file containing:

(a) reference data, which is normally altered (updated) infrequently; and also
(b) transactions data which is built up over time.

For example, in a system to record sales, the master file is the cumulative record of sales. This is a file consisting of 'standing' reference data for each product and transaction data for each sale, itemising goods sold, quantities and payments received. This transaction data is built up over time.

A *reference file* or index file is a file containing reference data, which is normally altered (updated) infrequently. It contains no transaction data. Examples of a reference file are:

(a) a price list;
(b) manuals of company regulations and procedures.

A database contains a bank of data, which can be used in a more flexible way than the files above. For example, a database of sales data might contain details of each sale and might allow a user to find out about all sales of a particular product, all sales to a particular customer or all sales worth over £500.

Temporary files and permanent files

Files might be temporary or permanent. Master files and reference files are usually permanent, which means that they are never thrown away. They will be updated from time to time, and so the information on the file might change, but the file itself will continue to exist.

A temporary file is one that is eventually scrapped. Many transaction files are held for a very short time, until the transaction records have been processed, but are then thrown away. The magnetic medium holding the file can then be re-used.

Exercise 6

A university keeps a file (A) of students' names and addresses, a file (B) of courses completed up to the end of the last academic year by each student and a file (C) of data on courses completed since the start of the current academic year waiting to be recorded in file B. Classify each of these three files as a master file, a transaction file or a reference file.

---

7   File organisation

File organisation refers to the way in which records are held on a file, with a view to the retrieval of data. File organisation may be sequential or non-sequential.

Sequential file organisation

A file's organisation is *sequential* if the records on the file are in a logical sequence according to their *key field*, for example in alphabetical order or in numerical order. The key field is the field chosen to identify each record. On a price list, for example, it could be the product number.

Sequential files must be maintained in sequence. New records must be placed into their correct position in the file, and records which follow 'pushed back' to make room for the new records. In computer systems this could lead to a large number of 'accesses', moving each record in turn one position back in the file. To get round this problem, it is usual to leave spaces on a sequential file, to allow room for new records. This is done by grouping records together in 'buckets' with each bucket starting part-filled with records and part-empty for new additions. After a while, when the empty spaces start to fill up, records will be regrouped into new buckets with spaces. This process of tidying up the file is called *housekeeping*.

Non-sequential file organisation

Where records are not in a logical sequence according to a key field, the file is organised *non-sequentially*. This does not, however, make it impossible to find records, as we shall see in a minute.

---

8 File access

File access means locating individual records on the file. The way in which a file can be accessed will depend on how the file is organised, but access might be serial, sequential or random.

Serial access

Serial access is simply reading through the records on a file in whatever order they happen to be in.

(a) With transaction files, serial access will often be suitable, because every record on the file has to be processed.

(b) With master files, serial access to locate records would be very time consuming and so very inefficient.

Sequential access

With *sequential access*, the records on the file must be organised sequentially. Sequential access is the access of records on a sequentially organised file, *without* using an index. Sequential access is faster than serial access for two reasons.

(a) Since records on a sequentially organised file are in key field order, once the particular record has been located, there is no need to check serially through the rest of the file, in case there is another record on file with the same key field number.

(b) There is a method of locating records on a sequential file, known as *binary search*, which means that individual records can be located more quickly than with serial access.

Random access

There are two methods of *random access*, indexed sequential access and direct access. They are methods of locating an individual record without having to look through any other records first.

Indexed sequential access

The term *indexed sequential access* is used to describe random access to records that are held in a key field order in file, that is filed sequentially, using an index to locate individual records. Both the records on file and the index must be held in sequence, and new records must be placed in their correct positions on the file, and their correct places on the index.

Indexed sequential access is often faster than sequential access, because any record can be located by reference to the index, which gives its address on file.

Direct access

Direct access refers to the retrieval of data from a file which is not sequentially organised. The method of random access will depend on the method used to put records on to the file in the first place. This may be done by calculating a key value from data about the record, or by reference to an index.

Exercise 7

The records in a telephone directory (names, addresses and telephone numbers) are organised sequentially by name. If you only had a directory in book form (and not in computer readable form), what method of access would you use:

(a)   to find someone's telephone number when you know their name;
(b)   to find someone's name when you know their telephone number?

---

9   File access with magnetic disks

The method of access on a disk may be one of the following.

(a)   *Serial* access is only used for temporary files, for example transaction files.

(b)   *Sequential* access may be suitable for master files in a normal batch processing system (one which processes a large batch of data at once), but depending on the hit rate (the proportion of records on the file which need to be accessed), random access may be preferable. If the hit rate is low (that is, only a few records need to be accessed for each batch), it may be useful to be able to access those records without working through other records.

(c)   *Random* access is useful where:

(i)   the hit rate is low;
(ii)   data cannot be conveniently batched or sorted;
(iii) a fast response is required.

Updating disk files by overlay

A disk file could be updated by *file copying* with each record being written to a physically different file. The old records are thus preserved. However, updating by *file overlay* is more common. The updated record is written back to its original address location after update, destroying the old record.

The procedure for *batch processing* (dealing with a whole batch of transactions at once) with update by overlay is as follows.

(a)   The transaction record is read into memory.

(b)   The relevant master record is located on the disk and read into memory.

(c)   The master record is updated in memory.

(d)   The next transaction record is read into memory.

(e)   The two record keys are compared. If they agree, the transaction data is used to update the master record (which is already in memory, updated with the first transaction). If the keys are different, the updated master is *written back* onto the disk.

(f)   The relevant master record (for the transaction record now in memory) is now read into memory and updated.

(g)   The whole process is repeated until all the transaction records have been processed.

The procedure for direct keyboard entry to update a master file for a single transaction is as follows.

(a)   The transaction record is keyed in.
(b)   The master file record is located by random access.
(c)   The master file record is updated and written back on to the same master file.
(d)   Any user output required is shown on a VDU screen or printed out.

There is a tendency for commercial files to expand and so in a sequentially organised file new records have to be placed in *overflow* areas. Also, when a variable length record has expanded to such an extent that it can no longer be accommodated in its own area, an overflow location must be used. The address of the overflow location is recorded in the original area and thus the records can still be accessed sequentially even though they are no longer physically held in sequence. This process of referencing is known as *chaining*. After a certain time, the structure of the file will become rather complex and it will have to be reorganised. *File reorganisation* (sometimes referred to as file maintenance) involves transferring the data on the disk onto a new disk, placing records back into sequence, deleting old records, rewriting the index and creating new (empty) overflow areas.

Exercise 8

A master file on disk of goods in stock is being updated by overlay. The master file contains records for products A, B, C, D, E and F. The transaction file contains four records, giving details of stock movements for products A, C, C (again) and F. Set out the sequence of readings of records from the master file, updatings of master file records and writings of records back to the master file, assuming that the transaction file records are processed sequentially but that random access to the master file is used.

---

10 File access with magnetic tape

With magnetic tapes, file access must be serial or sequential. It is impossible to have random access with magnetic tape, because the computer must work through the tape in order until it reaches the right place, rather than jumping straight to the middle of the tape.

It follows that magnetic tape is only usable in certain circumstances:

(a) for a transaction file, when every record on the file will be processed in turn. Since transaction data might not be pre-sorted when it is input to the computer, it must be sorted before the master file update. Sorting of transaction data would be done in a separate *sort program*, and the sorted data would be written to a new tape;

(b) for a master file, when the hit rate is high enough to make sequential access quicker than random access. The tape master file must be organised sequentially.

Another important feature of magnetic tapes is that it is usual to produce a new master file on a different physical tape from that used for the old master file.

The steps in master file updating with magnetic tape

The steps involved in updating a master file on magnetic tape are as follows.

(a) Read a transaction record into memory.

(b) Read a master record into memory.

(c) Compare the two *key fields*.

   (i) If they agree the master record is updated with the appropriate transaction record data and held in memory. Then read the next transaction record into the memory.

   (ii) If the record keys do not agree, write the master record to the new tape and read the next master record into memory.

(d) Compare the key fields of the two records now in memory (transaction record and master file record).

(e) If the keys agree, update the master record; if not, write the master record (which obviously does not need updating) to the new tape. The process continues repetitively until all the records on the transaction file have been processed.

Tapes are organised in blocks of records. As blocks are read into memory from both transactions and master files, a number of buffer areas (areas to hold data waiting to be dealt with or waiting to be written to the new tape) are allocated for all the records in each block. The updating procedure is as outlined above, each record being processed in turn until the whole block can be written to the new tape.

File maintenance (amending standing data, removing records or adding records) is carried out in a similar manner. As a completely new tape reel is produced each time, there is no problem in inserting records in the correct sequence, or in having variable length records, so there is no need for 'buckets' and file housekeeping.

Exercise 9

A master file on magnetic tape is being updated from a transaction file. The current master file record to be processed has a key field value of 75 (its serial number on the tape). The current transaction file record to be processed has a key field value of 183. What procedure should have been carried out to ensure that it is not now necessary to check through the transaction file for a record with a key field value of 75?

Chapter roundup

(a) Storage devices are used to hold data when it is not being processed.

(b) Magnetic disks may be exchangeable disk packs, smaller hard disks or floppy disks.

(c) PCs generally have an integral hard disk drive and one or two floppy disk drives.

(d) Magnetic tape can also be used to store large quantities of data.

(e) Optical storage devices have a very large capacity, but in most cases data cannot be erased.

(f) A file comprises many records, each of which has several fields.

(g) Master files are updated from transaction files.

(h) Data which is needed for processing but which rarely changes is stored in a reference file.

(i) Files can be organised sequentially or non-sequentially.

(j) Files can be accessed serially, sequentially or randomly.

(k) All methods of access are possible with magnetic disk files, and such files are usually updated by overlay.

(l) Only serial and sequential access are possible with magnetic tape files, and such files must be updated by producing a new tape.

Quick quiz

1   How is data laid out on a magnetic disk?

2   What is a cylinder on an exchangeable disk pack?

3   How may data on a small hard disk be dumped?

4   What are the two sizes of floppy disk, and how do they differ?

5   Why are files grouped into directories and sub-directories?

6   Why must a magnetic tape include inter-block gaps?

7   What does WORM stand for?

8   A file includes a record for each supplier to a company. What might the fields be?

9   When can a transaction file be discarded?

10 How can records be found in a file with random organisation?

11 Which method of file access should not be used for master files?

12 When is random access useful?

13 What are the steps in update by overlay?

14 How does chaining arise?

15 What are the steps in updating a magnetic tape file?

Solutions to exercises

1   A hard disk might be damaged or a PC containing a hard disk might be stolen.

2   Floppy disks should be used, because only about five disks would be needed and they can be taken out of one PC and inserted in another.

3   There might not be enough space in memory for the contents of a whole block.

4   Banks: it may be useful to be able to see how an account has been conducted over several years.

    Retailers: it may be useful to see how sales and stock levels fluctuate over time.

    Solicitors: it may be important to keep all drafts of a contract drawn up for a client, in case it is later alleged that the firm was negligent.

                                    BPP Publishing

5   Each record would represent an employee. Fields would include the following.

(a) Employee name
(b) Employee number
(c) National insurance number
(d) Tax code
(e) Weekly wage
(f) Gross pay for the year to date
(g) Tax for the year to date

There would probably be other fields, depending on how the payroll system worked and on whether overtime was paid.

6   A: reference file
B: master file
C: transaction file

7   (a) Indexed sequential access
(b) Serial access

8   Read in A, update A, write back A
Read in C, update C, update C (again), write back C
Read in F, update F, write back F

9   The transaction records should have been sorted into sequence, so that if a record with a value of 183 has been reached, any record with a value of 75 must already have been dealt with.

3 INPUT AND OUTPUT

Your objectives

After completing this chapter you should:

(a) know the stages of input;
(b) understand how a computer keyboard is laid out;
(c) understand the use of a VDU screen;
(d) know how to use menus;
(e) understand the WIMP user interface;
(f) know the advantages and disadvantages of direct keyboard input;
(g) know the stages in encoding to disk or to tape;
(h) know the main automatic document reading methods available;
(i) know the main types of card reading device;
(j) know the main types of printer available;
(k) know the methods of computer output on microform;
(l) be able to select a method of output appropriate to a given task.

1 The stages of input

The stages of data input are as follows.

(a) *Origination* of data (the business transaction that gives rise to data which needs to be recorded and processed).

(b) *Transcription* of data into a machine-readable form (which the computer can take in), if this is necessary.

(c) Data *input*.

Data origination and collection where transcription is not necessary is known as *data capture*.

2 VDUs and keyboards: direct data entry

The usual way to get data into a computer directly (without any intermediate stages) is to use a keyboard, with a VDU so that you can see what you are typing. VDUs and keyboards can be used for direct data entry as:

(a) terminals connected to a mainframe or minicomputer;
(b) an integral part of a microcomputer installation.

BPP Publishing

Keyboard layout and functions

You may be familiar with the basic QWERTY keyboard (a keyboard laid out in the standard typewriter pattern) which includes the alphabet, numbers 0 - 9 and some basic punctuation, plus other keys (such as space and shift). The shift key is used as follows.

K = k   [shift] K = K   [shift] 3 = £   [shift] / = ?

A typical keyboard is a development of the QWERTY design. A basic keyboard includes the following.

(a) *Ordinary typing keys* used to enter data or text. These may be used to denote *instructions* or *commands* if used with special keys called CTRL or ALT.

(b) A *numeric key pad* to use like a calculator or to enter lots of numbers. These keys may also double as cursor control keys, page-up and page-down (to move quickly through documents) and so on.

(c) *Cursor control keys*, which in compact keyboards may be incorporated into the numeric section. These are up/down/left/right keys to move the cursor or writing point on the screen.

(d) A number of *function keys* for use with software. These keys are numbered and preset to perform certain functions.

The actual positioning of these areas and what characters share certain keys may differ between keyboards. A typical keyboard, however, might look like this.

Exercise 1

Find an actual keyboard, and locate on it:

(a)   the function keys;
(b)   the cursor control keys;
(c)   the CTRL and ALT keys.

In addition to the function keys, there are special keys that must be used to let the computer know that you wish to enter or have finished entering a command, to correct a command and so on.

(a)   *Return key* or *Enter key*. All commands direct to the system must be 'entered' with this key, to let the machine know that you have finished typing your command and wish it to be executed.

(b)   *Escape (ESC) key*. This key can be used when, for example, you wish to stop using a procedure.

(c)   *Control (CTRL) key*. This alters the meanings of some keys. Thus in word processing, pressing the key 'P' would type the letter P, but pressing the control key at the same time as the key 'P' might make the word processor start a new page.

(d)   There may be another special key or combination which can be used to change the meanings of keys: there is no room on the QWERTY keyboard for characters such as accents, foreign alphabets, mathematical signs and so on. Such a key might change some letters to mean:

$\alpha \ \beta \ \gamma \ \delta \ \chi \ \Sigma \ \text{¿} \ @ \ \text{ç}$ etc.

The VDU screen

A VDU screen (or *monitor*) displays text and graphics. Monitors can be cathode ray tubes, liquid crystal displays or gas plasma display.

(a)   The screen's *resolution* is the number of pixels that are lit up. A pixel is a pictorial element, a 'dot' on the screen, as it were. The fewer the pixels on screen, the larger they will be: the resolution of any picture with large pixels will be low. More and smaller pixels enable detailed high-resolution display. *High resolution monitors* currently available include 1024 (horizontal) × 768 (vertical). Currently, many PCs have a resolution of 640 × 480. (This is the resolution offered by IBM's VGA standard). Higher resolution requires more processing power, but enables graphs and diagrams to be displayed.

(b)   The user must 'pan' up, down or sideways when he or she wants to view a different piece of text. Alternatively two or more bits of text which are in different places in the overall layout can be viewed on screen at the same time by making use of *windows:* a bit of text on screen is surrounded by a box, and two or more such boxes can be displayed at once.

(c) A *wrap-around* facility enables the computer to display a line of text that is too long to be displayed on the screen as one line in its entirety. The line appears on the VDU as two successive lines. *Scrolling* occurs when the screen is full of text: the computer moves each line of text up one line, thus removing the first line from view, so that text input can continue on the bottom line.

The screen is used to display text:

(a) to allow the operator to see what he or she has keyed in;

(b) to help the operator to input data by providing 'forms' on the screen for filling in (the screen's format can be specified by the program);

(c) to display output, such as answers to enquiries.

In addition, the screen can be used to give messages to the operator, and the operator can respond to messages by keying in new instructions.

Keyboard/screen dialogue

The design of the *keyboard* reflects the way in which the user communicates with the computer to direct its operating processes and to provide and manipulate the contents of its memory. The *screen* is the means by which the computer communicates with the user. The way the keyboard is used, and what you would expect to see on the screen, will therefore depend on the particular strategy for *screen dialogue* that the software adopts.

This dialogue between computer operator and computer might be a central feature of the running of a program, and the term *conversational mode* describes a method of operation in which the operator appears to be carrying on a continual dialogue with the computer, receiving immediate replies to input messages.

The cursor

You know exactly where your next character will be if you enter data on a page by hand or typewriter, and in the same way the cursor (an arrow, line or box) shows you on screen the point in your text that will be affected by your keyboard entries. It is basically a marker of where the computer's attention is at any given moment. It can be moved about the screen by direction keys on the keyboard or by a mouse. In WIMP systems (see below) the cursor is replaced by a pointer.

Exercise 2

A computer screen displays a form, with boxes to be filled in. When the operator has finished filling in a box, he or she can move to the next box simply by pressing the Return key. Why would it still be useful to have a cursor displayed on the screen?

Broadly speaking, there are two ways of using a *keyboard* with VDU to input data.

(a)   By selecting options from a menu. A menu is a display of a series of options, and the operator selects which option he or she wants by keying in an appropriate letter or number, or perhaps by moving the cursor to the required option and then selecting the option.

(b)   By using commands. Command codes or instructions are keyed in, to indicate to the program what it should do with the data that follows. The data is then keyed in, and the program processes it.

Menu selection

A menu is a list of items to choose from. A VDU screen might list a number of different options, from which the computer user must choose what he or she wants to do next. For example, a main menu for word processing functions might include:

    A -   edit a document;
    B -   create a new document;
    C -   print a document;
    D -   delete a document.

By selecting C, the operator will be specifying that he or she wants to do some printing. When C has been keyed in, *another* menu may be displayed, calling for the operator to narrow down still further the specification of what he or she wants to do (for example print the whole document or only part of it). A menu system is thus a hierarchical list of options.

Command codes

An alternative or supplement to menu selection is the keyboard entry of *coded controls* and typed *commands* to tell the computer what processing is to be done. Individual keys, or a combination of keys, can be used to enter the controls and commands. For skilled operators this is a quicker form of dialogue than a menu system.

Formatted screens

The main part of the screen area, of course, will be the 'page' on which you will be entering data or text. It is possible to have the screen laid out for specific user requirements. For spreadsheets, accounting applications and data files, there are suitable pre-formatted structures, into which items of data can simply be inserted. Formatting includes:

(a)   different colours for different screen areas;
(b)   reverse video (where colours in a selected area are the reverse of the rest of the screen);
(c)   flashing items;
(d)   whole forms laid out on screen, with boxes marked out for data to be entered.

BPP Publishing

WIMP and GUIs

It was felt by some manufacturers that the use of a typewriter keyboard to type in characters was not the most appropriate way. A useful mnemonic for one common alternative is **WIMP**. WIMP was designed to make PCs more user-friendly to people without experience of using computers, who might have difficulty in using a keyboard or who might resist the idea of becoming computer users.

WIMP involves the use of two design ideas and two operating methods.

(a) *Windows*. The screen can be divided into sections, 'windows' of flexible size which can be opened and closed. This enables two or more documents to be viewed and edited together, and sections of one to be inserted into another. This is particularly useful for word processed documents and spreadsheets, which are too large for the VDU screen.

(b) *Icons*. An icon is an image of an object used to represent an abstract idea or process. In software design, icons may be used instead of numbers, letters or words to identify and describe the various functions available for selection, or files to access. A common icon is a waste paper bin to indicate the deletion of a document.

(c) *Mouse*. A *mouse* is a small device which sits on the desk, and is plugged into the basic module of the micro, or into the keyboard. Underneath the mouse is a hard ball. The mouse is rolled by hand across the desk, and as the mouse moves a pointer (cursor) on the VDU screen mimics its movements. A mouse can be used to pick out an appropriate icon (or other option), to mark out the area of a new window, to mark the beginning and end of a block for deletion or insertion and so on. It has a button to execute the appropriate command when the pointer is in the right place.

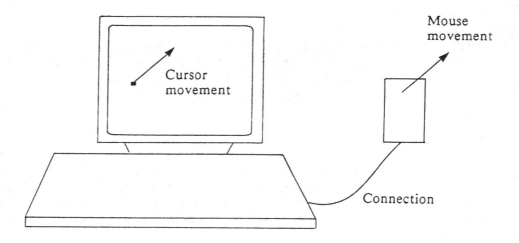

(d) *Pull-down menu*. An initial menu (or menu-bar) will be shown across the top of the VDU screen. Using the mouse to move the pointer to the required item in the menu, the pointer 'pulls down' a subsidiary menu, similar to pulling down a window blind in the room of a house. The pointer and mouse can then be used to select the required item on the menu pulled down.

Exercise 3

A word processor offers an initial menu which includes the following options.

1 Text feature; 2 Search; 3 Tabs; 4 Delete.

Which of the above would you expect to give you a subsidiary menu including the following options?

1 Subscript; 2 Bold; 3 Italic; 4 Underline.

Graphical user interfaces (GUIs)

WIMP is an example of a trend towards *user-friendliness* and ease of use for computer operators, many of whom are not computer professionals. WIMP is a 'graphical user interface' in that dialogue is conducted through images rather than just typed text.

WIMP is not used on all PCs: all the same operations can be performed by other means, using cursor control keys instead of the mouse, entering commands via codes or alphanumeric menu selection and so on. The WIMP strategy has several advantages, however.

(a) Icon selection is very easy to use, and less taxing for the user's memory than codes.

(b) The mouse/pointer/icon system means that the keyboard is not used for controls. This avoids confusion over keys which have different meanings in different modes and means that typing speed is no longer a constraint. It may, however, be more convenient during the typing of documents to have the necessary controls also at the typist's fingertips.

(c) The windows system is the only way of viewing the contents of two files simultaneously. It also provides a convenient alternative to panning around documents covering large areas, for example spreadsheets.

Manufacturers are now offering *pen-based systems*. In these systems, a 'pen' is used instead of a mouse; a sensor collects information about the strokes being formed and analyses the movements to identify the characters written. This is a development from mouse technology; however it has been criticised as being a backward step from the computer keyboard. However, they are proving popular with people who cannot type.

The advantages of direct keyboard input

By far the most significant advantage of direct input via a keyboard (with or without a mouse) is that a computer user can have interactive processing. Interactive processing is when data can be input to a computer, output information can be received quickly, further input can be keyed in and output received. The computer user gets the information he or she wants instantly.

Interactive processing is essential to some forms of data processing, and managers are increasingly need to obtain information rapidly from a computer that would take far too long to prepare manually. The use of financial models and spreadsheets are examples of how managers rely on computers for planning and budgeting. The modern trend is towards putting a PC on every manager's desk.

This major advantage of keyboard input is only an advantage, of course, when the computer user *wants* interactive processing. For some data processing applications, routine batch processing in particular, interactive processing is not needed.

The other advantages of keyboard input are as follows.

(a) The person keying in the data can be in a location far away from the computer itself, with the keyboard and VDU linked to the computer by telephone. In such a case, the keyboard and VDU are used as a *terminal* for the remote computer, which may be a PC or a larger computer. The terminal may be just a terminal, or it may itself be a PC able to carry out some computing itself.

(b) The person keying in the data can check it on the VDU screen before pressing the 'Enter' key to input it to the computer. Any keying errors, or even errors in the data itself, might be identified and corrected on the spot.

The disadvantages of direct keyboard input

Direct keyboard input is unsuitable for large volumes of transaction data. Keying in takes a long time, and a computer waiting for data to be keyed in is idle for much of the time. The speed of keyboard input depends on the typing speed of the operator. A typical speed might be 200–250 characters (bytes) per minute. This is slow in computer terms.

Keyboard input is error-prone because the only data verification that can be done before input is a visual check of the data on the VDU screen.

There might be security problems. Keyboard terminals are less secure than a computer centre: unauthorised users could gain access to a keyboard terminal in an office.

Exercise 4

A company inputs data from all of its 2,500 employees' weekly timesheets into its computer for payroll purposes, and the production director occasionally inspects this data to check on the amount of overtime being worked in each department. Why would direct keyboard input be valuable for the production director's enquiries, but not for the weekly input of data?

---

3 Encoding to disk or tape

Data can be copied from source documents and written on to a magnetic disk or a magnetic tape from a keyboard or terminal. This process is called *encoding*. In short the data is *transcribed* into a machine-readable form.

Encoding can be done in either of two ways:

(a) 'on line' to a computer, so that the keyboard input is encoded on to a disk (or possibly a tape) via the computer. A device is on line when it is connected to a computer, which can receive signals from it or send signals to it.

(b) 'off line' using special key-to-disk encoding equipment.

In both cases, the data (probably transaction data) that is encoded on to the disk will be sorted before input to the main processing program(s).

Generally, key-to-disk encoding systems are multi-station systems comprising a number of keyboard/VDU terminals on-line to a small computer. The system is controlled by the system's computer using a small library of programs. These are able to carry out some checks on the data as it is keyed in, and also control the encoding and verification processes. Checks may identify inconsistencies or logical errors.

The procedure is as follows.

(a) Data is keyed in, checked and shown on the VDU screen (detected errors are indicated on the screen) and when accepted, written onto the magnetic disk or tape.

(b) *Verification* is carried out by another operator. Verification is the process of checking that data input is *identical to source data*. The data is keyed in again by the second operator, and the system checks that both versions are identical.

(c) Completed batches are grouped together to create the complete transaction file which is written from the working disks to another disk (or a magnetic tape).

(d) This disk (or tape) is *then* used as the input for the main computer.

Key-to-disk encoding is suitable in systems where large volumes of data are input for processing.

Data may also be keyed in to a floppy disk, rather than to a big tape reel or disk pack. This may be used when a small amount of data is collected by each recording device. Examples include the recording of sales on cash registers, keying in stock level details (for example in a supermarket) and keying in household gas or electricity meter readings to a hand-held recording device.

Exercise 5

Give two examples of situations where preliminary encoding to disk or tape would be preferable to direct keyboard input.

---

4 Document reading methods

Transcribing manually-prepared data into a computer-readable form such as disk or tape is costly and jeopardises accuracy. Document reading methods of data collection involve the use of a source document that both humans and computers can read. The data on the source document might be pre-printed, or added later by manual processing, but in either case the source document itself is fed in to the computer. Data transcription and verification are reduced or eliminated. Although the on-line input speed of document reading devices is slower than that of magnetic tape or disk devices, the saving in data collection time is considerable.

Magnetic ink character recognition (MICR)

MICR is recognition of characters by a machine that reads characters printed in magnetic ink. Using ink which contains a metallic powder, highly stylised characters are printed onto documents. The documents must be passed through a magnetic field before the characters can be detected by a suitable reading device.

The largest application of MICR is in banking. Cheques are *pre-encoded* with the customer account number, branch code and cheque number and, after use, *post-encoded* with the amount of the cheque. The cheques are then passed through the reading device and details are stored on magnetic disk or tape. The cheque data is now on magnetic storage for processing, while the cheques (sorted by the reading device into branch code order) are returned to the appropriate branches. MICR is particularly well suited for cheques, since although they may become dirty, overwritten or crumpled, they are still legible to the reading device.

The main advantage of MICR is its accuracy, but MICR documents are expensive to produce, and so MICR has only limited application in practice.

Optical character recognition (OCR)

OCR involves a machine that is able to read characters by looking at their shapes. Optical scanners can read documents at up to 300 pages per hour. They recognise the characters, convert them into machine code and record them on to the magnetic medium being used. Most machines still require special typefaces, although some can cope with any printed letters and even with handwriting.

Mark sensing and optical mark reading (OMR)

Mark sensing is generally used for numeric characters, their values being denoted by pencilled lines in boxes on the preprinted source document. The document is then read by a device which senses the graphite marks in the boxes.

OMR is similar, except that the reading device uses an artificial light source and the marks can be made with ball point pen or ink as well as with pencil.

The data recorded must be of a fairly limited nature, for example yes/no responses on a questionnaire:

(a)   to avoid errors in recording data;

(b)   because the data must be numerical or capable of being represented by coded numbers. Trying to represent letters with marks on a form would make the documents too big and cumbersome since there would have to be 26 marking positions for each A - Z data character instead of just 10 for the figures 0 - 9.

Bar coding

Bar codes are groups of marks which, by their spacing and thickness, indicate specific codes or values. There is an example on the back cover of this book. Bar codes are now commonly used in shops. When a customer buys some bar coded items and takes them to the check-out to pay, the shop assistant uses a bar code reader which transmits the bar coded data to a central computer in the store. The computer then provides the price of the item being purchased and this is output to the cashier's check-out point. The total cost of all the purchases is similarly calculated, and the customer sees what he or she must pay on a small display screen, and receives a printed receipt. At the same time, the data about the purchases that has been read into the computer from the bar codes can be used to update the stock file (so that goods which have sold well can be re-ordered) and to record the sales data for management information purposes.

Turnround documents

OCR and OMR methods can make use of *turnround documents*. A turnround document is a document that is initially produced by computer. It is then used to collect more data and then re-input to the computer for processing.

Examples of turnround documents are as follows.

(a)   OCR: credit card companies include payment counterfoils with their computer-produced statements, which will then be used for inputting payment data to a computer.

(b)   OMR: multiple choice examination papers. An examining body that stores multiple choice questions on a computer file can produce examination papers by computer. Candidates are then asked to make marks to indicate their answers, and the positions of the answer marks are detected by OMR readers. The examination papers can thus be marked by computer.

Exercise 6

(a)   Why would a warehouse prefer bar codes to MICR as a system for marking goods?

(b)   Why is OMR used rather than OCR when a gas consumer fills in his or her own meter reading on a form provided by the supplier?

5 Card reading devices

Magnetic stripe cards

Magnetic stripe cards have been widely distributed over the past decade, so that almost every person with a bank or building society account can use one. The standard magnetic stripe card is rectangular in shape, about 8.5 cm by 5.4 cm in area, and about 1mm thick. One face of the card shows the name of the issuer, the payments system the card applies to (such as VISA), and often a hologram image (a bird on VISA cards) for security purposes. The customer's name, the card number and the card expiry date also appear (in embossed form, so that the details can be printed on to credit card payment slips).

However, none of this surface information is strictly necessary for data input to a computer system. All the machine-readable data is contained on the back, on a magnetic stripe. The stripe is divided into three tracks.

(a) Track 1 contains all the information (such as the customer name) that is found on the other side of the card.

(b) Track 2 contains a number which is unique to the customer; when used with the customer's PIN (Personal Identification Number), the customer's identity as the authorised user of the card is confirmed.

(c) Track 3 contains other information which can affect the customer's use of the card, such as a record of the most recent transactions, withdrawal limits and so forth.

The card is passed through a reading device which converts this information into directly computer-readable form.

Smart cards

Smart cards are similar to magnetic stripe cards in that information is held on a plastic card for the customer to use at will. However, the technology by which this is achieved is quite different. Smart cards are much more versatile than magnetic stripe cards. They are currently most widely used in France. A smart card is a plastic card in which is embedded a microprocessor chip. The microprocessor includes a memory which retains its contents even when there is no power supply to the card.

The smart card can contains a great deal more information than a magnetic stripe card. Not only does it contain basic account details, but also a memory and a processing capability. The smart card is used in a similar way to a magnetic stripe card for making payments.

One of the advantages of smart cards over magnetic stripe cards is that they are much harder to duplicate, and so are more secure. On the other hand, they are more expensive to produce.

Electronic point of sale (EPOS) devices

More and more large retail stores are introducing electronic point of sale (EPOS) devices which act both as *cash registers* and as terminals connected to a main computer. This enables the computer to produce useful management information such as sales details and analysis and stock control information very quickly. Many devices use bar coding, as described earlier, or direct keyboard entry.

A fully itemised and descriptive receipt can be produced for the customer, who will also feel the benefit of faster moving queues at the checkout. Management can obtain more information more quickly than was possible before, in particular:

(a) immediate updating of stock levels;
(b) identification of fast-moving items for reordering;
(c) sales information.

The provision of immediate sales information, perhaps analysed on a branch basis, permits great speed and flexibility in decision-making (certainly of a short-term nature), as consumer wishes can be responded to quickly.

Exercise 7

Suggest some applications for smart cards, where it is useful to be able to record data on the card as well as to read it.

EFTPOS

EFTPOS (Electronic Funds Transfer at Point of Sale) aims to handle, electronically, the high volume of low value transactions which banks would otherwise have to process in paper form. EFTPOS systems integrate the retailer's POS system with an electronic payment system. By this means, stock control, retailing and receipt of funds can be fully automated.

The plastic cards used in EFTPOS transactions are known as *debit cards*. This is because the payment is debited to the purchaser's bank account, usually within two or three days of the transaction's taking place. It is important that the distinction between credit cards and debit cards is understood. A debit card functions as an electronic cheque book, providing access to the holder's current account, and allowing instant electronic authorisation of the transaction by the paying bank. A credit card provides a means of charging purchases to the cardholder's credit card account, on which credit is provided by the card issuer.

The *Switch* consortium was set up by Midland, National Westminster and Royal Bank of Scotland in 1988 and has gained widespread acceptance in the UK; it is accepted as a means of payment at many large retailer groups.

A typical EFTPOS transaction

The steps in a typical payment by debit card at the retailer's terminal are as follows.

(a) The cardholder's card is swiped through the terminal.

(b) Data is captured: the sort code, the account number, the card's expiry date and the card number;

(c) The amount of the purchase is keyed in (unless already captured by a barcode reader).

(d)   The data, together with the retailer's identification, is coded and transmitted to a central electronic funds transfer switch.

(e)   The central switch forwards an electronic message to the cardholder's bank's computer system for authorisation.

(f)   The bank's computer computer decodes the message, checks the account balance and returns a coded approval (or refusal), logging the item against cardholder's account.

(g)   The central switch forwards a message to the retailer's terminal.

(h)   The cardholder and cashier are advised of the approval and an advice slip is printed for signature.

(i)   The customer signs the advice slip and the transaction is completed.

Settlement occurs two or three days later when the relevant bank accounts are debited and credited. There is no technical reason for the delay, but it is included because people are used to a short delay when they write cheques.

6   Printed output

Large-scale printers

Line printers are printers that produce one line of print at a time, but at very high speeds. Most large computer systems use line printers for the majority of printed output that the machine produces. The paper is in a continuous sheet, with perforations between 'pages', which is fed through the printer and can be separated into individual pages after printing. Such paper may be described as 'sprocket-fed' (moved by toothed wheels fitting into holes down the side of the paper) or as 'fan-folded' (because it is folded at the perforations). Chain line printers have characters embossed on the outside of a continuously revolving chain which moves past the print position.

Large-scale laser printers, like line printers, are used in large computer systems. However, they print whole pages at a time using an electrostatic process and have a greater range of print characters and styles. Although speeds of 30,000 lines per minute have been achieved, quality is reduced and lower speeds (say 15,000 - 20,000 lines per minute) are a more practical proposition. Like line printers, large-scale printers use continuous stationery, but, unlike them, make little noise.

Desk-top printers

Most minicomputers and PCs generally have no need of such fast print capabilities. Small desk-top printers, using continuous (or sometimes single sheet) stationery, are used in such systems. Desk-top printers can also be used in mainframe computer systems where high quality (letter quality) output is required.

Printers for PCs can be divided into two broad categories, impact printers and non-impact printers.

(a)   Impact printers work by means of the impact of a print hammer or pinheads on to a print ribbon and the paper, and they are therefore quite noisy.

(b)   Non-impact printers work with different technologies. They do not rely on the impact of a hammer or other device and so they are much quieter to use.

The choice between different types of printer involves balancing cost, speed and print quality, although noise can be an important factor too.

Impact printers

Daisy wheel printers

In a daisy wheel printer, fully formed print characters are positioned at the end of long stems, which protrude from a central wheel. This gives the impression of a daisy-like flower, with a solid round centre and petals sticking out all around it, hence the name of the printer.

(a)   The daisy wheel is inserted in the printer, and rotates until the desired character is in the right position. A hammer then strikes the end of the stem and the character appears on the paper.

(b)   Daisy wheels can be changed, if a different font is required (such as italics) but only one daisy wheel can be used at a time.

(c)   Daisy wheel printers print one character at a time, rather than one line at a time. Print speeds can range from 10 to 80 characters per second, depending on the make and quality of printer.

Dot matrix printers

A dot matrix printer has a head containing an array of steel pins. Characters are constructed by pressing a combination of these pins against the print ribbon, and so on paper each character appears as a matrix of small dots.

(a)   Most dot matrix printers have print heads with a matrix of 9×9 pins or 9×7 pins, and so there are noticeable gaps between the dots.

(b)   Like daisy wheel printers, dot matrix printers print one character at a time, rather than one line at a time. Dot matrix printers are faster than daisy wheel printers, printing typically 120 - 200 characters per second. They are also cheaper.

(c)   A further advantage is that the dots can be placed anywhere on paper, and so it is possible to produce *graphics* (of fairly low resolution) as well as characters.

(d)   Most dot matrix printers can also be used to print better quality print (known as NLQ: *near letter quality*). This is still not up to daisy wheel standard but it is acceptable for many users.

Exercise 8

A PC user needs to be able to print out about 25 pages of data a day, and has decided to buy an impact printer. Some of the pages are reports to the board of directors, and so as to make these reports easy to read they incorporate frequent changes of font for headings and sub-totals. None of the output goes to users outside the company. Recommend a suitable type of printer, explaining your choice.

Non-impact printers

Laser printers

Laser printers print whole page at a time, rather than printing line by line. They print onto individual sheets of paper (just as photocopiers do) and so they do not use continuous computer stationery (as daisywheel and dot matrix printers can).

(a) A laser printer works by means of a laser beam shining on to a photoconductive drum. Where the light strikes the drum, it becomes electrically charged. This then attracts toner which is fixed onto the paper by heat and pressure, to produce the printed page.

(b) The resolution of printed characters and diagrams with laser printers is very high.

(c) A desk-top laser printer will print between 8 and 15 A4 pages a minute.

(d) Laser printers have their own random access memory for storing data prior to printing, and also to store fonts. They can be used to combine different fonts, such as italics and bold characters and a wide range of other characters, including mathematical symbols and Greek letters.

(e) Laser printers are quiet, because unlike daisy wheel and dot matrix printers, laser printers are not impact printers which rely on the striking of hammers or pins.

(f) The cost of laser printers is higher than that of daisy wheel and dot matrix printers.

A development in laser printer technology is PostScript. PostScript is a new printer *protocol* (a set of rules for how instructions to printers are to be electronically encoded) which provides faster text printing and faster and more accurate graphic images than most other protocols can offer. It can support complex fonts such as Arabic with its precise encoding and positioning facilities, and is becoming accepted as the standard for laser printers.

Thermal printers

There are two types of thermal printer.

(a) Some work by heating thermally-sensitive paper with a printhead to form characters.

(b) An alternative form of thermal printer, a thermal transfer printer, uses a special printing ribbon with heat-sensitive ink, which melts on to the paper when either the hot printhead touches it, or an electric current is run through the ribbon.

A type of thermal printer for portable computers has been manufactured by Canon, and it is called a *bubblejet* printer. The print head heats up the ink and deposits it on paper. The inkhead and cartridge are removed when the ink runs out.

Inkjet printers

Inkjet printers, as their name suggests, work by sending a jet of ink onto the paper to produce the required characters. They are quiet and fast, but they need special paper that can soak up the ink as quickly as it is squirted on to it, to avoid smudging and produce good quality copy.

A more recent development is a solid inkjet printer, which uses a solid block of ink that melts on to a page to form characters, and is less messy than printers using liquid ink.

Buffering

Buffering is a method of storing output data in a printer, magnetic tape reader or other output device until the device becomes free and ready to accept it. By storing data in an output device, the processor is released for other work. The term 'buffering' can also be applied to cases where an input device feeds data to the processor, and the processor takes in more data than it needs immediately. Thus a block of records might be read in from a tape, and all the records but one would be put in a buffer area of memory.

This means that output devices, such as printers, need to have buffer storage areas for holding output data which they have not handled (for example have not printed) yet. In a microcomputer system, the size of a printer's RAM buffer area should be at least 8 kB.

Exercise 9

Why is a significant amount of buffering often needed when a processor is sending output to a printer, but very unlikely to be needed when a processor is receiving input from a keyboard?

---

7 Computer output on microform (COM)

COM is a form of computer output whereby instead of printing the output on to paper, it is projected on to a cathode ray tube and then photographed into a very much reduced form, a microform. Alternative methods of producing COM involve laser beam, electron beam or optical fibre technology.

(a) The microform is readable, but not by the naked eye, and a magnifying reading device (with a viewing screen) is needed by users. To assist the user in finding the records on the microform, 'eyeball' characters (letters or numbers visible to the eye without magnification) are shown on the microform.

(b) *Microfilm* is a continuous strip of film, with images in frames along the film. *Microfiche* on the other hand, consist of separate sheets of film (about the size of a postcard), each sheet containing over 100 frames.

Large volumes of information can be condensed into a very small physical space so that savings in storage space can be considerable where printed matter would otherwise have to be kept for fairly long periods of time. Microform therefore provides a suitable storage medium for *archive information* or *reference information*. Microform frames or pages can be reproduced on paper in an enlarged, readable form, if required.

Microform has the disadvantage of needing special reading devices, so that if the output is in regular use by various staff in a department, there might be 'bottleneck' problems for them in getting access to the information they need, as they queue up to use the reading device.

In comparing microfilm with microfiche, the advantages of microfilm are that:

(a) microfilm readers can scan microfilm images quickly, to locate the information required. In contrast, information on microfiche takes longer to locate;

(b) where the information held is updated regularly, it is probably more convenient to produce a new microfilm at regular intervals, rather than to produce new sheets of microfiche with the updated information, for inserting manually into the appropriate place in the file of microfiche sheets. The regular change in information would probably justify the cost of producing new reels of microfilm.

The advantages of microfiche over microfilm are that:

(a) where information changes slowly, it would probably be more economical to produce a new microfiche occasionally than to produce a new microfilm every time a change occurs;

(b) where information is held for archive purposes, sheets of microfiche can be produced with updating information and added to the back of the file manually. With microfilm, however, it would be uneconomic to produce new information until enough is available to fill up a reel of film. This means that there would probably be a longer delay with microfilm in updating the archive records.

Microfilm and microfiche output are not common, and because of the expense of COM output devices, this form of output is generally reserved for organisations with a relatively large expenditure budget or for libraries which would otherwise have to hold large quantities of bulky books and articles in paper form.

Exercise 10

Give three examples of data which might reasonably be stored on microfiche.

---

8 The choice of output medium

Choosing a suitable output medium depends on a number of factors, such as:

(a) is a hard (paper) copy of the output required? If so, what quality must the output be?

    (i) If the output includes documents that are going to be used as OCR turnround documents, the quality of printing must be high.

    (ii) If the information will be used as a working document with a short life or limited use (such as a copy of text for checking) then low quality output on a dot matrix printer might be sufficient;

(b) the volume of information produced. For example, a VDU screen can hold a certain amount of data, but it becomes more difficult to read when the information would more than fill a screen and can only be read a bit at a time;

(c) the speed at which output is required. For example, to print a large volume of data, a high speed printer might be suitable to finish the work more quickly (and release the processor for other jobs);

(d) the suitability of the output medium to the application:

    (i) a VDU is well suited to interactive processing with a computer;

    (ii) output onto a magnetic disk or tape is appropriate if the data is to be used in further processing;

    (iii) large volumes of reference data for human users to hold in a library might be held on microfilm or microfiche, and so output in these forms would be appropriate;

(e) the cost: some output devices would not be worth having because their advantages would not justify their cost.

Exercise 11

Suggest suitable input and output devices for a lending library which needs to record the issue and return of books, identify books already out on loan in response to readers' enquiries and issue letters to recall books which are overdue or which have been requested by other readers.

Chapter roundup

(a) Data must be originated and in most cases transcribed before it can be input.

(b) A computer keyboard includes the normal typewriter keys and some additional keys.

(c) A VDU screen displays both data as it is input and the output from processing.

(d) A computer user can either type in commands or select options from a menu.

(e) The WIMP interface uses windows to display information, icons and menus to set out options and a mouse to allow the user to make choices.

(f) Direct keyboard input is particularly useful when the user wants interactive processing, but it is wasteful of processor time when large amounts of data are to be input for routine processing.

(g) Data can be encoded to disk or to tape off line, and then processed in batches.

(h) MICR, OCR, OMR and bar coding can all be used to reduce the amount of keying in required.

(i) Card reading devices enable information about cardholders to be input directly to a computer.

(j) Large-scale printers are much faster than desk-top printers.

(k) Desk-top printers may be impact printers (daisy wheel or dot matrix) or non-impact printers (laser, thermal or inkjet).

(l) Buffering enables better use to be made of the processor.

(m) Computers can output data to microfilm or microfiche.

(n) The choice of an output medium depends in part on whether hard copy is required, on the volume of output and on the speed and quality required.

Quick quiz

1   What are cursor control keys?

2   What is the resolution of a VDU screen?

3   What items might be found on a menu for amending a personnel file?

4   How is a mouse used?

5   What is a GUI?

6   What is a key-to-disk system and how is one used?

7   What is the largest application of MICR?

8   What are turnround documents?

9   What are EPOS devices?

10   What are the main types of large-scale printers?

11   How does a laser printer work?

12   How does buffering enable better use to be made of the processor?

13   What are the advantages of microfiche over microfilm?

14   What form of output is appropriate for data to be used in further processing?

Solutions to exercises

1   The function keys, labelled F1 to F10 (or F12), are likely to be along the top or down the left hand side. The cursor control keys will have arrows on them and may double up as number keys. The CTRL and ALT keys may well be near one end of the space bar.

2   The operator needs to be reminded where he or she has got to on the form. Having a cursor also makes it easy to pick out a character to be changed (for example a mistyped letter in the middle of a name).

3   Option 1: text feature

4   The production director makes occasional brief enquiries, and is likely to want responses immediately. Instant processing of each item of routine weekly input is not needed.

---

5   Recording responses to several thousand market research questionnaires.

Keying in data from credit card vouchers.

6   (a)   Bar codes can be scanned quickly from a few inches away using a hand-held reader. MICR characters must first be magnetised and then read (requiring contact with the paper). This needs bulky equipment which it would be difficult to carry around a warehouse.

(b)   People would write digits in many different styles, making it much harder to read handwritten digits than simple marks.

7   An individual's medical details (including required regular medication, and any allergies) could be kept on a smart card.

Smart cards could be used as clock cards, to record hours worked in a factory.

8   A dot matrix printer should be used. The quality will be adequate for internal use, and it can handle changes of font easily.

9   A processor works much faster than either a printer or a keyboard operator, so it quickly generates enough output to keep a printer busy for a while, but can deal with data from a keyboard as soon as it is input.

10   (a)   Telephone directories

(b)   Library catalogues

(c)   Records of previous years' transactions which need to be kept for several years for tax purposes.

11   (a)   Recording the issue and return of books: bar code readers (with each book and each membership card showing a bar code)

(b)   Identifying books out on loan: a keyboard and a VDU

(c)   Issuing letters to recall books: a laser printer or a dot matrix printer

4 DATA COMMUNICATIONS, NETWORKS AND PROCESSING METHODS

Your objectives

After completing this chapter you should:

(a)   understand the need for data communication;
(b)   know the main data communication media;
(c)   understand the concept of data switching;
(d)   understand the difference between synchronous and asynchronous transmission;
(e)   know the main items of data communication equipment;
(f)   know the difficulties of direct links between computers;
(g)   appreciate how a multi-user system is arranged;
(h)   be able to distinguish between centralised and distributed processing;
(i)   be able to distinguish between local area networks and wide area networks;
(j)   be able to draw diagrams of some network topologies;
(k)   know the advantages of distributed processing and networks;
(l)   know the difference between batch processing and demand processing;
(m)   appreciate when on-line, interactive and real-time processing should be used.

---

1   Data communication

Data communication means sending data between computers or other data processing devices.

When all data processing is done in the same office, no serious problem should arise with the transmission of data between input and output devices and the processor. The equipment will be joined together by cables.

When the input or output device is located away from the computer, so that data has to be sent along a communications link (such as a telephone line), additional items of equipment have to be used.

A link might connect:

(a)   a computer and a remote terminal (keyboard and VDU). A computer may have a number of remote terminals linked to it;

(b)   two computers located some distance from each other (for example a mainframe and a PC, which would use the link to exchange data); or

(c)   several processors in a network, with each computer in the network able to send data to any other.

                                                                    BPP Publishing

Who provides the communications link?

In the UK, British Telecom and Mercury provide services to send data and can supply public or private lines for direct data links.

(a) *Public lines* use the ordinary telephone network and the cost depends upon the service used and the time for which the telephone link is maintained (as for any ordinary telephone call).

(b) *Private lines* also use the telephone network but a special line is provided at a fixed annual charge.

Private lines are sometimes referred to as *leased* lines. Many organisations will lease a number of lines to construct their own private networks. Sometimes, they will be happy to allow other users to access them.

Data transmission media

These are a variety of physical media through which links are established.

(a) Copper wire, as used in current telephone systems
(b) Coaxial cable, also copper, but more sophisticated than (a)
(c) Fibre optic cable, made out of thin glass strands, through which pulses of *light* are passed
(d) Microwave radio links
(e) Radio links via satellite

Bandwidth

The amount of data that can be sent over a line is in part determined by the bandwidth. The bandwidth is the range of frequencies that the channel can carry. Frequencies are measured in Hertz (cycles per second):

(a) narrow band (up to 300 Hertz);
(b) voice band (300-3,000 Hertz);
(c) broad band (over 3,000 Hertz).

The greater the bandwidth, the greater the rate at which data can be sent.

Bit serial and bit parallel transmission

Data transmission can be either *bit serial transmission* or *bit parallel transmission*. In bit serial transmission, the bits making up a character are sent one after the other down the line. In bit parallel transmission, eight lines are required as each bit in a byte is transmitted at the same time over its own channel. Bit serial transmission is the most common method. The number of bits transmitted per second is referred to as the *baud rate*.

Exercise 1

Computer user A has large quantities of data to transmit every day. Computer user B has far less data to transmit. Which of these users is more likely to use:

(a) a leased line?
(b) bit serial transmission?

2 Data switching

When the computer user has a number of computers (and terminals) which will transmit data to each other in an irregular and unpredictable way, it would be too expensive to rent dedicated private lines for direct data links. Instead, a data switching arrangement is used.

A *switch* is a device for opening, closing or directing an electric circuit. A telecommunications link is a circuit like any other: when you are speaking to someone over the telephone a circuit exists between the two devices. In the telephone network, switches connect one set of lines to another.

Circuit switching occurs when the connection is maintained until broken at one end. If data is sent simply by circuit switching, the line between the sender and the recipient must be open for the duration of the message.

Because much data transmission is irregular, this would be a wasteful use of the telephone line. Gaps in transmission of your message, when the line is idle, could be used by somebody else. Similarly, you may wish to transmit your data at a time when there is nobody on the other end of the line to receive it. *Packet switching* seeks to overcome these problems, and operates as follows.

(a) A data message is divided up into packets of data of a fixed length, usually 128 bytes, and transmitted through the network (many processors all over the country, or even the world, linked together by cables or radio) in these separate packets. Each packet contains control data, which identifies the sender of the message and the address of the recipient. The first packet opens a route (or *virtual circuit*) from source to destination, which the others will follow.

(b) Each processor in the network receives packets of data from another processor, and redirects them to the next processor along the chain to the eventual recipient.

(c) At the local end of the link (the end near the recipient of the message) the packets of data are reassembled into the full message, which is transmitted to the recipient. If terminals are asynchronous (see below), they will be connected to the packet switching network by a packet assembler/disassembler (PAD).

The packet switching system in the UK is called PDN (Public Data Network).

Notes

Packet switching systems transmit data in *digital* form, that is as a series of pulses representing bits. When circuit switching is used to transmit data over ordinary telephone lines, the digital data is first converted into analogue (wave) form using a modem (see below).

Simplex, half duplex and full duplex transmission

There are three modes of transmission each of which requires different types of equipment (at increasing cost). These are:

(a) *simplex*, allowing transmission in one direction only;
(b) *half duplex*, allowing transmission in both directions but not simultaneously;
(c) *full duplex*, allowing transmission in both directions simultaneously.

Synchronous and asynchronous data transmission

Data transmission can be asynchronous or synchronous.

(a) With *asynchronous transmission*, one character at a time is sent. Each character is preceded by a start bit and followed by a stop bit with the bits of the character coming in between. The receiving device at the end of the line recognises a start signal which activates a clock and then reads the bits that follow until it comes to the stop signal which turns the clock off. PCs normally use asynchronous transmission. Asynchronous transmission is efficient and economical provided that very large quantities of data are not being transmitted.

(b) With *synchronous transmission*, data is transmitted between the sending and receiving machines at a constant rate, and so there is no need for start signals and stop signals between the characters. The rate of transmission is controlled by a clock, which is usually the computer's internal clock. Synchronous transmission is less error-prone than asynchronous transmission. However, it needs more expensive equipment. Many *mainframes* normally use synchronous transmission, and can only communicate in the asynchronous mode by adding special items of equipment.

(c) One type of synchronous data transmission is BSC (binary synchronous communication) developed by IBM for communication between a mainframe and terminals. Special control characters are used to control the message. Synchronisation *characters* begin a message, followed by header, text and end of text characters.

Exercise 2

In a commonly used binary code for characters (ASCII), the code for '5' is 1010110 and the code for 'j' is 0101011. Use this example to explain why start and stop bits are needed in asynchronous transmission but not in synchronous transmission.

3 Data communication equipment

Equipment used to connect terminals to a computer some distance away includes modems and multiplexors.

Modems

Computer equipment stores and uses data in discrete *digital* (or 'bit') form. Much of the telephone network, however, still handles data in *analogue* or wave form. For data transmission in analogue form through the telephone network to be possible, there has to be a device at each end of the telephone line that can convert (modulate) the data from digital form to analogue form, and demodulate from analogue form to digital form. This conversion of data is done by devices called modems. There must be a modem at each end of the telephone line.

Multiplexors

In some computer systems, several terminals or local PCs share the same data link. A multiplexor is used where it is necessary to send data from several sources down a single line at the same time. It codes the data in a special way so that it can be sorted out at its destination. Where a number of terminals are linked to the central computer, the multiplexor is an essential piece of hardware handling the input/output and reducing line charges (as only one line, rather than several, is necessary).

One of the functions of a multiplexor is to stop the data from one source being mixed up with the data from another. In *time division multiplexing*, a device is allocated specific time slots in which to use the signal path. In *frequency division multiplexing*, the transmission medium is divided into a number of channels of smaller bandwidth.

4 Computer-to-computer links

One computer can be connected to another computer, or to several other computers (depending on the size of computer). These computer-to-computer links might be via cable, or via a data communication link so that geographically distant computers can be made to communicate directly with each other.

Why should computers need to communicate directly with each other?

(a) Two or more computers can share the data processing work.

(b) One computer can obtain data or programs from another computer's files.

(c) Database systems can be made more versatile and useful when several computers have access to the same database.

Mainframes can be linked directly to each other, but more common types of computer-to-computer links involve PCs, in some form of *network* configuration.

 BPP Publishing

Technical aspects of mainframe to PC links

Although many PCs used by large organisations are linked to a mainframe, there are problems with creating such a link which have to be overcome.

(a) *PCs normally use asynchronous transmission* whereas mainframes normally use synchronous transmission to transmit data.

(b) *PCs may use a different data alphabet to the mainframe.* A data alphabet is the combination of 0s and 1s used to represent each character. PCs use a data alphabet called ASCII whereas IBM and some other mainframe manufacturers use an alphabet called EBCDIC in their mainframes. To allow the PC and the mainframe to communicate, there must either be a special translation device (called a *protocol converter)* or special hardware and software added to the PC.

(c) *PCs have to be made to act like (emulate) mainframe terminals.* For example, an IBM PC might be linked to a mainframe and expected to act like an IBM 3278 terminal. This can be done by inserting an *emulation board* into the PC, and using this with an *emulation program* on a disk that comes with the emulation board. Even then, the computer user may have some problems because the keyboard on the PC will differ from the keyboard of a mainframe terminal, and so some keys may have to double up, with keys being used for two different purposes. This can make it difficult for the terminal user to learn which keys to use.

The reasons for wanting mainframe to PC links

There are three main reasons for wanting to link a PC to a mainframe computer.

(a) Opening a communications link between a PC and a mainframe allows the PC user to run programs on the mainframe, using the PC as a terminal.

(b) When the computer user writes software for the mainframe computer, a PC can be used to create and correct programs on the PC using its 'text editor' software, before it is actually put into use on the mainframe.

(c) *With the right software* to link the PC and the mainframe, data can be exchanged between them, giving the PC user access to the mainframe's database files and integrating the organisation's data processing system.

Exercise 3

A company has a data input office in London, linked to a mainframe computer in Glasgow. The input office is equipped with 25 PCs, all of which use ASCII, whereas the mainframe uses EBCDIC. All of the PCs are in use for data input to the mainframe at the same time, and only one line is available to transmit the data. List the various additional items of hardware and software that might be required.

---

5 Stand-alone computers and multi-user systems

A computer system might consist of a stand-alone computer (one not linked to other computers) with its peripheral equipment and one user, a computer whose peripheral equipment includes several terminals for several different users, or networks of inter-communicating computers with shared files.

Stand-alone computers are used:

(a) when the data processing requirements can be handled by one user with one computer. Office PCs are often stand-alone machines for use by individuals;

(b) when the data processing is centralised, for example with very large volumes of transaction data being handled by a mainframe, or with a centralised minicomputer being used for the processing requirements of a department.

With mainframe computers, minicomputers and larger PCs, several users, each with their own terminal (VDU and keyboard), might be connected to the same computer, with all the users able to carry out processing work simultaneously. Computer systems of this type are called *multi-user systems*. The terminals are *dumb* terminals, which means that they do *not* include a processor and so cannot do independent data processing. A dumb terminal relies on the central computer for its data processing power.

The terminals in a multi-user system might be:

(a) in the same room or building as the central computer, connected to the computer by internal cable; or

(b) geographically distant from the central computer, in which case the terminals are connected to the central computer by an external data link, usually provided in the UK by British Telecom.

Terminals can be used:

(a) for interactive computing with the central computer; or

(b) to input data into the computer from a remote location. *Remote access* describes access to a central computer installation from a terminal which is physically distant. The term *remote job entry* is used to describe a method of processing in which the computer user inputs his data from a remote terminal.

The benefits of multi-user systems are as follows.

(a) More departments or sections can have access to the computer, its data files and its programs. This improves the data processing capabilities of local offices.

(b) By giving departments more computing power and access to centralised information files, multi-access systems also make it easier for an organisation to *decentralise* authority from head office to local managers.

(c) The speed of processing, for both local offices and head office, is very fast.

(d) Local offices retain their input documents, and do not have to send them to a remote computer centre for processing.

Exercise 4

In what circumstances might a multi-user system encounter difficulties because the processor could not cope with the demands being made on it? How might such situations be prevented from arising?

6 Centralised data processing

Centralised data processing is carried out in a central location, such as a head office. The data for processing might be gathered from a wide area, for example from local offices or regional centres. The output will probably be distributed over a correspondingly wide area. But the actual processing of data is centralised.

Data might be fed in to the central processing system by:

(a) physically transporting data records from their source to the central location; or
(b) electronic means, for example from remote terminals linked to the central computer.

Similarly, output might be sent to local offices:

(a) physically, by post or courier (for example in printed form or on floppy disks); or
(b) electronically, to a remote terminal in the local office linked to the central computer.

7 Distributed processing and networks

In *distributed processing*, there are several autonomous but interacting processors and/or data stores at different locations linked by a communications network. The key features of distributed processing are as follows.

(a) A computer can access the information files of other computers in the system.
(b) Computers within the system can process data jointly.
(c) *Processing* is either carried out centrally, or at dispersed locations.
(d) *Files* are held either centrally or at local sites.
(e) *Authority* is decentralised as processing can be performed autonomously by local computers.

Exercise 5

What advantage does linking PCs to a mainframe in a distributed processing system have over linking dumb terminals to a mainframe in a multi-user system?

Local area networks

Distributed processing systems are usually referred to as networks. However, not all distributed processing systems are networks. In a network, each user is aware that there are other users with their own computers, which he can communicate with. It is possible to have a distributed processing system in which a user is unaware of the existence of other users, and the system automatically shares work between computers.

A local area network (LAN) is a system of interconnected PCs and other devices over a small area, typically within a few hundred metres, linked directly by cables. This use of cables distinguishes LANs from *wide* area networks, which may use telephone lines or radio links.

Most LANs include a *server* computer. As its name implies, it serves the rest of the network:

(a)   offering a shared hard disk file for all the other PCs (a *file server*);
(b)   sometimes offering other resources, such as a shared printer for the network (a *printer server*);
(c)   offering connections to long-distance communications links (a *communications server*);
(d)   offering access to a collection of software (a *library server*).

Network topologies

Basically, there are three types of LAN configuration: bus systems, rings and stars. A *network topology* is the physical arrangement of *nodes* in a network. A node can be a computer or a peripheral device such as a printer.

In a bus or tree structure, messages are sent out from one point along a single *bus*, and the messages are received by other connected computers. Messages identify the intended recipient, and a computer only accepts messages which contain its unique identifying code.

In a *ring system,* the cable in the network, and the computers in it, are joined in a ring. There may or may not be a server.

Ring system   *Star system*

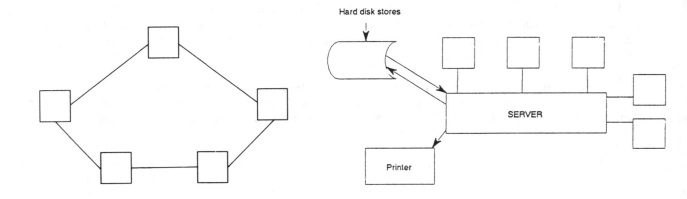

In a *star network*, there will be:

(a)   a central disk file and program store, controlled by a server computer;

(b)   cable linking the central computer to the other computers.

Why have LANs become so popular?

Local area networks have been successful for a number of reasons.

(a)   Networks have been made available to computer users at a fairly low price. Some computer users who could not afford a mainframe or minicomputer with terminal links have been able to afford a LAN with PCs.

(b)   Networks provide important advantages for the computer user.

   (i)   Data files can be shared by all the PCs in the network. With stand-alone PCs, each computer would have its own data files, and there might be unnecessary duplication of data. A system where everyone uses the same data helps to improve data processing and decision making. The value of information increases with its availability.

   (ii)   Each PC in a network can do the same work. If there were separate stand-alone PCs A, B and C, A might do job 1, B might do job 2 and C might do job 3. In a network, any PC (A, B or C) could do any job (1, 2 or 3). This provides flexibility in sharing workloads. In a peak period for job 1, say, two or more people can share the work without having to leave their own desks.

   (iii)   Peripheral equipment can be shared. For example, in a LAN, five PCs might share a single on-line printer, whereas if there were stand-alone PCs, each PC would need its own separate printer.

   (iv)   LANs can be linked up to external services via a communications server, thus adding to the processing capabilities in an office.

Exercise 6

Assume that a network is set up so that any user can read and work on files created by any other user. Give two reasons why this could sometimes be a disadvantage instead of an advantage.

Wide area networks (WANs)

Wide area networks (sometimes called long haul networks (LHNs)) are networks on a wide geographical scale. WANs often use minicomputers or mainframes as the 'pumps' which keep the data messages circulating, whereas LANs normally use PCs for this task. A wide area network is similar to a local area network in concept, but the differences are as follows.

(a) The geographical area covered by the network is wider.

(b) WANs will send data over telecommunications links. LANs, in contrast, will use direct cables for transmitting data.

(c) WANs will often use a larger computer as a server.

WANs will often be larger than LANs, with more computers linked to the network.

The advantages and disadvantages of distributed processing and networks

The advantages of using a distributed processing system compared with having a stand-alone centralised mainframe computer are as follows.

(a) There is greater flexibility in system design. The system can cater for both the specific needs of each local user of an individual computer and also for the needs of the organisation as a whole, by providing communications between different computers in the system.

(b) Since data files can be held locally, data transmission is reduced because each computer maintains its own files which provide most of the data it will need. This reduces the costs and security risks in data transmission.

(c) There is faster processing for both local offices and the central (head) office.

(d) There is scope for a *distributed database*. Data is held in a number of locations, but any user can access all of it for a global view.

(e) The effect of breakdowns is minimised, because a fault in one computer will not affect other computers in the system. With a centralised processing system, a fault in the mainframe computer would put the entire system out of service.

(f)   The fact that it is possible to acquire powerful PCs cheaply enables an organisation to dedicate them to particular applications. This in turn means that the computer system can be more readily tailored to the organisation's systems, rather than forcing the organisation to change its systems to satisfy the requirements for a mainframe computer.

(g)   Decentralisation allows for better local control over the physical and procedural aspects of the system.

(h)   Decentralised processing may facilitate greater user involvement and increase familiarity with the use of computer technology. The end user must accept responsibility for the accuracy of locally held files and local data processing.

Distributed processing has certain disadvantages, some of which might be overcome by future technological developments. These are that:

(a)   PCs have not had a large storage capacity in the past, and the programs needed for distributed processing have used up much of the storage capacity available. This disadvantage is now being eliminated by the development of more powerful PCs;

(b)   there may be duplication of data on the files of different computers. If this is the case, there may be some unnecessary storage costs;

(c)   a distributed network can be more difficult to administer and to maintain;

(d)   the items of equipment used in the system must be compatible with each other.

8   Processing methods

There are many different ways in which data can be processed, and we will end this chapter by considering the main ones. Different methods make different demands on communications links.

Batch processing

Batch processing means processing a group of similar routine transactions at the same time in one operation. The input transactions might be entered into the computer system all at once, or over a period of time, but computer processing does not begin until they have all been collected together in a transaction file. Much *bulk volume* routine processing is done on a batch processing basis.

Payroll work for salaried staff, for example, will usually be done in one operation once a month. To help with organising the work, the payroll office might deal with each department separately, and do the salaries for department 1, then the salaries for department 2, and then department 3, and so on. The batch processing would be carried out by dividing the transaction records into smaller batches, one batch per department.

Some delay in processing the transactions must be acceptable for batch processing to be used. For example, in a purchase ledger system it must be possible to pay invoices once a month (say) without provoking complaints from creditors.

Demand processing (transaction processing)

Demand processing (also called *transaction processing*) is carried out when batch processing would be inconvenient or undesirable and the user wants to process transactions on demand. It requires that the input device is *on-line* to the computer, that is connected to it and under its control.

Transactions for processing might arise infrequently, and so it would take too long to build up a batch for processing at the same time. Alternatively, the user might not be prepared to accept the delay implicit in batch processing. For example:

(a) if a final demand to pay an invoice is received, perhaps because the invoice had been overlooked, it might be decided to pay it at once;

(b) if a manager asks for some information from the data files, such as a statement of monthly sales figures for the past year, he will usually expect to have the work done on demand.

Exercise 7

A company makes several sales on credit each day. The input documents are batched and processed at the end of each week, when invoices are printed and posted. Customers are allowed 30 days from the invoice date (which is the same as the date of printing) to pay. Why might the company prefer this method to daily batch processing or demand processing, despite the longer credit period allowed to customers who buy early in the week?

Interactive processing

Interactive processing is a form of demand processing where:

(a) data is input to the computer;
(b) the data is processed immediately by the computer;
(c) the computer produces processed output.

An example of interactive processing is as follows.

(a) An operator inputs details of a transaction into the computer from a remote terminal.

(b) The computer processes the transaction and then outputs the results of the processing, usually on to a visual display screen.

(c) The operator notices an error in the output, or decides that some further processing is needed on the data, and so inputs more data.

(d) The computer processes the new input or amendment and displays the results, and so on until the operator is satisfied that the transaction has been fully and correctly processed.

Another example of interactive processing is a situation in which an operator wants to carry out several data processing operations on some input data, and the processing is divided into small stages. After each stage of processing, the computer will show the operator the results so far and sometimes even ask the operator in a message on the screen what he or she wants to do next. In effect, the processing is carried out by means of the operator and the computer talking to each other, and this form of interactive processing dialogue is referred to as *conversational mode* of data processing.

Real-time processing

Real-time processing is a form of interactive processing.

When a data processor wants to process transactions one at a time, and receive output information from the processing, he might simply want to get the job over and done with, and there is no other reason why he wants the processed output straightaway.

In other situations, however, the data processor might want the output so that he can use the information at once. The information would have an immediate effect on what is done next. There is real-time processing when the computer's response affects the immediate situation.

Examples of real-time systems

Real-time systems are invariably expensive, and the larger the system and the faster the response times required, the more expensive it is going to be. However the use of real-time systems is rapidly increasing and examples include the following.

(a) The *British Airways Booking System (BABS)*, which is operated by a central computer at Heathrow linked to British Airways agents in the UK and overseas via a communications network (telephone and satellite). An intending passenger may enquire at an airline office or travel agent for a flight to a particular place on a certain day. The reservation clerk is able to ascertain immediately if there is a vacancy, and then make a booking if required to do so. If no seats are available the computer will indicate possible alternatives for the customer's consideration. Thus the response to the original enquiry is received sufficiently quickly for the customer to await it, and make a decision based on that response.

(b) *Stock control in shops*. As a sale is made and details are recorded (perhaps by reading a bar code), the stock records are updated in real time. Any customer wishing to buy a product can be informed as to whether the item is available or not (if not, an alternative might be offered). Although the stock files are maintained in real time, other files (such as a sales analysis or a file of debtors) may be batch processed at a later stage with the accumulated sales details from each terminal. The computer can automatically order goods from suppliers should stocks fall below replenishment level.

Exercise 8

How might a customer of a bank use an automated teller machine in a way which would be an example of real-time processing?

Chapter roundup

(a) Data transmission occurs whenever data is sent from one data processing device to another.

(b) Communications links may include electrical cables, fibre optic cables and microwave and satellite links.

(c) Packet switching methods may be used to ensure efficient use of the available transmission media.

(d) A link may be simplex, half duplex or full duplex. Data may be transmitted synchronously or asynchronously, depending on the sending and receiving computers.

(e) Modems may be used to change the form of data before transmission.

(f) PCs may need to be modified before they can communicate with mainframe computers.

(g) In a multi-user system, dumb terminals cannot do their own data processing but PCs can.

(h) In distributed processing, data processing can be done by several computers.

(i) In a local area network, there are several computers linked to each other and to a server computer.

(j) Possible network topologies include buses, rings and stars.

(k) Wide area networks are spread over a large area, and generally use fairly large computers as servers.

(l) Distributed processing reduces data transmission and makes a system less vulnerable to breakdown, but it can lead to unnecessary duplication of data.

(m) Batch processing involves a delay in processing individual transactions, unlike demand processing.

(n) Interactive processing involves the computer promptly processing input and producing output.

(o) In real-time processing, output affects the immediate decisions of the computer user.

BPP Publishing

Quick quiz

1   How does a public line differ from a private line?

2   Why is the bandwidth of a telecommunications link important?

3   What is packet switching?

4   What type of transmission requires start and stop bits, and why?

5   Why are modems needed?

6   What is an emulation board used for?

7   What is a stand-alone computer?

8   What are the advantages of multi-user systems?

9   What is a server computer?

10   What is a bus structure?

11   How can a network enable work to be distributed more efficiently?

12   What is conversational mode?

Solutions to exercises

1   (a)   A would be more likely to use a leased line.
    (b)   B would be more likely to use bit serial transmission.

2   The first six bits of '5' are the same as the last six bits of 'j'. Thus it is necessary to know exactly where each ASCII character starts, either from a start bit or because sender and receiver know that they are in step, so that '5' and 'j' are not confused.

3   Hardware: modems, multiplexors, emulation boards.
    Software: emulation program.

4   There might be, say, 200 terminals but the processor might only be designed to handle 100 terminals at any one time. If all terminals were in use at once, the processor would have too much to do. A rationing system, in which some users are denied access to the computer at peak times, might be needed.

5   Some processing can be done by the PCs themselves, thus reducing demands on the central mainframe and on the communication links.

6   Some files would be confidential.

One user might be unaware that another user has altered the contents of a file.

7   The cost of the extra credit period might be greater than the extra cost of daily processing.

8   The customer could request his or her account balance, and then based on that balance decide how much cash to withdraw.

5 SOFTWARE

Your objectives

After completing this chapter you should:

(a) understand the need for programming languages;

(b) be able to distinguish between low level and high level languages;

(c) know the names of several languages, and the main uses of some high level languages;

(d) understand why programs in high level languages need to be compiled or interpreted;

(e) understand the role of fourth generation languages;

(f) know what tasks are performed by an operating system;

(g) be able to give a list of utilities normally provided with an operating system;

(h) understand the benefits of multitasking and multiprogramming;

(i) understand the concept of open systems, and be aware of the main features of Unix;

(j) be aware of recent developments in microcomputer operating systems;

(k) know the difference between applications software and general purpose software.

1   What is software?

A computer operates under the control of instructions normally collected in a program. All programs used by computers are known as *software.*

Some software is built into the computer's ROM memory. Other software must be loaded into the computer's RAM memory from elsewhere, for example from a disk.

2 Programming languages

Programming languages are the various languages that programs are written in. There are many different languages. A programming language is neither the normal written language of human beings, nor is it usually the strings of 1s and 0s used by processors. This might seem odd. Why is it necessary to invent new languages for programming a computer?

A computer can only deal with data and program instructions which are in *binary* form (the 1 and 0 corresponding to the ON and OFF states of an electronic component). So every program must be in a computer's *machine code* (which only uses 1s and 0s) before the computer can do anything with it. Writing in machine code is difficult, because it takes a long time to learn, and is therefore usually restricted to programs developed by the computer manufacturers themselves. A program in a programming language can be translated *into* machine code. The programming language is easier for humans to use, being more condensed and displaying a logic that human beings can understand.

Source programs and object programs

The program written in a programming language is called the *source program* or *source code*. The translation into machine code is done by a specialised translation program. The translated program in its machine code (or machine language) version is called the *object program* or *object code*.

3 Machine code

A program instruction in machine code defines a particular machine operation that the computer can obey. A typical machine code instruction consists of two parts:

(a) one or more *address fields*, which specify the addresses in the computer's memory where the data can be found; and

(b) an *operation code*, which states what operation should be carried out on the data.

The programmer writing in machine code has to know the operation codes used in the particular computer, and the physical locations in store and physical lengths of data items. Because the machine code is determined by the computer hardware design, machine codes are said to be *machine specific*. Machine code application programs could be written, but this would normally be too complex and time consuming.

4 Assembly languages

Assembly languages (also known as *low level languages*) are a development from machine code. They are also machine specific, but the task of learning and writing the language is made easier than with machine code because they are written in *symbolic* form. Instead of using machine code operation numbers, the programmer is able to use easily-learned and understood operation mnemonics (for example, ADD, SUB and MULT), and *symbolic data locations* (names allocated by the programmer and used to refer to particular data areas in the program) instead of addresses.

BPP Publishing

For the most part one instruction must be written in an assembly language program to create one instruction in machine code, but this is not always necessary. There are some *macro instructions* in any assembly language which, when translated into machine code, become several machine code instructions. Macro instructions make programs written in an assembly language shorter than machine code programs.

Assemblers: translation programs for assembly languages

The assembly language must be translated into machine code. Computer manufacturers will supply an *assembler program* which translates the operation mnemonics and replaces the symbolic data locations by the addresses reserved for them. The assembly language source program is thus *assembled* into the machine code object program, the process involving translation, the allocation of storage space and the detection of errors in the program.

Once the source program has been assembled into the object program in machine code it is on file and can be used for data processing. The program has to be assembled only once.

An assembly language for a computer is designed to make full use of the *particular* computer's processing capabilities and so is designed to give the most efficient coding to each part of a computer program.

Exercise 1

Why would a computer manufacturer be unable to write an assembler program in assembly language?

5   High level languages

To overcome the low level language difficulty of machine dependency, *high level* (or machine independent) languages were developed. Such programming languages with an extensive vocabulary of words and symbols are used to instruct a computer to carry out the necessary procedures, regardless of the type of machine being used.

The main purposes of a high level language are as follows.

(a)   Improving the productivity of programmers.

(i)   An instruction written in a high level language may produce many machine code instructions when it is translated into machine code. There is no clear visible relationship between a high level language program and the machine code that it eventually becomes. High level language source programs are shorter than low level language source programs, and programs can be written comparatively quickly.

(ii)   New programmers can be trained more quickly as they need only learn the language, not the detailed layout of the processor.

(b) Enabling programs to be used on different types of computer without having to re-write them. A program written in COBOL, for example, can be moved from one make of computer to another simply by re-translating the source program into a new object program. This is not the case with low level languages, because each low level language is specific to a particular make or range of computers.

(c) Speeding up testing and error correction.

(d) Making programs easier to understand.

Some high level languages are said to be *problem-oriented*, because they have been created to deal with particular types of data processing problem. Thus FORTRAN is designed for scientific applications and COBOL for commercial applications. Some high level languages are more general purpose, and have been developed simply to make the task of programming easier (for example BASIC). When a high level language is problem-oriented, it will handle other types of problem (for which it was not designed) inefficiently or not at all.

Some examples of high level languages are:

(a) COBOL, used for business data processing;

(b) BASIC, designed for beginners, particularly on microcomputers. Several enhanced versions of BASIC are available;

(c) FORTRAN, a scientific language;

(d) CORAL, a language well-suited to on-line real time systems;

(e) PASCAL, well-suited to the structured programming technique;

(f) C, a language developed for the Unix operating system, which combines high-level language capabilities with the ability to address hardware (like an assembly language).

The main disadvantage of using a high level language as opposed to a low level language is that high level languages cannot usually take advantage of specific facilities on individual machines. Programs written in high level languages are therefore unlikely to be as efficient in terms of processing speed and the use of memory as programs written in machine code or in assembly language. However, with recent falls in the cost of memory and improvements in processing speed, this disadvantage is becoming less significant.

Compilers: translation programs for high-level languages

As with a program in assembly language, a high level language program has to be translated into machine code before it can be used. This is done by a *compiler program*, supplied by the manufacturer as software which *compiles* the source program into the object program. This involves translating the program, identifying errors and storing the object program in a storage device. Once compiled and tested the object program is ready for operational use. As with the assembly process, once a source program in a high level language has been compiled, the object program in machine code is filed and can be used whenever it is required for data processing. The source program has to be compiled only once.

An *interpreter* does the same sort of job as an assembler or compiler, but in a different way. It takes a program written in a high level language and executes it, instruction by instruction, during the running of the program. With an interpreter, there is no need for a compiler to produce machine code in advance. On the other hand, the program must be interpreted afresh each time it is run.

The *advantage* of an interpreter over a compiler is that it is suitable for *interactive work*, where the programmer wishes to test (or amend) the program segments on-line, as the results can be seen immediately.

The *disadvantages* of an interpreter are:

(a) it is slow;

(b) it uses up more memory, because although the high level language program in memory is shorter than its machine code equivalent, the interpreter program must also be in memory at the same time.

An interpreter is useful for those who wish to write small programs for their own use. BASIC is interpreted rather than compiled.

Exercise 2

A company wishes to write its own (large) program to prepare detailed weekly management accounts, and then to recoup the cost of writing the program by selling copies of it to other companies. Why would COBOL be a better choice of programming language than either BASIC or an assembly language?

---

6 Programming aids and fourth generation languages

Programming aids or programming tools are programs which are provided to help programmers to do their work. The term 'tools' is a fairly recent one, and is used loosely to mean any software productivity aid for programmers. Examples of programming tools are:

(a) *program development systems* which help users to learn programming, and to program in a high level language. Using a VDU and keyboard terminal under the direction of an interactive program, users are helped to construct application programs;

(b) a *program generator* or *applications generator*. This is a program which assists users to write their own programs, by expanding simple statements into full programs;

Fourth generation languages

Fourth generation languages, or 4GLs, are intended to help computer users or computer programmers to develop their own application programs quickly and cheaply. A 4GL, by using a menu system for example, allows users to specify what they require, rather than describe the procedures by which these requirements are to be met. The 4GL produces a program in a high level language to meet the user's needs, and that program can then be compiled.

A 4GL is therefore a *non-procedural language*. The programmer decides what he or she wants, but does not specify the procedures to achieve the desired result.

4GLs arose partly in response to the *applications backlog*. A great deal of programming time is spent maintaining and improving old programs rather than building new ones. Many organisations therefore have a backlog of applications waiting to be developed. 4GLs, by speeding up the process of application design and by making it easier for users to build their own programs, help to reduce it.

Exercise 3

A user of a 4GL may get a computer to achieve the desired results without understanding the procedures the computer uses to do so. Could this be a disadvantage of the use of 4GLs?

---

7 Operating system software and utilities

As computer systems developed over the years, and processors became more powerful and operated at higher speeds, it became apparent that inefficient use was being made of processors by human operators. The problems arose because of the *set up times* required to load the peripheral units (with tapes, paper and so on), the manual intervention required to investigate problems and the slowness of peripheral units in comparison with processors. It became apparent that the handling of most *computer operations* could best be done by means of stored programs. A whole package of control programs makes up an *operating system* (OS). An operating system provides the interface between the computer hardware and both the user (via the keyboard and VDU) and the other software. Leading operating systems include MS-DOS and Unix.

An OS will typically perform the following tasks.

(a) Initial set-up of the computer, when it is switched on. This is achieved by the boot (or *bootstrap*) program, which is normally resident in ROM. It summons the rest of the OS from backing storage into RAM.

(b) Checking that the hardware (including peripheral devices) is functioning properly.

(c) Calling up program files and data files from external storage into memory.

(d) Opening and closing files, checking file labels and so on.

(e) Assigning program and data files from memory to peripheral devices.

(f) Maintaining directories in external storage.

(g) Controlling input and output devices, including the interaction with the computer user.

(h) Controlling system security (for example monitoring the use of passwords).

(i)   Handling interrupts (program abnormalities or machine failures).

(j)   Applying checkpoint procedures. If there is some catastrophe, the entire contents of memory can be recorded *(dumped)* in a storage device and printed for investigation. Sometimes checkpoint programs will be implemented dumping memory contents onto a disk as a matter of routine, so that if processing is interrupted, it can be continued from the most recent checkpoint.

(k)   Managing multitasking and multiprogramming (see below).

(l)   *Spooling*. This means collecting data which is waiting to be processed or waiting to be output (for example printed) in a storage device, until it can be processed or output. Thus spooling is a form of buffering, but instead of (for example) sending output into the printer's own buffer memory, it is kept within a storage device under the processor's control. When the printer is free, it is taken from that storage device by the processor and sent to the printer.

Software companies writing software packages (such as word processing programs) must write each software package for a specific operating system. A PC user must be aware of what operating system his PC uses in order to establish whether a particular software package will run on it. More packages have been written for MS-DOS than for other operating systems. However, the more popular off-the-shelf software packages are available in different versions, one for each of the leading operating systems.

Utilities

A utility program does routine jobs which frequently arise. Whilst strictly speaking a utility is not part of the OS, utility programs are provided with the OS software. MS-DOS, for example, includes a number of utilities.

Examples of utilities include:

(a)   file conversion (transferring data or program files from one output or storage medium to another);

(b)   file copying (producing back-up files). MS-DOS, for example, allows you to copy files from hard disk to tape;

(c)   memory dumping, as part of a checkpoint program;

(d)   listing files;

(e)   comparing the contents of two disks, if one has been copied from another;

(f)   deleting files;

(g)   sending files to a printer or other output device;

(h)   renaming files;

(i)   sorting data by key field sequence.

Multitasking and multiprogramming

As the processor works much faster than any peripheral device, processor time is wasted to the extent that processing times depend on the speeds of these peripheral units. Wasted processor time can be reduced by the simultaneous use of more than one peripheral device (simultaneity), so that the processor can be receiving some input A from one peripheral device, processing data B and sending output C to another peripheral device all at the same time.

In spite of simultaneity, a computer's processor is still idle for a large part of the time. Multitasking and multiprogramming enable several programs to share the use of the processor and take up the under-used capacity.

In multitasking, one user does more than one thing simultaneously (for example print one document while editing another). In multiprogramming, the processor runs several programs at once, executing bits of each in turn.

Some programs will be *peripheral bound*, requiring considerably more input/output time than processor time, while others will be *processor bound*, requiring more processor time than input/output time. The programs used in a multiprogramming or multitasking operation should ideally comprise a mix of peripheral bound and processor bound programs which can be put in an order of priority.

With a large number of programs and peripheral units, the processor can be kept occupied for almost 100% of the time. This needs a suitable operating system, whose functioning in turn requires:

(a)   sufficient memory to hold all programs and the data to be processed by each program;

(b)   *memory protection* (a user must not be allowed access to parts of memory not allocated to his program and data);

(c)   *a priority rating* for each program. The highest priority program (usually the most peripheral bound) is allowed to use the processor whenever it can (for example after an input/output transfer). When the program can no longer use the processor, the operating system allocates processing time to the next program in line. Whenever a higher priority program is ready to use the processor, the operating system *interrupts* the lower priority program and gives processor time to the higher priority one.

Operating systems and the user interface

The operating system controls how the user relates to the computer system and the processing operation.

Readers familiar with DOS will be aware of the fact that the user interface is based on a series of commands, and in most DOS manuals, a long list of commands can be found to enable the user to manipulate the system, access the utilities provided with the system software and so forth. For example, if you are using a PC with a hard disk that is called drive C and you wish to delete a text (or document) file named MTI, then after the prompt C> you will type in DELETE MTI.DOC and then press return.

This type of screen dialogue is being overtaken by more user-friendly techniques, as we have seen, including the *graphical user interface*. IBM's operating system designed for 32-bit PCs uses Presentation Manager as its graphical user interface. Microsoft *Windows* can be used with MS-DOS. Machines using the Unix operating system can be run with X Windows. Apple computers tend to have their own graphical user interfaces, as the Apple operating system is only used by Apple computers.

Exercise 4

A computer runs two programs for two different users at once. Program A requires 15 seconds of processor time and five minutes of printer time. Program B requires one minute of processor time and one minute of printer time. In both cases, some of the printing can be done when only part of the program has been executed by the processor. Which of the two programs should be given priority if both of them request processor time simultaneously?

---

8 Developments in operating systems

Operating systems in a network environment

So far, the discussion of operating systems has been limited to consideration of the interaction between one processor and the peripheral devices attached to it. An OS is also needed to control the interaction and communication between the various computers and peripherals in a LAN or WAN. There are two approaches to this problem.

(a) A separate networking operating system can be put in charge of the operating systems of the individual computers. As MS-DOS was designed purely for personal computing, this is the solution necessary when machines using MS-DOS are to be linked. An example of network OS is Novell's *Netware*.

(b) An operating system in which networking facilities are an integral part of the design can be used. An example of such an operating system is Unix.

Open systems

Open systems aim to ensure compatibility between different makes of equipment and software, enabling users to choose on the basis of price and performance.

It is arguable that in the PC market there is already a sort of *de facto* open systems arrangement, given that there are so many makes of PC using MS-DOS. However, whilst MS-DOS is ideal for stand-alone PCs, it had a number of limitations, in that:

(a) it has limitations when it comes to multitasking;

(b) it is basically single-user;

(c) it was developed originally for the IBM PC, and it may not be powerful or flexible enough to make full use of the more recent 32-bit PCs.

Until recently many computer users have not given a great deal of though to their operating system. Purchasers of mainframes and PCs are supplied with a proprietary system by the hardware manufacturer and that is usually the end of the story. IBM users have OS/VS, ICL users have VME and each machine will only run on its own system. Recently, the market has changed. Mainframe and mini users are talking of Unix and PC users, instead of accepting MS-DOS, can choose the new systems OS/2 or Windows NT. Suddenly, there is consumer choice in an area where users have traditionally had to use what they were given.

Unix

The Unix operating system was developed by AT&T in 1969 as a multi-tasking operating system that could be used on computers with different architectures. It is an example of an *open system*. It first gained popularity in universities, where many computer science students needed to be able to work at the same time, but was seen as lacking in user-friendliness and uneconomic by commercial suppliers and users. However, its popularity among those who used it ensured that it survived and by the 1980s it had been developed far enough for commercial users to take an interest in it.

Unix works equally well in a network environment as in a multi-user system. Particular areas where Unix has already demonstrated its capabilities are communications, where the ability to accommodate other operating systems in the Unix environment supports the use of electronic mail, and engineering, where Unix's capabilities are suited to running high-resolution graphics systems.

The strategic decision is whether, in the long term, an organisation should change to open systems. In principle, there seems little to be said against it. It has government support. The UK Department of Trade and Industry is encouraging firms to take an interest. It might also be noted that ICL, the UK's major indigenous computer company, took the open systems route many years ago. The European Community is also encouraging open systems. The hardware is reputedly cheaper and much easier to upgrade than that of most proprietary systems.

Unix is perhaps best able to satisfy another trend towards managerial workstations. Unix allows a user to carry out a number of tasks concurrently, at the same terminal (a different window appearing for each task), or to use computing resources on other machines in the network.

On the other hand, many users have already invested large amounts in other systems. If these are working well, there is little point in changing over, at least in the short term.

Open systems may be a sensible choice for an organisation which:

(a) is contemplating a major change in its computer systems in any case;

(b) is contemplating a substantial increase in the use of information technology throughout the organisation;

(c) requires multiuser, multitasking computers.

Exercise 5

A company decides to change to an open system. Why is the change likely to be of greater benefit to managers than to staff carrying out routine data input?

PC operating systems

Just when Unix looks set to become the standard choice for mainframes and minicomputers, the operating system which has been the natural choice for PCs is under threat from two new systems. *OS/2* was developed jointly by IBM and Microsoft to replace the latter's MS-DOS. Microsoft have now ended their involvement with the project and so IBM have released OS/2 alone. Microsoft have followed a different route, developing *Windows NT*.

OS/2

The feature of OS/2 which is likely to be most popular is its multitasking capability. The user can switch between computer applications without being forced to follow long exit procedures from one and entry procedures to the other.

Like Windows, OS/2 offers a graphics-based interface rather than MS-DOS's text-based approach. Graphical interfaces can be tailored to meet the needs of the organisation, and standard icons can be replaced with graphics created by the user or imported from any of a number of packages now on the market which offer a wide range of alternatives.

Windows NT

Windows was originally developed to use within the MS-DOS operating system, but Microsoft have recently launched Windows NT, a complete operating system in its own right. This will place it in direct competition with OS/2. Windows NT offers a full graphical user interface, so that the user, instead of having to memorise commands to type in after the 'C prompt', can either pull down menus and select commands from them or point to icons to make selections.

Windows NT provides a comprehensive working environment, managing both programs specifically written for it (WordPerfect for Windows, Lotus 123 for Windows and so on) and those which were written for DOS (WordPerfect, Lotus 123 and so on).

Exercise 6

Explain how a finance director preparing a report for the board of directors might benefit from the multitasking facilities offered by OS/2 and Windows NT.

9 General purpose software and applications software

A distinction can be made between general purpose software and applications software.

(a) *General purpose software* can be used for processing of a general type, but the computer user can apply the software to a variety of specific uses of his own choice. Spreadsheets are an example.

(b) *Applications software* will carry out a specific processing application: for example, sales ledger software would enable a computer user to do sales ledger processing work and payroll software would be specific to payroll processing.

General purpose packages provide ready-made general purpose software. *Application packages* are ready-made programs written to perform a particular job. The job will be common to many potential users, so that the package could be adopted by all of them for their data processing operations.

As an alternative to using packages, software of either type can be specially written. However, specially written applications software is far more common than specially written general purpose software.

In the next chapter we will look at general purpose packages, and in the following chapter we will look at applications software.

Chapter roundup

(a)   A computer can only execute instructions in machine code, which is unintelligible to most people.

(b)   To bridge the gap between everyday language and machine code, programming languages are used.

(c)   Assembly languages are low level, machine specific languages.

(d)   High level languages, which can be used with several makes of computer, include BASIC, COBOL and FORTRAN.

(e)   Programs must be assembled, compiled or interpreted in order to convert them into machine code instructions.

(f)   Fourth generation languages enable users to specify their requirements, which are then automatically converted into programs in high level languages.

(g)   An operating system is in overall charge of a computer, supervising the execution of programs and the running of peripheral devices.

(h)   Utilities operate on files as a whole, without regard to their contents, performing commonly required tasks.

(i)   Multitasking and multiprogramming are responses to the fact that peripheral devices work much more slowly than processors.

(j)   Open systems are designed to allow users a free choice of hardware and software, and facilitate networking.

(k)   Recent developments in PC operating systems include OS/2 and Windows NT.

(l)   Applications software carries out specific tasks, whereas general purpose software can be used for a wide variety of tasks.

Quick quiz

1 Why is an assembly language easier to use than machine code?

2 Give some examples of problem-oriented high level languages, and the corresponding types of problem.

3 How does a compiler differ from an interpreter?

4 Why are fourth generation languages described as non-procedural?

5 List the tasks typically performed by an operating system.

6 What utilities are commonly supplied with an operating system?

7 What tasks must an operating system perform in order to allow multiprogramming?

8 In what situations might an organisation do best to change to open systems?

9 What are the significant features of Windows NT?

Solutions to exercises

1 An assembly language program cannot be assembled into a form which a computer can use until an assembler program has been written. The assembler program must therefore be written in machine code.

2 COBOL is compiled whereas BASIC is interpreted, so COBOL is better for large programs. COBOL is machine independent (unlike assembly language), so copies of the program could be sold to users with other types of computer.

3 Yes: someone who does not understand how a program works may fail to understand its limitations.

4 Program A should have priority, because it is the more peripheral bound.

5 Routine data input requirements are likely to change only slowly, and the work done by the staff can be standardised. Managers, on the other hand, often want new ways of analysing and presenting information, and want good communication links to each others' computers.

6 The finance director might type some text, draw up a table and prepare a graph. On looking at the graph he might decide to change the text, and then amend the table. Thus several different types of job would need to be done in quick succession.

BPP Publishing

6 GENERAL PURPOSE PACKAGES

Your objectives

After completing this chapter you should:

(a) know how a spreadsheet is used for financial calculations;

(b) appreciate the use of spreadsheets in sensitivity analysis;

(c) be aware of additional features available with some spreadsheet packages;

(d) appreciate the usefulness of word processors;

(e) be aware of word processing facilities which can enhance the appearance of documents;

(f) appreciate the sophisticated presentation facilities available in desktop publishing;

(g) know the ways in which data can be presented graphically by a computer;

(h) know the main output devices for computer graphics;

(i) appreciate the uses of financial modelling packages.

---

1 Introduction

There are several types of package usually classified as general purpose packages. They can be tailored by the user for a wide range of applications. In this chapter we will examine the features and uses of:

(a) spreadsheets;
(b) word processing (WP);
(c) desk top publishing (DTP);
(d) graphics;
(e) modelling packages.

2 What is a spreadsheet?

A spreadsheet is a type of software package for financial modelling. The computer's VDU monitor displays a sheet divided into rows and columns, and figures or text can be inserted into the boxes on the sheet. Examples of spreadsheets are Supercalc, Lotus 123 and Excel.

Uses of spreadsheets

Some of the more common uses of spreadsheets are:

(a)   cash flow analysis/forecasting;
(b)   inventory records;
(c)   job cost estimates;
(d)   market share analysis and planning;
(e)   profit projections;
(f)   tax estimation.

What all these uses have in common is that they all involve data processing with:

(a)   numerical data;
(b)   repetitive, time-consuming calculations;
(c)   a logical processing structure.

The great value of spreadsheets derives from their simple format of rows and columns of data, and the ability of users to have direct access themselves to their spreadsheet models via their own PCs. For example, an accountant can construct a cash flow model with a spreadsheet package on a PC in his or her office: he or she can create the model, input the data, manipulate the data and read or print the output directly. He or she will also have access to the model whenever it is needed.

What does a spreadsheet look like?

When a blank spreadsheet is loaded into a computer, the VDU monitor will show lines of empty rows and columns. The rows are usually numbered 1, 2, 3 ... and the columns lettered A, B, C ... . Typically, it will look like this.

Each box in the table, for example column A row 1, column A row 2 or column B row 1, is referred to as a *cell*.

The screen will not be able to show all the columns and rows: Lotus 123 contains 230 columns and 8,192 rows. The spreadsheet will 'scroll' in any direction when the user operates the cursor keys on the keyboard, to find the rows and columns that the user wishes to look at. If the user wishes to look at two different parts of a spreadsheet on the screen at the same time, there is a command in all spreadsheet packages which enables the user to split the screen. It is usually called a 'window' command, and enables two separate parts of a large spreadsheet to be viewed at the same time on the screen.

A spreadsheet, then, consists of a large number of cells, each identified by a reference such as A4, D16 or AA20. (After Z, we have AA, AB and so on.) The screen cursor will highlight a particular cell: in the illustration above, it is placed over cell B1. At the top or bottom of the screen, the spreadsheet program will give you such information as:

(a)   the reference of the cell where the cursor lies;

(b)   the width of the column where the cursor lies (you can alter column widths to suit yourself, up to about 100 characters, without changing the total number of columns available on the spreadsheet);

(c)   the contents of the cell where the cursor lies, if there is anything there.

The contents of any cell can be one of the following.

(a)   *Text*. A text cell, or label cell, contains words or numerical data that cannot be used in computations (such as a date) providing it is so designated. Lotus 123 requires you to insert an apostrophe before a number if that number is to be read as an item of text.

(b)   *A value*. A value is a number that can be used in a calculation.

(c)   *A formula*. A formula refers to other cells in the spreadsheet, and performs some sort of computation with them. For example, if cell C1 contains the formula +A1-B1 this means that the contents of cell B1 will be subtracted from the contents of cell A1 and the result displayed in cell C1. If the amount in A1 is changed, the amount in C1 will change as well. (The + sign before A1 indicates that cell A1 contains a number or a formula, and is not a text cell.)

(d)   *A macro*. Macros are automated commands (see below).

Exercise 1

In a spreadsheet, cell A1 contains the number 2. Cell A2 contains the formula +A3-A1. Cell A3 contains the formula +A2-A4. Cell A4 contains the number 5. What is wrong with this spreadsheet?

---

3   Spreadsheets in practice

The user constructs a model in rows and columns format, by:

(a)   identifying what data goes into each row and column and inserting text, for example column headings and row identifications;

(b) specifying how the numerical data in the model should be derived. Numerical data might be:

   (i) inserted into the model via keyboard input;

   (ii) calculated from other data in the model by means of a formula specified within the model itself. The user must insert these formulae into the model; or

   (iii) occasionally, obtained from data on a disk file.

Example: constructing a profit and loss account model

Suppose that you wanted to set up a simple profit and loss account, in such a way that you could use it to estimate how the net profit will change in total when any individual item is altered. You know that cost of sales is 40% of sales, but that distribution expenses do not vary over a reasonable range of sales.

Inserting text

The first job is to put in the various headings that you want. It is usually convenient to start at row 1 and column A, although this is not essential.

At this stage, your screen might look as follows.

	: A	: B	: C
1:			
2:		£'000	£'000
3:			
4:	Sales		
5:	Less cost of sales		
6:	Gross profit		
7:			
8:	Administration expenses		
9:	Distribution expenses		
10:	Finance expenses		
11:	Total expenses		
12:			
13:	Net profit		

The 'A' column has been widened so that long titles will fit into it and not spill over.

Inserting formulae

The next stage in constructing a model is to put in the calculations you want the computer to carry out, expressed as formulae. For example, referring back to our example, in cell C11 you want total expenses, so you put in the formula + B8 + B9 + B10. This could also be written as
@ SUM (B8..B10).

Other formulae required for this example are:

(a) in cell C5:   +C4 * 0.4 (* is used for multiplication)
(b) in cell C6:   +C4 – C5
(c) in cell C13:   +C6 – C11

Unlike the text, these formulae will not be shown on the spreadsheet itself, but at the top or bottom of the screen when the cursor is over the relevant cell. So at this stage, the spreadsheet looks just the same as it did after setting up the headings, except that when the cursor is on a cell where a formula has been input, that formula is shown at the top or bottom of the screen.

Our example only uses plus and minus functions and multiplication, but most spreadsheets offer several functions including:

(a) division;
(b) multiplication of items by a constant factor;
(c) square roots;
(d) logical functions (such as true or false);
(e) financial analysis (such as discounted cash flow);
(f) statistical functions (such as standard deviation).

Inserting numerical data

The last stage in setting up a spreadsheet is to input data. In our example, suppose that sales are £17m. This would be input as a figure into cell C4 and the computer would automatically show the cost of sales in cell C5 and the gross profit in cell C6, using the formulae already specified in the model. Other data would be input to cells B8, B9, and B10.

The completed profit and loss account might look like this.

	: A	: B	: C
1:			
2:		£'000	£'000
3:			
4:	Sales		17,000
5:	Less cost of sales		6,800
6:	Gross profit		10,200
7:			
8:	Administration expenses	600	
9:	Distribution expenses	1,200	
10:	Finance expenses	800	
11:	Total expenses		2,600
12:			
13:	Net profit		7,600

Using spreadsheet model for sensitivity analysis

Whenever a forecast or budget is made, management should consider asking 'what if' questions, and so carry out a form of sensitivity analysis.

With our example, 'what if' questions for sensitivity analysis might be:

(a) what if the cost of sales is 43% of sales?

(b) what if administration expenses rise by 25%?

Using the spreadsheet model, the answers to these questions, and others like them, could be obtained simply and quickly, using the editing facility in the program. Managers could then work out what changes might lead to budgeted profit not being achieved.

Exercise 2

Returning to the above example of a profit and loss account, suppose that you want to show in cell C15 the sum of the cost of sales and the administration and distribution expenses. What formula would you put in that cell?

---

4   Features of spreadsheets

Spreadsheets are versatile tools. Different spreadsheets will offer different facilities, but some of the more basic ones which should feature in all spreadsheet programs are as follows.

(a) *Print* commands. You should be able to print the contents of the spreadsheet in total or in part, with or without the spreadsheet row and column labels.

(b) *File* commands. You should be able to *save* the spreadsheet model for further use as a *file* on your disk, either all of it or just part of it. Other file commands allow you to *combine* data from another spreadsheet model with the present one (for example, the prior year's profit and loss account could be inserted alongside the current year's).

(c) *Cell editing facilities*. The program should allow alteration of anything shown on the spreadsheet. This is particularly useful for *'what if?'* calculations. For instance, in our example, you might want to know what net profit would be if the cost of sales were 43% of sales. Using the editing facility, you would only have to change the formula in cell C5 to + C4 * 0.43, then ask the computer to recalculate the entire spreadsheet on the basis of the new figures.

(d) *Facilities to rearrange the spreadsheet*

   (i)   *Insert* a row or column at a desired spot. For example, you might wish to split finance expenses into overdraft interest and long term loan interest. The insert command facilitates this, and the formulae in the spreadsheet are adjusted automatically.

   (ii) *Move* or *copy* a cell, row, column or block of cells elsewhere.

   (iii) *Delete* a row or column.

(e) *Sort*. A spreadsheet package will usually provide a facility for sorting data alphabetically or numerically.

(f) *Copy* a formula. For example, suppose you wanted to have a cumulative total of a list of numbers, as follows.

	A	:	B	:	C	:
1:						
2:	9		9			
3:	10		19			
4:	14		33			
5:	3		36			
6:	86		122			
7:	9		131			

The numbers in the A column are data. The cumulative numbers in the B column are calculated from the formulae B2 = A2; B3 = +B2 + A3; B4 = +B3 + A4 and so on. Clearly it would take a long time to input all these formulae individually, and so to save time it is possible to input +B2 + A3 in the B3 cell, and then *copy* the formula down the column. It is usually possible to copy downwards or sideways throughout the spreadsheet, and the computer will automatically change the formula to give the right cell addresses, in this instance the cell above plus the cell to the left. This is described as treating the cell addresses in the formula as *relative* cell addresses. *Absolute* cell addresses can also be specified, so that when a formula is copied into another cell the cell addresses do not change.

(g) *Format.* This command controls the way in which headings and data are shown, for example by altering column widths or changing the number of decimal places displayed. You can format a selected *range* of cells, or the whole spreadsheet.

(h) Many spreadsheets offer a *graphics* facility, so that data can be displayed as bar charts or pie charts.

(i) *Macros.* Many spreadsheet facilities are provided as *commands* in a menu. Some procedures require a number of commands to be executed. This is often time consuming.

For example, if you wish to print some or all of your spreadsheet, you will first execute the *print* command.

You may then see a menu which asks you to specify for example:

(i) what part of the spreadsheet you wish to print;
(ii) the length of the pages you are using in the printer, what you wish the size of the margins to be and so forth.

Many spreadsheets provide a *macro* facility. This allows the user to automate a sequence of commands, executing them by pressing two keys.

(j) Some spreadsheets offer a *search and replace* facility to highlight and alter individual formulae.

(k) Some spreadsheets offer a *protect* facility, to ensure that the contents of a specified range of cells cannot be overwritten.

Three-dimensional spreadsheets

One of the problems with using spreadsheets for financial modelling is that spreadsheets work only in two dimensions (columns and rows). Combining information in three dimensions is difficult. For example, you might wish to produce financial statements for a number of companies in a group, as well as the consolidated results for the group as a whole, analysed over a number of months. In a normal two-dimensional spreadsheet you would have, say, the months across the top as columns, and the income and expenditure down the side as rows. If there is more than one company involved you would have to repeat this design separately for each company.

Lotus 123 version 3, released in 1989, has a facility that permits working in *three* dimensions, as 256 *sheets* can be held in memory at one time. A filing cabinet is perhaps a good analogy, as the user can flip between different sheets in a file. Cells in one sheet may refer to cells in another sheet. In our example, the front sheet would be the consolidated results, and the other sheets the results for the constituent companies. The formulae in the cells in the front sheet could refer to the cells in the spreadsheets behind it.

Exercise 3

In a spreadsheet, the formula in cell D8 is @SUM(A2..A6)*(+B4-C2). All addresses are relative. This formula is copied to cell G22. What will the resulting formula in cell G22 be?

---

5 Word processing (WP)

Word processors are computers which provide a system for storing letters and text on disk, recalling them at a later time and possibly amending them so as to reproduce them with slight variations (such as a change of name and address on a letter). Corrections are easily keyed in. Word processors may be dedicated machines, for word processing only, or may be general purpose computers (normally PCs) using word processing software packages. Leading packages include Word and WordPerfect.

Certain features of word processing are worth emphasising.

(a) Text which is keyed in can be merged with other text already held on a file (such as common text for standard letters). The facility to merge some keyed-in text with text on file enables the user to produce personalised standard letters quickly and with few keying-in errors.

(b) Word processing enables the person preparing the text to check the input visually on the VDU screen as it is being keyed in, and to correct errors immediately (some spelling checks can be built into the word processing software).

(c) The user can easily make amendments to the original text.

BPP Publishing

(i)   If the contents of the text are discussed and as a result of these discussions, changes are agreed, the changes can be made quickly and simply. For example, contracts under negotiation can be amended in this way.

(ii)   Text can be held on file and subsequently updated. For example, a company might hold its rules and procedures books, or its price lists on a file and update them just before they are to be reprinted. Updating can be done quickly and with a low error rate.

6   Using WP

Different word processing packages have been developed with different design philosophies as to the user interface.

(a)   Some packages use a system of *commands* whereby the operator remembers a number of keystrokes (or consults a list of commands in a *help* facility) and uses them appropriately.

(b)   Some packages use a *menu system,* whereby, at the top or bottom of the screen, a number of options are listed. Some packages operate several menus.

(c)   Finally, some packages employ a WIMP interface (for example using an icon of a pair of scissors for 'cut and paste' editing). Some packages are available in versions which run with Microsoft's *Windows*. They can be identified by their titles, for example Word for Windows and WordPerfect for Windows.

The WYSIWYG (What You See Is What You Get) facility is another helpful feature for users who wish to see on screen exactly the format and typeface they will get on paper. Thus italics would actually appear on screen as italics rather than being indicated by a code.

Document creation

When saved onto backing store, a word processed letter, for example, is a file of data, like any other file. So creating a document requires giving it a name and setting it up as a file. In some word processors, setting up a document may also involve filling in a formatted screen giving basic details about the document (such as the originator, the destination or the date).

There is a limit to the number of characters which can be held in the processor's memory at any one time. When the document is longer than memory allows, part of it must be saved on disk as a file in its own right, rather like a chapter in a book. However it should be relatively easy to move between these subdocuments.

The word processor screen is first of all given all the characteristics of a sheet of paper. The operator is able to specify the *width* and *length* of the area the text is to cover on the page, taking into account desired margins when the text is printed on to paper. If the text area is larger than the screen can accommodate, the operator can scroll up and down or to pan from side to side in order to view a page.

Editing

Once the text in its basic form has been keyed in, the editing facilities of the software come into their own. The functions of *erasure, correction* and *insertion* are all available on screen. Text can be *moved* or *duplicated*. Moreover, text can be *justified* (given straight left and right hand edges) automatically within preset margins.

Single characters, words, lines or specified blocks of text can be removed from the screen, to be erased, replaced, or moved elsewhere. Keying-in can be set to *type over* existing text, or to *insert* text immediately to the left of the cursor.

Repeated errors or items for updating can be found, and corrected automatically if desired, using a *search and replace* function, for example 'search for TYPEWRITER ... replace with WORD PROCESSOR'. The *search* facility is also useful for moving quickly to required points in the text.

Layout can be altered with equal ease.

Commands to indent, tab, centre, right align,
close up or widen vertical gaps can be inserted
into a block of text.

       All adjustments entailed by the move will be carried out
       automatically.

Blocks of text can also be either moved from their original positions to specified points in the document, or copied to one or more positions.

Exercise 4

Give some examples of business letters, other than those used in direct mail selling, which would be worth saving on disk for re-use with changes of detail.

---

7 Features of a WP package

Other valuable aids in producing documents include the following.

(a) *Page headers* (such as chapter headings) can be keyed in only once, but inserted by the program at the top of every page.

(b) *Footers* can be added at the foot of each page. An 'input' point may be inserted so that the appropriate page number within the document will be printed automatically.

(c) *A spell-checker* program can check a specified word, page or file against its own dictionary and call attention to any word it cannot recognise: the operator then has the choice of ignoring the word (if it is unfamiliar to the machine, but correctly spelt), adding it to the dictionary (if it is unfamiliar, correctly spelt and much used) or correcting the error (by substituting a word offered by the machine from its dictionary, or by typing afresh).

(d) *Typescript variations* can be used for emphasis or appearance. These are entered as controls in the text, or selected from a menu, as instructions to a printer, and may or may not appear on screen as they will on paper. For example:

Underlining, *italics*, **emboldening**, different type sizes **and type faces**.

(e) *Proportional spacing* is available with some packages. This means that each character is printed in a space proportional to its size. Letters like 'i' take up less room than 'w' or 'm', and so would have too much space around them if all the characters, for example in a word like wimp, were given 'm'- or 'w'-sized spaces.

Calculation facilities may be included, including automatic totalling of columns and rows of figures. The calculator program may also be used to check and correct paragraph numbering. A code is entered with each number, and the calculator can then be asked to check and match sequences.

Form design and graphics software packages are increasingly added to basic word processing. Graphics facilities enable lines to be drawn on screen (directed by cursor movement from the keyboard or by means of a mouse), areas to be shaded, points to be plotted and even colour to be applied in advanced graphics systems.

For users of word processors, perhaps the most useful application of a graphics-related program is in the design of forms and documents of camera-ready quality for bulk printing and use.

Lines and boxes, which can be moved and/or duplicated as required, can be 'drawn' on screen, with a mouse or by marking relevant points with the cursor. Lines can be of varying density and areas can be shaded in various tones. Operations are usually selected from a series of easily-assimilated menus, offering options such as draw, edit, move, copy, shade or delete, within which there are further options, such as shade 1, 2, 3 or 4.

Once a graphic format has been designed to the user's satisfaction, it can be 'downloaded' or overlaid onto a separate text file (with the form headings, document contents and so on) which has been appropriately laid out: the two are printed together to create the finished document.

Work flow management is facilitated by 'background printing' which allows the operator to continue keying in and editing material while the printer carries on printing documents put into its own memory. This also allows for queuing of tasks: an urgent printing task may override routine or held-back tasks, which are made to queue up in order of importance.

Communications facilities are important. Any computer running a particular package should be able to communicate with other computers running the same or compatible software: they may be close enough to be linked by a cable, or they may be linked by telephone using a modem. This means that documents or disk files can be sent or read across from one computer to another, with complete confidence that the text will be sent and received correctly.

Some word processing packages allow tables of figures taken directly from spreadsheets to be included in a text without re-typing. Graphs prepared using other software *(graphics packages)* may also be added to documents.

Macros are automated sequences of commands which can be executed with single keystrokes. If a text editing function is repeated over many pages, it can be automated and executed easily. *Stylesheets,* a feature more commonly used by desktop publishing systems, enable a selected font and page layout to be given a name and stored for later use.

Many packages enable *pagination* to be achieved, especially useful for long documents.

Two of the most valuable specialist applications often included in packages are:

(a)   record keeping (indexing of all correspondence);
(b)   mailing (preparation of address labels).

The widespread use of word processing by businesses might suggest that it has few, if any, disadvantages. There are two points, however, that are worth noting.

(a)   Operators might suffer physical injury (such as eye strain or repetitive strain injury) from continually looking at a VDU screen or using a keyboard.

(b)   There can be some vexing delays and inactive periods for operators.

   (i)   When an operator is correcting or editing a lengthy text, there may be a considerable waiting time, with some packages, between keying in a command to call up a certain page of text, and the page eventually appearing on the screen.

   (ii)   In some systems, when the printer is producing printed output, the operator cannot insert new text on another job because the printer ties up the word processor.

   However, these are problems related to stand-alone PCs of limited power rather than word processing in principle.

Exercise 5

A long report on a new project is to be prepared, incorporating text, graphs and tables of figures. The report must be attractively presented, because it is to be shown to external providers of finance for the project. Which features of a sophisticated word processing system would be particularly useful in the preparation of the report?

---

8   Desktop publishing (DTP)

Desktop publishing is the use of office computers to implement computerised typesetting and composition systems. A desktop publishing package has at its root a word processing package, but it is more sophisticated than a work processing package. A word processing package produces high quality text, suitable for letters and some reports. However, if the text so produced is to be embellished with, for example, graphs, diagrams, photographs or tables, the text may require further (manual) manipulation prior to publication. A DTP package allows pages to be made up on screen and printed in the required format. The need for a messy cut-and-paste exercise is avoided and the package will produce pages of the type found in books, magazines or newspapers. It is used to produce output which is well finished, professional and above all well designed. It is likely that, with time, DTP and word processing will move closer together as word processing becomes more sophisticated.

These capabilities mean that organisations wishing to produce a wide range of documents no longer require outside typesetters. Annual reports, sales catalogues, marketing brochures, reviews of the business, newsletters, press releases and other documents for which a high quality finish is required can be produced in-house. The only equipment required is a PC and a laser printer. DTP packages are becoming increasingly user friendly, so that any operator can learn how to use a package without difficulty. The lead time necessitated for sending documents to external typesetters is eliminated and documents can be produced to extremely tight deadlines.

Desktop publishing software packages vary in complexity. Some are suitable for the general user producing an occasional document; others are appropriate for specialist DTP departments, producing brochures, company reports and advertisements, with sophisticated photography and artwork for output on professional typesetting printers.

The finished page can be made to resemble any newspaper, magazine or brochure page, with boxes, ruled lines and frames delineating or emphasising areas of text. Text can be spread right across the page, or in two or more columns; it can be wrapped round diagrams or presented in blocks. However, with one or two exceptions, DTP programs are not good programs with which to *create* text or graphics.

DTP's main function is that it enables the page, both graphics and text, to be seen as the 'artwork' image for editing and production. A space for a picture can be moved around the page, like 'cut and paste' artwork.

DTP software should:

(a)   offer WYSIWYG: what appears on the screen should look like what will be printed;

(b)   support PostScript for output (PostScript is software which enables users to work with a variety of printers);

(c)   be able to import text from a wide variety of word processing and graphics software, including high quality graphics;

(d)   support colour output;

(e)   provide standardised style sheets for typeface and layout, which can save time in determining the look of a document;

(f)   be able to work with a document scanner for the input of photographs and diagrams.

DTP is likely to need a powerful computer, as it requires lots of memory and processing.

Exercise 6

Which features of desktop publishing might make it the best way to produce a staff magazine for a large organisation?

---

9   Computer graphics

One use of computers is the production of information in the form of pictures, diagrams or graphs (collectively known as *graphics*).

Graphics software

Graphics software comes in a variety of forms and may provide any of the following facilities (in ascending order of sophistication):

(a)   the facility to interpret and present data in graphical form;

(b)   presentation graphics;

(c)   free-form graphics (in which any required output can be drawn, even if it is not in the form of a recognised type of graph).

The presentation of data in graphical form

Some programs with a graphics facility allow the user to display data in graphical form, as:

(a)   line graphs (for example a time series graph, perhaps showing profits over time);
(b)   bar charts;
(c)   pie charts;
(d)   scattergraphs which plot the value of one item against the corresponding value of a second item, for a number of pairs of data;
(e)   maps;
(f)   time series charts;
(g)   architectural drawings;
(h)   organisation charts.

Most graphics programs are menu-driven, allowing the computer user to select the type of graph that is required. The numerical data must be input or produced by other parts of the program's operations. The software then produces a graph automatically.

Presentation graphics

Programs for presentation graphics allow the user to build up a series of graphical displays or images which can be used for presentation. With additional hardware, this type of software can be used to produce 35mm slides for an on-screen slideshow or storyboard (which can be synchronised with a sound track). The VCN Concorde software package is an example: this includes a library of over 200 icons, symbols and images for inclusion in presentations.

Graphics hardware: processor, input and output equipment

All graphics packages accept commands from the standard keyboard terminal, but other useful input devices are a light pen, a mouse and a digitiser. A powerful processor and a colour monitor are essential for implementation of an advanced graphics package.

For a computer to be able to produce graphics, it must have the appropriate processor hardware. With a PC, a *graphics card* can be inserted into the PC (there are monochrome graphics cards and colour graphics cards). This hardware is used with suitable software to produce graphics.

Graphics, like letters and numbers, can be displayed on a VDU screen by lighting up tiny dots called pixels (which stands for picture elements). The quality of the graphics (whether high or low resolution) depends on the size of the individual pixels. A program can instruct the VDU screen to light up a pixel on any x and y co-ordinate, and this is how computer graphics are formed on a screen.

Types of graphics

(a) *Line graphics* are created on screen by specifying two points on the screen and instructing the computer to light up all the pixels between them. In this way, several lines can be created to build up a full line drawing.

(b) *Animated graphics* simulate motion by creating a whole series of 'frames'. By deleting one frame and replacing it with the next in quick succession, the impression of movement is given.

(c) *3-D graphics* give the illusion of a three-dimensional object. One way of doing this is to create a 'wire frame drawing' in which all the lines which make up the picture are shown even if they would be hidden if the object were really solid. Here is an example.

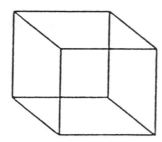

(d) *CAD* stands for computer aided design, which is the use of computer graphics to help professional designers in industry in their design of new products.

Exercise 7

A presentation (to be shown on VDU screens) is being prepared for the board of directors of a company which is considering relocation of its head office. The presentation is to be about a new office building, and is to include drawings of the overall space available and of individual rooms. The presentation will also include graphs of costs, divided between rent, business rates, gas, electricity and so on, and projected over the next five years. Explain how computer graphics might be used in the presentation.

Hard copy output of graphics

A graphics software package will be of limited value if the images it produces can only be displayed on a VDU screen. There ought to be a way of producing the image either:

(a) on paper; or
(b) on photographic film.

Dot matrix printers can be used to print graphics, using the pins on the print head to build up a picture in dots. Higher quality graphics are available from the newer dot matrix printers with 24×24 pins on the print head (instead of the 9×9 pins on many printers). These printers can print in monochrome (black on white paper) but colour options are available for them, even though not many graphics software packages currently support colour printing options. Not every make of dot matrix printer is compatible with a particular graphics software package, because not all printers obey the same set of commands.

Laser printers can produce graphics output more quickly and of better quality than dot matrix printers.

Plotters are output devices which actually draw on paper or transparencies, using pens held in a mechanical arm. Unlike dot matrix printers, they can draw unbroken straight lines, and so are particularly useful for computer aided design work. They can be very slow output devices, so they are often unsuitable for normal office applications.

Photographic output is often useful. Graphs on a VDU screen can be photographed, but the quality of picture that this produces is variable. A fairly recent development is a special item of hardware, the Polaroid Palette, which can be used to make 35mm slides by taking data from the graphics program itself rather than from the image on the screen.

Improvements in the quality of computer graphics

There have been some significant improvements in the quality of colour display graphics recently. Some graphics packages provide the following facilities.

(a) Different *colours* can be used, either chosen from a fairly limited selection or generated by mixing the desired colours from a palette. ArtWorks Paint offers in theory 16 million colours.

(b) *Multi-level masking* enables images to be superimposed on each other, with the image behind still visible.

(c) *Colour cycling* allows colours to be animated to suggest movement, such as water flowing through a pipe.

(d) *Video feed* enables pictures from a video tape to be displayed on screen with computer graphics at the same time.

(e) The stages of image creation can be saved and replayed *as a sequence*.

(f) Images can be drawn freehand, using a mouse. Alternatively, some packages offer stencils to help you draw. A 'rubberband' feature might be offered, so that circles or ovals can be pulled to the required shape.

BPP Publishing

(g) Three dimensional graphs with shading can be generated automatically.

Scanners

Computers can read words and pictures on a sheet of paper using a special input device called a scanner. A scanner looks at a whole printed page of input, and records and stores a pattern of dots. Users can therefore put illustrations into a scanner. The image will be fed into the computer, where it can be enlarged or reduced, and put into position alongside text.

A different sort of scanner actually reads printed or typed text, recognising the letters. Thus if text is not already in computer-readable form it can be converted into that form without the need to key it in. The text can then be edited using a word processing package.

Exercise 8

Why might a graphics package suitable for an engineer be unsuitable for an advertising agency?

---

10 Modelling packages

The purpose of a financial modelling package is to allow the computer user to develop a model for financial forecasting. For example, credit terms, interest rates and the rate of inflation can be projected across a forecast time period to see how variations in these will affect company performance. Such forecasts help managers to make decisions, so financial modelling packages are often referred to as *decision support systems*.

Financial models can be developed using spreadsheets, and often are. But a spreadsheet is a blank matrix of cells into which the user inserts formulae and data. All the instructions for column formats and titles, all the formulae to compute the values in given cells and all the original data are keyed into the blank matrix. In contrast, with a financial modelling package, there is a spreadsheet for holding the data, but:

(a) there are *command files* which contain the program instructions about entering, manipulating and formatting the data; for example, there will be commands for the column headings and row titles and for the formulae (specified by the user when the model is first set up) for calculating data values (on a *logic file* or job file). There will also be a *report generator* file of commands to format output reports;

(b) other data might be extracted from a *data file* (whereas with a spreadsheet model the data would usually have to be keyed in). Packages may well use data which has been extracted from a database onto a data file, for example. On the other hand, input data may be keyed in, just as with a spreadsheet package.

Examples of financial modelling packages are:

(a) Micro FCS (for PCs);
(b) Microfinesse (for minicomputers);
(c) EPS (which has a PC version and a mainframe version);
(d) Plusplan (a financial modelling package for accountants).

Financial modelling packages and spreadsheet packages

Although financial modelling packages often include built-in 'what if?' functions for sensitivity analysis, they do not work interactively with the computer user. In this respect, they differ from spreadsheet packages where the user can key in 'what if' questions and receive answers more or less immediately.

Financial modelling packages have an *advantage* over spreadsheet packages, however, in that they are better suited to the creation of large and complex models with many different formulae, for example, models which consolidate divisional accounts and budgets. The problem with spreadsheets is that formulae have to be entered into each cell individually.

The other advantages of financial modelling packages over spreadsheet packages are as follows.

(a) They have more complex programming capabilities.

(b) More sophisticated reports can be produced.

(c) They can be used by several different users. Spreadsheets are single-user models for PCs.

Financial modelling packages such as Micro FCS can be linked in easily to other packages, such as a database or a word processing package. Output can be written onto a text file rather than being output on to a printer or screen. The text file can then be fitted into other text in a word processing operation, or used as input to a database or statistical package. This can be a big advantage, for example, when there is a need to add explanations to figures in a report. There are also some, but not many, packages which provide a spreadsheet with database and word processing facilities, for example Lotus Symphony.

Forecasting packages

Software packages that prepare forecasts from historical data are available for all sizes of computer, from mainframes to PCs, varying in complexity and cost. These packages take historical data fed in by the computer user, and conduct correlation analysis and regression analysis to produce forecasts and information about the degree of confidence that can be placed in them.

Some packages include a Box-Jenkins model, which analyses source data and produces a forecasting model which best fits the historical data. A firm might use a package to forecast future results from past trends.

BPP Publishing

Risk analysis packages

Spreadsheets and financial models are not particularly good at dealing with uncertainty. 'What-if' analyses are unwieldy if the number of variables becomes large, as the number of possibilities increases. For example, assume you are manufacturing a product whose profitability depends on four variables:

(a) materials cost, which can either be high or low, depending on the market;
(b) exchange rates, which can be high or low;
(c) the market which can be tough or easy;
(d) the world economy which can be good or bad.

You would need 2^4 = 16 models to analyse every situation.

Risk analysis software aims to cope with this uncertainty, by using a probability distribution. Rather than using a large number of separate models, these situations are represented on a graph.

Predict! a package developed in the oil industry is used by the Post Office Counters Division to simulate arrival patterns of customers. Service demands, and so appropriate staffing levels, can be planned in advance.

With such a package, not only is factual uncertainty dealt with, but it is possible to build in the potentially conflicting objectives of a number of different strategies.

Exercise 9

A company is considering the future profitability of an existing product, which has been sold for the past five years. Increases in both the selling price and production costs are possible, and competitors might enter the market. List the data you would expect to be needed by a financial modelling package in order to predict the product's future profitability.

Chapter roundup

(a)   A spreadsheet package effectively gives the user a large worksheet, on which text and numbers may be entered.

(b)   Calculations may be performed automatically, and reperformed if any numbers are changed, by the use of formulae.

(c)   Facilities available with spreadsheet packages include cell editing, rearrangement of the spreadsheet, copying of formulae, formatting and macros.

(d)   Word processing is a sophisticated form of typing with many additional facilities.

(e)   Word processing facilities include editing of existing documents, headers and footers (with page numbers if required), variations in typescript and shading.

(f)   Macros, stylesheets and communication between computers may also be available with word processing packages.

(g)   Desktop publishing offers more sophisticated presentation techniques than word processing, including the preparation of complete page layouts with both text and photographs.

(h)   Computers can present data in a variety of graphical formats, and can output graphs to VDU screens, to paper or to photographic slides.

(i)   Financial modelling packages can build up models using historical data, probability distributions and other statistical methods. They can predict different outcomes and the risks involved.

Quick quiz

1 Why are window commands useful when working with spreadsheets?

2 What mathematical functions are commonly available with spreadsheets?

3 How do relative cell addresses differ from absolute cell addresses?

4 What sorts of user interfaces are used in word processing packages?

5 How is a spell-checker used?

6 What, in a word processing package, is a macro?

7 What are the important features which desktop publishing software should have?

8 What are graphics cards used for?

9 What is CAD?

10 How does a plotter work?

11 What does a command file in a financial modelling package contain?

12 What are the advantages of financial modelling packages over spreadsheet packages?

Solutions to exercises

1 The computer cannot work out the value in A2 until it knows the value in A3, and it cannot work out the value in A3 until it knows the value in A2. Furthermore, the value in A2 must be 2 less than the value in A3, but the value in A3 must also be 5 less than the value in A2, which is impossible.

2 +C5+B8+B9

3 @SUM(D16..D20)*(+E18−F16)

4 Requests for suppliers' catalogues
Letters to confirm appointments
Contracts for major sales
Debt collection letters

5 Typing facilities, including spell-checking, correction of text, typescript variations and proportional spacing

Page headers and footers

The ability to incorporate tables of figures taken from spreadsheets, and to perform simple calculations

Graphics facilities and the ability to incorporate graphs prepared using graphics packages

6   The magazine could be produced quickly and entirely under the organisation's control.

Pictures (for example of staff sports teams) could be incorporated easily.

Contributions from throughout the organisation could be submitted on disk and incorporated directly, thus avoiding re-typing.

7   There would probably be a wire frame drawing of the whole building, and then line graphics plans of individual floors and rooms.

Overall costs over five years could be shown on a line graph or a bar chart. Such graphs could also be used for individual items of expenditure (such as rent over the next five years). Pie charts could be used to show the elements in the total cost for each year.

8   Engineers require precisely drawn lines, but usually only need drawings in one colour. Advertising agencies need to be able to use photographs, in full colour.

9   Sales data for the past five years
Expected inflation rates for selling prices and costs
Expected changes in the size of the market
Expected changes in the company's share of the market

7 APPLICATIONS SOFTWARE

Your objectives

After completing this chapter you should:

(a) be able to analyse a business into subsystems by function;
(b) appreciate the effect of integrating the data processing parts of subsystems;
(c) appreciate how computers can be used in the marketing function;
(d) be able to list the files, input and output for a typical computerised sales ledger;
(e) appreciate the uses of computers in the production function;
(f) be able to list the files, input and output for a typical computerised purchase ledger;
(g) know the main features of computerised stock control and payroll systems;
(h) be aware of the functions of the nominal ledger and of budgeting systems.

---

1   Subsystems by function

In this chapter, we will look at software for specific business applications. Before we do so, however, we need to identify the different areas of a business which might need applications software.

A business consists of many parts or subsystems, and each part will be divided into further smaller parts, or sub-subsystems. Each subsystem or sub-subsystem should be:

(a) clearly distinguishable as a recognisable unit, function or operation; and

(b) related to other subsystems within the overall system, so as to achieve good co-ordination and co-operation between all the subsystems.

Co-ordination between subsystems will be achieved by the flow of relevant information between them.

Subsystems analysed by function include:

(a) sales and marketing;
(b) production, including purchasing and stock control;
(c) personnel, including payroll;
(d) finance and administration.

The data processing part of each subsystem may be integrated with those of the others, so that data entered in one subsystem will be passed automatically or by simple operator request through into any other subsystem where the data is of some relevance.

For example, if there is an input into the invoicing subsystem authorising the despatch of an invoice to a customer, there might be automatic links to:

(a) the sales ledger, to update the file by posting the invoice to the customer's account;

(b) the stock subsystem, to update the stock file by:

   (i) reducing the quantity and value of stock in hand;
   (ii) recording the stock movement;

(c) the nominal ledger, to update the file by posting the sale to the sales account;

(d) the job costing subsystem, to record the sales value of the job on the job cost file;

(e) the report generator, to update the sales analysis and sales totals which are on file and awaiting inclusion in management reports.

2 The sales and marketing function

Marketing is not simply the task of selling goods which are produced or services which are offered; if is a means of trying to ensure in advance that the goods produced or services offered are what potential customers want and will buy. Selling is only one aspect of the marketing process. Marketing is concerned with events before the act of selling (such as research and product development) and after the act of selling (after-sales service).

The principal functions of marketing management are market research, advertising and sales promotion, public relations, selling, servicing and methods of payment and credit. The organisation of marketing management is fairly standard across industry. Marketing directors will usually report directly to the chief executive or managing director. Reporting to the marketing director himself there may be a sales manager, a merchandising manager (responsible for advertising and public relations) a market research manager and a service manager.

Many of the data processing needs of the marketing function are suitable for computerised methods. Typical data requirements within the department would include:

(a) data for market research, including the results of surveys, needed to determine marketing strategy. Widely used databases to giving information on potential customers include Mosaic and Acorn.

(b) data relating to the success or failure of advertising. You may yourself have been asked where you heard of a product or service which you have ordered;

(c) data relating to sales and distribution. This may include:

   (i) customer orders and enquiries;
   (ii) sales made by each salesperson and commission earned;
   (iii) sales per outlet, per geographical area or per product;
   (iv) comparisons with budget;

(d) data relating to after-sales service and warranty work.

A typical use of computer systems in marketing and market research would be a *customer database*. Details of customers would be accessed based on a variety of different criteria, such as age. This means that various types of customers can be targeted for direct mail. To reach a small market by direct mail is much cheaper than advertising on television. Knowing who your potential customers are is likely to save money in the long run.

Exercise 1

What criteria might be used to select customers from a database for a direct mail campaign?

---

3 The sales ledger

While a marketing system ensures sales are made, there should always be a system to record and process them, and to ensure that invoices are correct and that customers pay up. The sales ledger system:

(a) keeps the sales ledger up to date;

(b) produces output such as statements, sales analysis reports and responses to customer file interrogations. The output might be produced daily (day book listings), monthly (statements), quarterly (sales analysis reports) or as required (responses to file interrogations, or customer name and address lists printed on adhesive labels for despatching catalogues).

The *input data* must be sufficient to allow the user to keep the sales ledger *file* up to date and, together with the data on this file, it must be capable of producing the desired *output*. The file data, output and input might be as follows.

(a) *The sales ledger file*

   (i) *Standing data for each record (one record for each customer)*

      (1) Customer account number
      (2) Customer name
      (3) Address
      (4) Credit limit
      (5) Account sales analysis code
      (6) Account type (open item or balance forward)*

      * Where the number of invoices for a customer each month is small, and the customer usually pays promptly, the customer's account may be processed by the balance forward method. With this method, there is no attempt to identify individual invoice debts; instead, the customer's balance is maintained in total. The only check on the customer is that he does not exceed his total credit limit. In contrast, the open item method identifies specific invoices, and credits individual payments against specific invoices. Late payments of individual invoices can be identified and chased up.

(ii) *Variable data relating to transactions*

    (1)   Transaction date
    (2)   Transaction description
    (3)   Transaction code
    (4)   Debit
    (5)   Credit
    (6)   Balance

(b) *Output*

(i) *Day book listing:* a list of all transactions posted each day. This provides an audit trail. Batch and control totals will be included in the listing.

(ii) *Invoices.*

(iii) *Statements*, produced monthly for customers.

(iv) *Aged debtors list.* Probably produced monthly.

(v) *Sales analysis reports.* These will analyse sales according to the sales analysis codes on the sales ledger file.

(vi) *Debtors reminder letters.* Letters can be produced automatically to chase late payers when the due date for payment goes by without payment having been received.

(vii) *Customer lists* (or perhaps selective lists). Lists might be printed onto adhesive labels, for sending out circulars.

(viii) *Responses to enquiries*, perhaps output onto a VDU screen rather than as printed copy.

(ix) *Output onto disk file for other modules.*

(c) *Input data*

(i) *Amendments*

    (1)   Amendments to customer details, for example changes of addresses or credit limits
    (2)   Insertion of new customers
    (3)   Deletion of old customers

(ii) *Transaction data*

    (1)   Sales transactions, for invoicing
    (2)   Customer payments
    (3)   Credit notes
    (4)   Adjustments (debit or credit items)

BPP Publishing

Exercise 2

Which other parts of a computerised accounting system might receive data directly from the sales ledger?

4 The production function

The function of the production director is to provide an agreed volume of products within an agreed delivery plan and at a pre-planned cost and level of quality, and also to achieve a planned return on assets employed.

Production systems involve the following.

(a) The organisation and operation of the manufacturing department and assembly department.

(b) The provision of a production engineering capability to plan manufacturing methods, the use of tools, the design of machine tools and so on.

(c) The provision of a purchasing activity capable of buying the raw materials, components, tools and equipment necessary for manufacturing.

(d) The provision of a quality control department to ensure adequate quality commensurate with cost, by inspection at various stages of manufacture and assembly and by testing finished products.

(e) The provision of a production control department. The problems of economic machine loading and the satisfaction of customers' requirements is one of the most complex in modern factory management. Most large companies now handle this complicated activity with the help of computers.

(f) Maintaining the efficiency of the company's plant, buildings and tools by establishing and controlling a maintenance department.

(g) The provision of economic and efficient storage of consumable goods, raw materials and components, with records capable of ensuring that quantities held in stock are within the predetermined budgets.

Production management information systems provide information to help with the planning and control of production. Computer systems are being used in a number of contexts in advanced manufacturing environments.

Just-in-time (JIT) systems are used to monitor, in detail, the flow of stock and components through the system, to minimise inventory levels. This is done to reduce the costs (such as warehousing costs) of high stock levels. *Material requirements planning* (MRP) systems are used to plan backwards from expected output to materials and subassemblies required, taking into account purchase delivery and production lead times. *Computer integrated manufacture* (CIM) is the integration of a number of manufacturing systems so that stock control is integrated with process control.

Computer aided design (CAD) is the use of advanced computer graphics in product design. In particular this reduces the amount of time needed to be spent on technical drawing.

Exercise 3

Outline how computers could be used in production planning by a printing company, which has several presses and receives orders for a wide variety of sizes and numbers of copies of books.

---

5   The purchase ledger

Purchasing is one of the necessary support services provided by the accounting function to the production function. At the same time, management of creditors is important in managing an organisation's working capital. If creditors are not paid, then they might cease to make supplies. If they are paid too soon, this might cost overdraft interest.

The simplest purchases system is one where the computer is used to maintain the purchase ledger and produce a purchase analysis. The file data, input and output might be as follows.

(a)   *Purchase ledger file*

    (i)   *Standing data for each record (one record for each supplier)*

        (1)   Account number
        (2)   Name
        (3)   Address
        (4)   Credit details
        (5)   Bank details
        (6)   Cash discount details, if appropriate

    (ii)   *Variable data relating to transactions*

        (1)   Transaction date
        (2)   Transaction description
        (3)   Transaction code
        (4)   Debit
        (5)   Credit
        (6)   Balance

(b)   *Input data*

    (i)   *Amendments*

        (1)   Amendments to supplier details, for example changes of addresses
        (2)   Insertion of new suppliers
        (3)   Deletion of old suppliers

BPP Publishing

(ii) *Transaction data*

(1) Purchase transactions and invoices received
(2) Payments made
(3) Credit notes received
(4) Adjustments (debit or credit items)

(c) *Output*

(i) Lists of transactions posted, produced every time the system is run.

(ii) An analysis of expenditure for nominal ledger purposes, may be produced every time the system is run or at the end of each month.

(iii) A list of creditors' balances together with a reconciliation between the total balance brought forward, the transactions for the month and the total balance carried forward.

(iv) Copies of creditors' accounts.

(v) Details of payments to be made, for example:

(1) remittance advices (usually a copy of the ledger account);
(2) cheques;
(3) credit transfer listings.

(vi) Other special reports for:

(1) costing purposes;
(2) updating records about fixed assets;
(3) comparisons with budget.

Exercise 4

A foundary works on a small number of different projects, all specifically ordered by customers, at any one time. How might information from the production planning system be used to check the accuracy of information on the purchases ledger?

---

6 Stock control

Computerised stock control systems vary widely. The simplest types involve just updating a stock file from movement records. In a manufacturing company it is necessary to distinguish between different categories of stocks (raw materials, work in progress, finished goods and consumable stores) and appropriate internal movement documents will be required. In on-line computer systems it would be possible to give customers up to date information on stock availability. A good stock control system should reduce working capital that would otherwise be tied up in stocks.

The main features of a simple stock control system are:

(a) inputs, which would include data about:

    (i)   goods received notes;
    (ii) issues to production;
    (iii) production to finished goods store;
    (iv) despatch notes;
    (v) adjustments;

(b) outputs, which would include:

    (i)   details of stock movements, produced every time the system is run. Summary movements listings may also be produced less frequently as management reports;
    (ii) stock balances produced as required, perhaps weekly;
    (iii) stock valuation lists, produced at the end of each accounting period;

(c) files used. The main file is the stock ledger. There would be a record on file for each stock item, and record fields might include:

    (i)   stock number;
    (ii) description;
    (iii) standard cost;
    (iv) quantity in stock.

If summary movements schedules are produced it will also be necessary to maintain the appropriate details on file.

Another important role common to many stock control systems is the identification of slow moving items. A print-out will be obtained of all materials and products whose turnover has failed to reach a predetermined level over a specified time.

It is also normal for the results of physical stock counts to be matched against the stock file so that a list of differences can be printed out. This should be done as often as necessary to enable wastage and pilferage to be identified and to allow the stock files to be corrected.

Stock control systems can be automated so that stock movements are recorded by bar codes. Bar code readers used in shops can alter stock files as transactions occur. Shops depend on good stock control systems to ensure that they are able to respond swiftly to changes in consumer requirements.

7 Payroll

The main features of a payroll system are:

(a) inputs, which include:

    (i)   clock cards or time sheets (sometimes both are used). Details of overtime worked will normally be shown on these documents;

(ii) amounts of bonus or appropriate details if the bonus is calculated by the computer;

(iii) annual salary, where appropriate.

(b) outputs, which include:

(i) payslips;

(ii) the payroll;

(iii) a payroll analysis, including an analysis of deductions (tax, national insurance and so on) and details for costing purposes;

(iv) a notes and coin analysis, cheques or credit transfer forms as appropriate;

(v) in some cases, a magnetic tape, cassette or floppy disk with payment details, for despatch to the bank and payment through the BACS system;

(c) files used. The master file will hold two types of data in respect of each employee:

(i) standing data, including personal details, rates of pay and details of deductions (including a tax code);

(ii) transaction data, including gross pay to date, tax to date and pension contributions.

Exercise 5

When a new employee joins a large organisation, why should it not be possible for the ordinary payroll clerks to add the employee's details to the payroll master file?

---

8 The nominal ledger

The nominal ledger is the nucleus of any accounting system. It contains details of assets, liabilities, capital, income and expenditure, and consequently profit or loss.

Some nominal ledgers are structured as stand-alone systems, so that every transaction or group of transactions has to be input as a separate process. Others are posted automatically from related accounting subsystems.

9 Budgeting

The budgeting process is a key activity in any organisation. It is usually co-ordinated by the finance department. Larger organisations might set up a budget committee.

The budget committee does not *prepare* budgets. This is done by functional departments, with the finance function usually taking responsibility for central costs. The traditional approach to budgeting starts by assuming that last year's activities will continue at the same volume, and that next year's budget can be based on last year's costs and revenues amended to allow for expected expansion, contraction and other factors like inflation.

Budgets prepared at departmental level are consolidated centrally, in the same way as actual results are consolidated at the end of each management or financial reporting period.

Exercise 6

What inputs and outputs would you expect to find in a budgeting system?

Chapter roundup

(a) The data processing parts of a business's subsystems may be integrated, so that transactions need only be entered once.

(b) Computers can be used to conduct market research, to design products to meet customers' requirements and to facilitate the distribution of promotional literature.

(c) The sales ledger keeps track of sales made and payments received. A record is kept for each customer, and the master file is updated with transactions data.

(d) Computers can be used to schedule and control production, to ensure that raw materials are available when needed and that finished goods are ready when required by customers, and to design new products.

(e) The purchase ledger keeps track of purchases and payments made for them. A record is kept for each supplier.

(f) A stock control system both records stock movements and provides the information needed for managers to control stock levels.

(g) A payroll system records details for each employee and computes the amounts to be paid on each payday.

(h) The nominal ledger collects together all the information on income, expenses, assets and liabilities and thus enables the business's profit or loss to be calculated.

> **Quick quiz**
>
> 1　List some functional subsystems of a business.
>
> 2　What sorts of data will a marketing department collect?
>
> 3　What fields are likely to be contained in records for individual customers in the sales ledger?
>
> 4　What is MRP?
>
> 5　List the typical outputs from a purchase ledger system.
>
> 6　List the typical inputs to a stock control system.
>
> 7　List the typical outputs from a payroll system.

Solutions to exercises

1　Age, area of residence, likely cost of house or flat, whether a car owner, likely income, credit cards held and so on.

2　Stock control, so that goods which are selling well are re-ordered.
Cash recording, so that payments by customers can be followed through to the company's bank account.

3　The company will want to keep all its presses busy, or at least not have work waiting to be done while a press is idle. A computer could maintain a work schedule for each press. On being given details of a new book, it could search the work schedules for a space on an appropriate press, taking into account the customer's deadline.

4　Goods should only be bought for particular orders. Thus it should be possible to relate all purchases (as shown in the purchases ledger) to products recorded in the production planning system.

5　If it were possible, the clerks could use the same procedure to add fictitious employees to the payroll, diverting the net pay into their own bank accounts.

6　*Inputs*
Last year's budgets
Last year's actual results
Estimates of changes in sales volume
Estimates of changes in selling prices
Estimates of changes in costs

Outputs
Detailed budgets for separate departments
An overall budgeted profit and loss account

8 MANAGEMENT INFORMATION SYSTEMS

Your objectives

After completing this chapter you should:

(a) know the differences between strategic, tactical and operational information;

(b) know the differences between planning, control and operating information;

(c) appreciate how management information systems for the different levels of information differ;

(d) be aware of the general characteristics of information;

(e) be aware of the different ways in which management information can be presented;

(f) know the features of decision support systems, executive information systems and expert systems;

(g) appreciate the different roles of the different types of management information system.

---

1   Information

Management information systems (MIS) are systems to gather, process and distribute information within an organisation, in order that management can take informed decisions. The development of information technology means that management information can be provided quicker and cheaper than before, and that managers can have greater involvement in information production and report design.

Levels of information

Information *within* an organisation (as distinct from information provided by an organisation to external users, such as shareholders, the general public, pressure groups, competitors, suppliers and customers) can be analysed into three levels.

(a) *Strategic information* is used by senior managers to plan the objectives of their organisation, and to assess whether the objectives are being met in practice. Such information includes overall profitability, the profitability of different segments of the business, future market prospects, the availability and cost of new funds, total cash needs, total manning levels and capital equipment needs. Much of this information must come from outside sources, although internally generated information will always be used. Strategic information is used in *strategic planning*.

(b) *Tactical information* is used by middle management. Such information includes productivity measurements (output per man hour or per machine hour), budgetary control or variance analysis reports, and cash flow forecasts, manning levels and profit results within a particular department of the organisation. A large proportion of this information will be generated from within the organisation and is likely to

---

BPP Publishing

have an accounting emphasis. Tactical information is usually prepared regularly, perhaps weekly or monthly (whereas strategic information is communicated irregularly) and it is used in *management control*.

(c) *Operational information* is used by 'front-line' managers such as foremen or head clerks to ensure that specific tasks are planned and carried out properly within a factory or office. In the payroll office, for example, operational information will include each employee's hours worked each week, rate of pay per hour, details of deductions, and for the purpose of wages analysis, details of the time spent on individual jobs during the week. In this example, the information is required weekly, but more urgent operational information, such as the amount of raw materials being input to a production process, may be required daily, hourly, or in the case of automated production, second by second. Operational information is used in *operational control*.

The amount of *detail* provided in information is likely to vary with the purpose for which it is needed, and operational information is likely to go into much more detail than tactical information, which in turn will be more detailed than strategic information. What is information to one level of management or one department may be raw data (needing to be processed) to another. A foreman, for example, will check the output of each worker within the area of his responsibility but his superior may only wish to know about the performance of the section as a whole.

Planning, control and operating information

Another way of categorising information is into planning, operating and control information.

(a) *Planning information* is information needed to formulate plans and consider alternative courses of action. It will include:

(i) forecasts (such as demand forecasts or forecasts of increases in prices and wages);

(ii) estimates of environmental conditions, such as likely actions by competitors or possible legislation.

Planning information may be based on historical data, but is essentially forward-looking, and so inevitably, it will be subject to *uncertainty*. When plans depend on environmental information, there is also likely to be some difficulty in obtaining all the relevant information.

(b) *Control information* is information which provides a comparison between actual results and the plan. Control information cannot exist without a plan or target. Feedback is the key concept in the use of control information. The value of control information in an organisation will depend largely on the qualities of the information - its relevance, accuracy, comprehensiveness, timeliness and who receives it. Frequent criticisms of control information are that:

(i) it arrives too late to be of any use;

(ii) it contains information about matters outside the control of the person who receives it;

(iii) the person receiving it does not rely on it, perhaps because he or she suspects it of being inaccurate or incomplete.

(c) *Operating information* is information which is needed for the conduct of daily operations. It will include much transaction data, such as data about customer orders, purchases, cash receipts and payments. Operating information must usually be consolidated into totals in management reports before it becomes management control information.

Exercise 1

How would you classify each of the following pieces of information as strategic, tactical or operational?

(a)   27 cars were painted yesterday morning.
(b)   The company will need to raise £5m in new capital over the next two years.
(c)   2,000 cars should be sold next month.

---

2   MIS and levels of management

Operational level MIS

We have seen that operational decisions are essentially small-scale and programmed, and that operational information is often highly formal and quantitative. Many operational decisions can be made automatically by computers.

At operational level, MIS are used for processing transactions, updating files and so forth. The inputs will be basic transaction data, and outputs will be simple reports, which have sorted or listed the input data, or documents as records of transactions, or further instructions.

Tactical level MIS

A variety of MIS can be used at the tactical level, and there may be a greater reliance than at operational level on:

(a)   exception reporting;
(b)   informal systems;
(c)   investigation and analysis of data acquired at operational level;
(d)   externally generated data.

Tactical information may be generated in the same processing operation as operational level information. For example, tactical level information comparing actual costs incurred to budgeted costs can be produced by a system in which those costs are recorded.

Functional MIS at tactical level are typically linked to other functional MIS. Information from the sales MIS will affect the financial accounting system, for example.

Strategic level MIS

At strategic level the MIS is likely to be informal, because it is not always possible to quantify strategic information, and much of the information will come from outside sources. The MIS will, however, obtain summary level data from transactions processing.

A comparison of the three levels

A table showing typical inputs, processes and outputs at each level of a management information system is provided below.

	INPUTS	PROCESS	OUTPUT
Strategic	Plans, competitor information, overall market information	Summarise, investigate, compare, forecast	Key ratios, ad hoc market analyses, strategic plans
Management/ Tactical	Historical and budget data	Compare, classify, summarise	Variance analyses, exception reports
Operational	Customer orders, stock control levels, cash receipts and payments	Update files, output reports	Updated files listings, invoices

In a finance subsystem, to take just one example, the *operational level* would deal with cash receipts and payments, bank reconciliations and so forth. The *tactical level* would deal with cash flow forecasts and working capital management. *Strategic level* financial issues are likely to be integrated with the organisation's commercial strategy, but may relate to the most appropriate source of finance (such as equity or long-term debt).

Other general characteristics of information

Information has certain other general characteristics.

(a)   *Purpose*. Information must have a purpose, otherwise it is useless. It might have an immediate purpose or it might be filed away for future use, even if it is just being held because it might be needed one day.

When information is used, it should be good enough to fulfil its purpose. Whether information fulfils its purpose adequately will depend on:

(i)   whether it is relevant;

(ii)   whether it is complete;

(iii) how accurate it is;

(iv) whether it is clear to the user;

(v)   whether the information user has confidence in the information or is inclined to mistrust it.

Since information should have a purpose, the information users ought to be identifiable. The information should be designed for their needs.

(b) *Volume.* The information available to an information user might vary in volume as well as scope. It is difficult for manual data processing systems to cope with very large volumes of information.

(c) *Timeliness.* Information might be communicated when it is needed, or it might be delayed. Some information is needed at once whereas other items of information are not needed for some time and so must be filed away until later.

(d) *Channel of communication.* Information can be communicated in a number of different ways. A path or medium by which information is transmitted is known as a channel of communication. Some examples are:

(i)   written reports;

(ii)   graphs or visual displays;

(iii) sheets of figures;

(iv) telephone conversations;

(v)   management meetings;

(vi) informal discussions;

(vii) transfers of data by computer;

(viii) information obtained simply by looking around to see what is happening;

(ix) TV or videos;

(x)   broadcasting or announcing systems;

(xi) factory noticeboards;

(xii) company journals.

(e) *Cost.* Data costs money to collect and process. Information costs money to communicate and file away. The cost of having information is therefore an important characteristic of an information system because each feature or part of an MIS should not cost more than it is worth.

Exercise 2

A computer sales company, which employs representatives who visit clients in their offices, uses a computer system to record all sales made by its representatives. What output from this system would you expect to see as:

(a) operational information;

(b) tactical information?

---

3 The presentation of management information

One of the qualities of good information is *clarity*. This has implications for MIS design, in that modern technology has greatly expanded the techniques for displaying management information. Management information can be presented in a number of ways.

(a) *Computer printouts*. Management information can be presented in printed computer reports. For relatively simple information these are cheap and easy to prepare. Once the information becomes complicated, rows of figures become harder to use.

(b) *Desktop published*. More advanced printing technology has greatly expanded the flexibility of visual presentation of management information. Graphs, charts, maps and so on can be used.

(c) *On a VDU*. Much management information is computer generated. Managers can access information with a VDU and keyboard. The advent of powerful graphics software means that the information can be manipulated, converted into graphical format and made easier to understand.

(d) *Orally*. Remember that management information, especially of the more unstructured nature, can be distributed on the grapevine.

Some management information can be presented in a group context.

(a) If senior management wish to communicate, say, a change in strategy to middle management, this can be achieved by group presentations. Videos, for example, can be used to present this type of information. Moreover, some computer graphics packages are able to manipulate video-based information so that a combination of graphics and pictures can be prepared.

(b) Another source of information is the computerised 'bulletin board' so that managers can communicate information to *all* their colleagues. This is a good way of sharing ideas. Computers are arranged in a network, and everybody has access to the bulletin board, which any user can put messages on.

(c) Videoconferencing can be used. PCs can be supplemented by video cameras and special hardware and software, so that managers in separate offices (perhaps in several countries) can discuss issues and can see each other on their PC screens.

4 Decision support systems (DSS)

Decision support systems are a form of management information system. Decision support systems are used by management to aid in making unstructured decisions, where it is not obvious how to work out the answer.

These complex problems are often very poorly defined with high levels of uncertainty about the true nature of the problem, the various responses which management could make or the likely impact of those actions. These highly ambiguous environments do not allow the easy application of many of the techniques or systems developed for more well defined problems or activities. Decision support systems are intended to provide a wide range of alternative information gathering and analytical tools with a major emphasis upon flexibility and user-friendliness.

The term 'decision support systems' or DSS is usually taken to mean *computer* systems which are designed to produce information in such a way as to help managers to make better decisions.

(a) They are now often associated with information 'at the touch of a button' on a manager's PC.

(b) DSS can range from fairly simple information models based on *spreadsheets* to *expert systems* which review data and themselves suggest solutions.

Decision support systems do not make decisions. The objective is to allow the manager to consider a number of alternatives and evaluate them under a variety of potential conditions. A key element in the usefulness of these systems is their ability to function interactively. This is a feature, for example, of spreadsheets. Managers using these systems often develop scenarios using earlier results to refine their understanding of the problem and of possible responses.

Some decision support computer systems are composed of three elements:

(a) a language subsystem used by the manager to communicate interactively with the decision support system;

(b) a problem processing subsystem which provides analytical techniques and presentation capabilities; and

(c) a knowledge subsystem which holds internal data and can access any needed external data.

Many decision support systems have been developed so that they can be implemented on a wide range of hardware: fully featured systems require mainframe or minicomputers while less powerful or specialised applications may quite comfortably be used on PCs. The most common implementation is on distributed processing systems with all types of hardware so that several users may easily use the system.

A decision support system integrates many of the functions supplied by information systems so that managers may use them more easily and on a wider range of both structured and unstructured problems.

Exercise 3

In which subsystem of a decision support system would you find each of the following?

(a) Monthly sales figures for the past six months
(b) Software to translate instructions such as 'compute budgeted profit' into machine code
(c) Software to compute probabilities of different outcomes

---

5 Executive information systems (EIS)

An EIS is a type of DSS, and takes the form of PCs on executives' desks linked to the organisation's other computer systems. An EIS is likely to have the following features.

(a) Provision of summary-level data, taken from the organisation's main systems.

(b) A facility which allows the executive to 'drill down' from higher levels of information to lower levels (for example from total sales to sales of particular products).

(c) Data manipulation facilities, such as comparison with budget or trend analysis.

(d) Graphics, for user-friendly presentation of data.

(e) A template system. Using this, the same type of data (such as sales figures) is presented in the same format, irrespective of changes in the volume of information required.

A good EIS should:

(a) be easy to use, as it may be consulted during a meeting, for example;

(b) make data easy to access, so that the EIS describes the organisation from the executive's point of view, not just in terms of its data flows;

(c) provide tools for analysis (including ratio analysis, forecasts, what-if analysis and trends);

(d) provide presentational aids so that information can be conveyed in a readily comprehensible form.

Many of the features described can be provided by spreadsheets. However, an EIS is not only a tool for analysis, but also a tool for interrogating data (drilling down, as mentioned above).

6 Expert systems

Expert systems are computer programs which allow users to benefit from expert knowledge and information, and also give advice.

An expert system is therefore a program with access to a large amount of specialised data, for example on legal, tax, engineering or medical matters. The user keys in certain facts and the program uses its information on file to produce a decision about something on which an expert's decision would normally be required. For example:

(a) a user without a legal background can obtain guidance on the law without having to consult a solicitor;

(b) doctors can use an expert medical system to arrive at a diagnosis.

Applications of expert systems include:

(a) locating the most relevant data;

(b)   identifying the causes of problems, for example in production control systems or in medical applications;

(c)   credit scoring.

Expert systems can be written from scratch, in specialised artificial intelligence programming languages such as PROLOG or LISP. Alternatively, an expert system can be bought off-the-shelf as a 'shell', that is a package which is empty of information but with a rule structure already in place.

An expert system has four parts.

(a)   The *knowledge base* contains facts (such as 'a rottweiler is a dog') and rules (such as 'if you see a dog, then run away').

(b)   The *knowledge acquisition program* is a program which enables the expert system to learn new facts and rules.

(c)   The *inference engine* is the software which executes the reasoning. It needs to discern which rules apply, and allocate weights to different factors.

(d)   The *user interface* is the means by which the expert system communicates with the user. The expert system may be designed to accept enquiries in something very close to everyday English.

Exercise 4

How might an expert system be useful to a credit controller?

---

7   MIS and decision making

Problems requiring decisions can be:

(a)   structured (the decision is almost automatic);
(b)   semi-structured (not all knowledge is available);
(c)   unstructured (there are few rules, procedures or guidelines to help the decision maker).

You will also recall the division into information at strategic, tactical and operational levels.

Given that the aim of any management information system is to provide managers with information, we have to assess how well a formal MIS can do so. The diagram below illustrates the contrast between information at the different levels.

Management layer   Types of information

Strategic

Tactical

Operational

Subjective, incomplete

Routine   Summary, unstructured

Short term   Ad hoc

Structured

Detailed   Long-term

Complete

Computational

Which information system is appropriate?

A management information system cannot realistically provide for all of the information needs of management, but tools for decision support can be provided in the format of a computer system.

(a) Executive information systems are used at *strategic* level, for *unstructured* problems, or perhaps even to identify problems rather than solve them.

(b) Decision support systems are not often used by top executives, being less user friendly and requiring more expertise. They are used by middle managers for routine modelling, but also to analyse unstructured problem situations for senior executives.

(c) Normal MIS provide structured information from transactions data, for all levels of management.

Chapter roundup

(a) Strategic information is used in strategic planning, tactical information in management control and operational information in operational control.

(b) Planning information is used in planning, control information in comparing plans with actual outcomes and operating information in conducting daily operations.

(c) Management information systems for different levels of information differ in their inputs, processes and outputs.

(d) For any information, we can consider its purpose, its volume, its timeliness, its cost and the channel of communication used.

(e) Management information may be communicated on paper, on VDU screens or orally.

(f) Decision support systems provide information in a form which helps managers to make decisions.

(g) Executive information systems give the user access to data at all levels, and allow that data to be analysed.

(h) Expert systems have their own knowledge bases and methods of inference, and can make recommendations.

(i) In selecting an appropriate management information system, it is important to distinguish between structured, semi-structured and unstructured decisions.

Quick quiz

1 Where is strategic information likely to be obtained?

2 List some frequent criticisms of control information.

3 What are the typical outputs of strategic, tactical and operational management information systems?

4 List some channels of communication for information.

5 For what decisions are decision support systems appropriate?

6 What are the main features of an executive information system?

7 What are the main components of an expert system?

8 How do semi-structured decisions differ from unstructured decisions?

BPP Publishing

Solutions to exercises

1   (a)   Operational
    (b)   Strategic
    (c)   Tactical

2   (a)   Sales made each day by each representative

    (b)   Sales made each month by each representative, in each geographical area and by the company as a whole.

3   (a)   The knowledge subsystem
    (b)   The language subsystem
    (c)   The problem processing subsystem

4   It could consider a defaulting customer's recent payment record, and suggest whether an ordinary statement, a reminder letter or a letter threatening legal action is most likely to lead to prompt payment. It could also consider financial information about a prospective customer, and suggest how much credit, if any, should be allowed to him.

9 DATABASES

Your objectives

After completing this chapter you should:

(a) be able to distinguish between application specific files and databases;
(b) be able to state the advantages and disadvantages of a database system;
(c) be aware of some of the uses of the database approach;
(d) understand the concepts of data independence and data redundancy;
(e) know how a database is administered and operated;
(f) be able to distinguish between the three different types of database;
(g) be aware of some of the general features of database packages.

1 Application specific files versus databases

Any organisation will keep a large amount of information in files, whether manual or computerised. If an organisation uses a system of *application specific files*, this means that there is a set of files dedicated to each business function, with each set being accessed by a separate program. For example, the sales function will use its own files to process orders and record sales, the stock control department will maintain its own files and the purchasing department will maintain purchase ordering and bought ledger records.

These files are likely to have some data in common. This is called *data redundancy*.

(a) The sales files will have customer details, despatch notes and invoices.
(b) The stock control file will have details of goods despatched, customers and goods inwards.
(c) The purchasing files will contain details of goods ordered and goods received.

Application specific files are common:

(a) where computerisation is patchy. With islands of automation, application-specific files will develop inevitably;

(b) where information technology is widely used in an organisation, but where there are a variety of competing systems, perhaps using incompatible hardware and/or software;

(c) where the use of stand-alone computers has encouraged the growth of application-specific files.

The main problems with such files are as follows.

(a) Different functions of the organisation are kept artificially separate.
(b) They are not easily accessed by other applications.
(c) Two files which should contain the same data might come to contain different data.

BPP Publishing

In the *database* approach, there is only one set of data, which is accessed by all applications.

Exercise 1

Give some examples of how two application specific files could come to contain conflicting data.

---

2 Databases for management information

The database approach can be used for a wide variety of functions. A database is built up, updated and accessed using a program called a database management system (DBMS). dBase IV is a leading DBMS for PCs, and ORACLE is one for larger systems.

The advantages of database systems

The advantages of a database system are as follows.

(a) Unnecessary duplication of data is avoided. Data can be used for many purposes but only needs to be input and stored once. For example, the code number and name of each raw material item will be input and stored once, instead of several times for a stock control system, a production control system and a purchase ledger system. The *drawback* to single entry input is that one department must accept responsibility for the accuracy of the input.

(b) A database provides data for the organisation as a whole, not just for individual departments. The database concept encourages management to regard data as a resource that must be properly managed just as any other resource. The installation of a database system encourages management to analyse data, relationships between data items and how data is used in different applications.

(c) The organisation of data into a database, rather than into separate files, encourages the integration of data and makes data more widely available.

(d) Because each item of data is only held in one place, it is easier to ensure that it is up to date, so that no department in an organisation uses out of date data, or data that differs from the data used by other departments.

(e) Data is independent of the user programs that access the data. This allows greater flexibility in the ways that data can be used. New programs can be easily introduced to make use of existing data in new ways. A database can also be easily extended and then more user programs can be developed for these additions, without affecting existing application programs. In other words, a database can be evolved as the user's data needs evolve.

(f) Developing new application programs with a database is easier than developing them without one, because the programmer is not responsible for the data organisation, which is already taken care of by the DBMS software.

(g) 'Off-the-shelf' DBMS software packages can be obtained, and so the cost of installing a database can be reduced.

The disadvantages of database systems

The disadvantages of database systems are being reduced as DBMS become more sophisticated. However, they are as follows.

(a) There are problems of data security and data privacy. (Data security is preserving data from alteration by unauthorised people and data privacy is preserving the confidentiality of certain data). Forms of control include control of terminal access, user identification and restrictions on access by certain users to certain programs or certain parts of the database. However, because of the widespread access by a variety of users to the same database, the potential for unauthorised access to data creates a serious problem. Problems of data security are increasingly handled by DBMS software. Even so, administrative procedures for data security must supplement software controls.

(b) Since there is only one set of data, it is essential that the data should be accurate and free from corruption. The responsibility for ensuring the integrity of the data might have to be delegated to a data administration manager.

(c) Since data is held once, but its use is widespread, there are potential problems of recovery of data in the event of a system failure. DBMS software increasingly looks after data recovery, but management must consider the consequences of a system failure, how serious these consequences might be and how the damage could be minimised.

(d) A database implies a central store of data, but access might be required over a wide geographical area. The data itself could be spread around several computers on a single network system (a *distributed database*), but this might add to the problems of access. A system that has users over a wide geographical area must rely on a communications network, which can be both expensive and unreliable.

Using the database approach

The database approach can be used at strategic, tactical and operational level. Just as a single database system contains data relating to, say, sales and purchase applications, so, too, information relevant to strategic, tactical and operational decisions may be contained on a single database system. This does not necessarily mean that all data is available to every user, as there can be restrictions on access to parts of the database.

Databases can be used to provide strategic information. A database cannot hope to capture all the necessary information, but it is very useful for analysing and abstracting data from current operations. An *executive information system* can only really be useful if the executive can 'drill down' into the company's database to analyse those bits of information which are of interest.

An organisation's use of databases need not be limited to the databases created by the organisation itself. Some organisations make it their business to provide information to their subscribers or to the general public. These *public databases* are becoming more common, and may provide useful strategic information.

A database approach enables more management control information, useful at both tactical and operational levels, to be produced for three reasons.

(a) The database can be used to provide key indicators about performance as a matter of routine.

(b) The database can be used to present the information it contains in new ways. For example, it would be a relatively easy task to change a report in a sales database from debtors analysed by size of debt, to debtors analysed by region. There is flexibility in the way that existing data can be presented. This means that new indicators can be developed, or new relationships established between variables.

(c) Many databases, especially the more advanced ones, can easily be amended, so that additional categories of information can be added. This flexibility means that management can ensure that its control measures maintain their relevance.

Databases can introduce flexibility into the *identification* of possible control information, the *presentation* of that information and the *updating* of the control measures used.

The banks use a database approach in marketing. They used to operate data processing on an *account* basis. This meant that it was not really possible for the information system to give information about *customers:* a customer who had a current account and a mortgage would appear on two accounting systems, with different codes. Barclays' Customer Information System takes a database approach to address this problem by ensuring that a financial profile of the customer can be drawn up by the computer. This is a valuable aid to marketing.

Exercise 2

In a database system, might there be reasons for preventing senior executives from having access to operational information?

---

3 Data independence and data redundancy

Two important and related concepts in database design are *data independence* and *data redundancy*.

Suppose that you wish to store four records, A, B, C and D in a storage device which has a maximum storage capacity of four records. This means that there are only four positions (1, 2, 3 and 4) where records can be stored.

You wish to access the records in alphabetical order. If this is the case, on a sequentially organised file, record A would be stored in position 1, B in position 2 and so on. On a non-sequential file, however, the records could for example be stored with C in position 1, B in position 4, A in position 2 and D in position 3. However, as far as you, the user, are concerned, this makes no difference at all, as you can still access the data in the logical order by providing the software used to access records with an index to where records A, B, C and D are stored. Even if you decide to change the order in which you wish to use the data (perhaps to D, C, B, A) this need not affect their physical position on the storage medium.

The point of this example is to indicate the difference (which is particularly important in the design of databases, although not exclusive to them) between *logical data structures* and *physical data structures*. The logical relationship between items of data need have no bearing on where they are physically stored.

The independence of logical structures from physical structures, and the independence of data items from the programs which access them, is referred to as *data independence*.

Additionally, we might wish to use information from several records. Where this is the case, it is desirable to create *logical records* that access the relevant data but avoid having to duplicate it within separate physical records. The use of logical records then permits data to be organised and manipulated without disturbing the physical records.

The use of *database systems* has permitted programmers and users to focus on the logical relationships which are of importance in using information. The database system takes over the mechanics involved in handling the physical storage of data and accessing it as needed.

With application specific files, data items are likely to be duplicated in for example separate sales, stock control and purchases system. This duplication of data items is referred to as *data redundancy*. It can have damaging effects if two records referring to the same transaction are inconsistent. This problem is generally avoided by a database system, using logical records to avoid duplicating data for different applications.

Exercise 3

A company keeps all accounting records in a single database. The credit control department decides that it would like to have information on debts arranged by size of debt, instead of (as hitherto) by time since the invoice was issued. However, the finance director still wants to be provided with the information arranged by time since the invoice was issued. Explain why the database approach is particularly helpful in a case like this one.

---

4 Database systems

The objectives of a database system

A database should have four major objectives.

(a) It should be *shared*. Different users should be able to access the same data in the database for their own processing applications, and at the same time if required. This removes the need to duplicate data on different files. Database systems need not be multi-user (multi-access) systems, but they will be much more useful if they are. A database on a stand-alone PC can only be used by one person at a time.

(b) The *integrity* of the database must be preserved. This means that one user should not be allowed to alter the data so as to spoil the database records for other users. However, users must be able to update the data.

(c) The database system should provide for the needs of different users, who each have their own processing requirements and data access methods.

(d) The database should be capable of *evolving*, both in the short term (it must be kept updated) and in the longer term (it must be able to meet the future data processing needs of users, not just their current needs).

Administration of the database

The contents of the data records will be continually changing, and the types of data and the relationship between the items will also occasionally change. The DBMS will automatically re-index the records according to the changes made and provide the interface with the application programs which use and update the database. The application programs should be independent, as far as is possible, of the actual organisation of the database. The DBMS has to protect data from unauthorised access and from corruption during processing. By keeping a record of data items accessed the DBMS can identify redundant items that should be removed from the database.

A *database administrator* will often be appointed to look after the structure, physical storage and security of the data in the best interest of all users. He or she is responsible for:

(a) maintaining the database, including setting out procedures for the addition of new data (liaising with users, the systems analysts and programmers) and ensuring that there is no duplication;

(b) maintaining a *data dictionary* describing the data items;

(c) maintaining manuals for users telling them how to use the facilities of the database;

(d) overseeing the security of the database and ensuring that individual privacy is not eroded;

(e) ensuring that the requirements of the Data Protection Act 1984 are complied with.

Operating a database system

The four main operations in using a database are:

(a) creating the database structure, that is the structure of files and records;
(b) entering data on to the database, and amending and updating it;
(c) retrieving the data, manipulating it and using it in a variety of applications;
(d) producing reports.

Creating a database structure

The database user must begin by specifying what records (entities, such as employees) will be held in the database, what fields (items of data about the entities, such as salaries) they will contain and how many characters there will be in each field. The fields must be named, and the characteristics of particular fields (such as all-numeric or all-alphabetic) should be specified.

Entering and amending data

When the database structure has been established, the data user can input data and create records.

The data must be kept up to date, and so there will be subsequent insertions of new records, deletions of unwanted records and amendments to existing records. With the dBase IV package, for example, commands which are used to do this include:

(a) APPEND, which allows new records to be inserted on to the file;
(b) EDIT, which allows records to be accessed and amended;
(c) BROWSE, which allows several records to be viewed at the same time;
(d) DELETE, which is for deleting individual records in a file, or for deleting a whole file.

Another amendment function allows the same field in every record, or all records with certain characteristics, to be amended in the same way by means of a single command. For example, a single command could arrange for all customers whose accounts have never been settled late to have their credit limits raised by 5%.

The retrieval and manipulation of data

Data can be retrieved and manipulated in a variety of ways.

(a) Data can be retrieved by specifying the required parameters. For example, records of all employees in the sales department who have been employed for over 10 years and are paid less than £12,000 a year could be extracted. If certain search and retrieve parameters are used regularly, they can be stored on a search parameters file for future use.

(b) Retrieved data can be sorted on any specified field (for example for employees, sorting might be according to grade, department, age, experience or salary level).

(c) Some calculations on retrieved data can be carried out, such as calculating totals and average values.

Report production

Most database packages include a report generator facility which allows the user to design report structures so that information can be presented on screen and printed out in a format which suits the user's requirements and preferences. Report formats can be stored on disk, if similar reports are produced periodically, and called up when required.

Exercise 4

Give some examples of calculations a human resource manager might want to carry out on employee records selected from a database.

---

5 Database software packages

The scope for many organisations to construct and use database systems has been considerably enhanced by the availability of database software packages. A user of the software package can insert data into a database framework that the package contains, and then use the database.

There are three broad categories of database package: hierarchical databases, network databases and relational databases.

Hierarchical databases

A hierarchical database has a simple tree structure. For example, a database of students at a university might have a record for each faculty (Business School, Sciences, Arts). A faculty record would be linked to a record for each course within that faculty (so the Business School record might be linked to a record for the Accounting course, a record for the Economics course and so on). Each course record would be linked to records for the individual students on that course.

Network databases

In a network database, each record may be linked to other records, but in a more flexible way than the tree structure required in a hierarchical database. Thus our example of a university there might be a record for courses with an information technology element, linked to both the Computer Science course in the Sciences faculty and the Business Studies course in the Business School. A user could thus obtain access to the records for all students studying information technology.

Relational databases

In a *relational database*, all records are effectively arranged in a table, with columns for the different fields and a row number for each record. Any record may be identified by its row number, and records meeting any specified criteria may be selected (for example, in a database of customers, all customers who spent over £15,000 last year and who are entitled to a 2% discount on the company's normal prices this year). The structure of the data inside the database (as opposed to what the user sees) may be made more sophisticated than the table, to reflect the relations between different field values. For example, if all customers who spent between £20,000 and £29,999 last year are entitled to a 4% discount this year, and all customers who spent £30,000 or more last year are entitled to a 5% discount this year, a table of amounts spent and discount rates could be drawn up. The records of the individual customers would then only need to record the amounts they

---

spent last year, and not the discounts they are now entitled to. If the system were to be called upon to display full details of a customer, it could use the table of discount rates to look up what discount rate to display.

Exercise 5

Give another example of how a relational database package might set up a subsidiary table, showing the relationship between two variables, so as to reduce the amount of information which has to be stored in the records for the individual entities.

General features of a database software package

The database software is software that sees to the administration and use of the database files, providing a bridge between the data files and the user's application programs.

All database packages ought to have certain basic features. The recent trend in database software has been away from the traditional complex software to user-friendliness, with pull-down menus, graphical user interfaces and other features that make them easier to learn and use.

(a) For interrogating the files, DBMS should allow the user to construct queries, either single queries or multiple queries chained together. Queries are put to the DBMS in a *query language*.

(b) The database must be capable of being restructured and reorganised without losing data. The DBMS should automatically re-index records according to changes that are made.

(c) The package must allow the user to print out information, for example onto address labels or in reports.

(d) Report writers enable users to define and format the output.

(e) Security features are needed if data is to be shared.

Different database packages have other features which vary from package to package.

(a) Some packages limit the number and size of the fields that are permitted in records. For example, an address field might be limited to 60 characters. Others allow much more flexibility in the number of fields, and also allow variable length fields.

(b) Some packages limit the number of allowable key fields, that is fields which are used to speed up sorting and searching.

(c) Some packages allow the user to update records in batches.

(d) Packages vary in the way they handle and store data, and in the degree of control the user has in retrieving information.

(e)   Some packages allow a database to be multi-user, that is accessible from several terminals. Others do not.

(f)   For data security, some packages offer a system of passwords for restricting access to specified records or fields.

(g)   Some packages allow the user to define his own menus and help screens.

Chapter roundup

(a)   Application specific files are not shared between different applications. With a database, all applications use the same set of records.

(b)   A database ensures that all applications use the same data, and avoids duplication of data.

(c)   Holding all an organisation's data in one database can be risky.

(d)   A database can provide all levels of information, and can provide a wider variety of control information than application specific files.

(e)   In a database, the logical structure of the data is independent of its physical structure.

(f)   The integrity of a database should be protected, while allowing its widespread use within the organisation.

(g)   A database administrator is responsible for maintaining a database, although several users will be able to enter and update data.

(h)   There is normally great flexibility in the ways data may be retrieved and manipulated and reports prepared.

(i)   Hierarchical databases use a tree structure, whereas network databases are more flexible.

(j)   Relational databases can take account of the relationships between values in different fields.

(k)   Database software offers the ability to put queries in various forms to the database and to restructure the database.

(l)   Other facilities include report writing, passwords to limit access and user-defined menus.

Quick quiz

1   In what sorts of organisation are application specific files likely to be found?

2   Does the fact that data need only be entered once in a database system have any disadvantages?

3   How may databases be used for marketing purposes?

4   What is data redundancy?

5   What are the duties of a database administrator?

6   Give some examples of commands for entering and amending data in a database.

7   Distinguish between a hierarchical database, a network database and a relational database.

8   What is a query language?

Solutions to exercises

1   Cash received from a customer who bought goods on credit might be recorded in the cash control system but not in the sales ledger.

Goods received might be recorded in the stock control system but not in the system for payment of suppliers' invoices.

2   Yes: some information, such as salaries, might be confidential; and it might be better to prevent senior executives from getting immersed in detail, so as to encourage them to focus on broad strategic issues.

3   Only one record is needed for each debt. The DBMS can take information from these records in order of size of debt for the benefit of the credit control department, or in order of time since the invoice was issued for the benefit of the finance director, without disturbing the records themselves.

4   Average length of service
Average basic pay
Total cost of overtime
Percentage of hours worked which are overtime hours

5   Products for sale might be subject to any one of several different delivery charges, including fixed charges (say £10 per delivery) and variable charges (say 3% of selling price). These charges could be given names (say charge A, charge B and so on), and the record for each product would just record the name of the appropriate charge. A table would show what charge each name referred to. If the £10 charge were increased to £12, only the table would need to be amended, not the records for all the products subject to that charge.

10 THE ELECTRONIC OFFICE

Your objectives

After completing this chapter you should:

(a) understand the scope of office automation;
(b) be aware of modern techniques for handling correspondence;
(c) know several different ways of communicating information electronically;
(d) know how funds may be transferred electronically;
(e) be aware of the main electronic public information services;
(f) understand the document image processing technique;
(g) appreciate the effects on business of office automation.

---

1 What is office automation?

Office work is generally a matter of information handling and information processing. In spite of the widespread use of the telephone, and even early developments in computer technology, office work has always been associated with paperwork. However, the advance of information technology has brought nearer the coming of the *electronic office*, in which paper is less central than it used to be.

Technology has developed to the point where an office might have a PC on every desk, with data processed and transmitted by cable links rather than by means of paper and internal mail. 'Workstation' is a term used to described an office manager's desk which has its own PC, together with readily available application software.

However, automation means more than simply having a PC on every desk. For example:

(a) a number of PCs can be linked in a small *local area network*;

(b) office switchboards and *telephone systems* might offer sophisticated features. Private Automatic Branch Exchanges (PABX systems) provide features such as automatic message switching, automatic dialling and call repeating (when a line is engaged) and conference calls;

(c) office users can access information provided by an information-supplying organisation using, for example, the Prestel service of British Telecom;

(d) office automation software (such as IBM's *Officevision*) combines electronic mail and word processing applications.

BPP Publishing

The development of the electronic office has meant that office workers do their jobs in a different way. Technological change has brought about job changes and changes in organisational structure. These in turn affect the way that office workers communicate with each other. The social life of office workers and the group behaviour of office workers are also changing.

2 Correspondence: changing techniques

The old fashioned office in which correspondence is typed has been superseded by more modern methods of preparing and transmitting correspondence.

(a) *Word processing* and *desktop publishing* make it easy to produce high quality correspondence.

(b) Some correspondence may not need to be on paper at all. It might be appropriate to hold much information on computer, whether in word processed form or as part of a *document image processing* (DIP) system which allows a user to read a document by calling it up onto a VDU screen. Alternatively, records can be held on *microfilm* or *microfiche*.

(c) *Fax machines* allow correspondence to be sent instantaneously.

Electronic mail (e-mail)

The term *electronic mail* describes various systems of sending data or messages electronically via the telephone network or other data network. It has the advantages over paper correspondence of:

(a) speed (transmission, being electronic, is instantaneous);

(b) economy (there is no need for stamps);

(c) security (access can be restricted by the use of passwords, although a committed hacker might breach access controls);

(d) the ability to retrieve documents from or store them in word processing packages.

One form of electronic mail popular in the office environment is a system of sending letters and information over a telecommunications network, whereby the information is posted by the sender to a central computer which allocates disk storage as a mailbox for each recipient. The information is subsequently collected by the recipient from his or her mailbox at a time to suit his or her convenience. This sort of service is also called a *message handling service*.

Each user will typically have password protected access to his own mailbox. He can prepare and edit letters and other texts using word processing, and send mail using standard headers and identifiers to an individual or to a group of people on a prepared distribution list.

British Telecom's e-mail service is known as Telecom Gold. The sender prepares his information on a PC and transmits the message via the telephone network to a central mailbox. This is a part of a large BT computer's information store, which is assigned to the Telecom Gold subscriber. The subscriber also picks up any messages in his mailbox.

Exercise 1

A report on a company's Manchester branch is prepared locally. It is then amended by a manager at the head office in Cardiff, and finally incorporated into a report on prospects for the north of England being written by the marketing director at the head office. Explain how modern techniques for document handling might be used to facilitate this process.

---

3 Communication

In spite of the increasing popularity of e-mail, the telephone is still the most important method of communication in the office, and even in this area, there have been major advances in technology, for example in mobile communications (cellular radio telephones and telepoint phones) and office switchboards (PABX).

Telex

Telex is a service which enables users to transmit and receive printed messages over a telephone line. Users have to be telex subscribers, with their own telex equipment and code number, in order to send or receive messages. The telex service started in the 1930s, and from the mid-1970s it developed significantly as an international message transmission system.

As a communication system, it has certain disadvantages. Data transmission speeds are very slow compared with other methods such as leased telephone lines, and only a restricted set of characters can be used in messages. However, the great strength of telex is the number of telex users, around 100,000 in the UK and 2,000,000 worldwide. Advances in telex technology have made it possible for a telex user to connect PCs to the telex system. A user's PC can also:

(a) store a large number of commonly-used telex addresses;
(b) store messages for transmission at a predetermined time;
(c) re-dial numbers automatically if the addressee's line is busy;
(d) send the same message to a large number of users.

Telex, in spite of earlier predictions to the contrary, therefore continues to be an important communication facility for businesses. BT and Mercury are investing in a digital telex network. However, telex is likely to be superseded by fax machines where the quality of communications links permits (fax needs higher quality links than telex).

Voice mail

Voice mail systems enable the caller's spoken message to be recorded at the recipient's voice mailbox, similar to a mailbox in an e-mail system. The main advantage of the system is that it only requires a telephone to be used. No typing or keying in is necessary.

The advantage of voice mail messages, compared to cellular radio or mobile communications, is that it is relatively cheap. However, it is not suitable for conversations. Voice mail can be used:

(a) to leave messages in departments in different time zones;
(b) in organisations where employees might be working away at a client's premises.

Computer conferencing (teleconferencing)

A computer conferencing system is similar to e-mail but more expensive, in that there is a large central mailbox on the system where all persons connected to the system can deposit messages for everyone to see, and in turn read messages which other people have left in the system. Computer conferencing can be appropriate for a team of individuals at different locations to compare notes. It becomes a way of keeping track of progress on a project between routine team meetings.

Computer conferencing systems can become organisation-wide *bulletin boards,* where members can leave messages of general import. A bulletin board system can be a way of reestablishing some of the social ties of office life which may suffer from computerisation. The management problem is recognising the importance to employee morale of informal communication systems outside the management hierarchy or chain of command. A bulletin board might encourage new ideas to be developed informally, and so is a way by which companies can tap their employees' creativity and expertise.

Videoconferencing

Videoconferencing is the use of computer and communication technology to conduct meetings whereby several participants, perhaps in different parts of the world, are linked up via computer and a video system. Conference calls on a telephone system, whereby several people can converse at the same time, are a precursor of videoconferencing.

The most expensive videoconferencing systems feature a separate room with several video screens, which show the images of those participating in a meeting.

Whilst the technology might be expensive, it is arguable that it is far cheaper than the management time and air fares spent on business travel.

Exercise 2

Which methods of communication would be suitable in each of the following cases?

(a) A company's head office and clients need to be able to leave messages for sales representatives who, although they have telephones in their cars, are often out of their cars and in other clients' offices.

(b) A company's regional managers in London, Paris and Berlin need to discuss business strategy for the coming year.

(c) Occasional, brief but urgent messages need to be sent to overseas offices which are often unstaffed for periods of up to an hour.

Facsimile (Fax)

Facsimile transmission or fax involves the transmission by data link of *exact duplicate copies* of documents. An original is fed into a fax machine, which scans it and converts it into electronic form so it can be transmitted over a telephone line. It is printed by the recipient's fax machine. *PC fax* systems do not even require the document to be input in *hard copy* form to the sender's fax machine. The computer communicates directly with the receiving fax machine.

It was thought that fax might be particularly beneficial to the legal profession, because speed in sending documents (with signatures) might reduce the time needed to make contracts or settle cases. However, the service has much more widespread appeal, and the use of fax is growing rapidly.

Electronic data interchange (EDI)

Electronic data interchange is a form of computer-to-computer data interchange. The general concept of having one computer talk directly to another might seem straightforward in principle, but in practice there are three major difficulties.

(a) Each business wants to produce documents (and hold records on file) to its own individual requirements. Thus a computer of X Ltd might not be able to transmit data to a computer of Y Ltd because the data transmitted might not be in a format to suit Y Ltd.

(b) Different makes of computer cannot easily talk to each other. The problem of compatibility between different makes of computer is a serious one, and some form of interface between the computers has to be devised to enable data interchange to take place.

(c) Businesses may work to differing time schedules, especially when they are engaged in international trade. For example if a computer in London wants to send a message to a computer in San Francisco, the San Francisco computer might not be switched on and able to receive the message.

A way of ensuring that electronic communication is possible is to have an agreed format for electronic documents so that they can be recognised by all parties to the transaction. A standard which is widely adopted in the UK and Europe is *Edifact* (Electronic data interchange for administration, commerce and transport).

Joining an EDI network (there are several) is quite expensive. Many smaller companies are encouraged to do so by their suppliers and/or customers. Many of Marks and Spencer's suppliers use EDI. Tesco now has 400 trading partners across Europe connected to it by EDI. Alternatively one or two low cost services are offered, such as Ethosfax offered by

INS for small companies dealing with the UK National Health Service. However, it is possible that these services could be challenged by the Public Data Network provided by the telecommunications companies.

In 1991 the five largest UK banks offered for the first time a *financial* EDI service for their corporate customers. This allows companies to send payment instructions electronically, along with electronic remittance advices to their bank, for onward transmission to companies with which they do business.

Until this development, payments (typically through cheques, CHAPS or BACS transfer) have been separated from remittance advices. The new service, called IDX, ties the payment instruction to the remittance advice. The certainty of payment and the saving in clerical time spent on reconciling incoming payments to invoices should bring considerable benefits to payee companies.

The advantages of EDI also extend to purely *internal* uses.

(a) If an organisation is decentralised, EDI can speed up internal billing.
(b) If an organisation's paperwork is intricate and complex, EDI can speed it up.
(c) EDI can be used to create files of historical information.

Electronic funds transfer (EFT)

In electronic funds transfer, a computer system is used to transfer funds, for example make payments to suppliers, pay salaries into employees' bank accounts or transfer funds from one bank account to another, by sending electronic data to a bank.

Since businesses keep most of their cash in bank accounts, electronic funds transfer must involve the banks themselves.

(a) A system for the electronic transfer of funds internationally between banks themselves is known as SWIFT II (the Society for Worldwide Interbank Financial Telecommunications; 'II' indicates that the current system is a replacement for the original system). If X Ltd in the UK wishes to make a payment to a company in, say, Germany, and if X Ltd's UK bank and the German company's bank are members of the SWIFT II network (all the UK clearing banks are members), the settlement between the banks themselves can be made through the SWIFT II system.

(b) Interbank settlements amongst clearing banks within the UK are also made by electronic funds transfer, using CHAPS (Clearing House Automated Payments System). Many large companies now pay the salaries of employees by providing computer data to their banks, using the BACS (Bankers' Automated Clearing House) or BACSTEL services. Originally, the banks could only process magnetic tapes sent by employers, but with the BACSTEL service, they can now process salary data sent by telecommunications link, and in addition will accept floppy disks or magnetic tape cassettes from customers.

Exercise 3

What are the advantages of electronic funds transfer over more traditional methods of payment?

5   Public services

Teletext

There are a number of teletext systems in the UK. The most widely received are provided by the BBC (Ceefax) and the independent television companies (Teletext on 3, Teletext on 4). Users must have a television set with a teletext facility; otherwise they pay no fee for use of the service. The information is broadcast on pages as part of the television signal, and includes weather reports, news, sports reports, subtitles for certain television programmes, cooking hints and other items of general interest. Teletext on 3 and Teletext on 4 carry some advertisements.

Viewdata/Videotex

Viewdata (also known as *videotex*) is the name for systems which provide information through a telephone network to a television or terminal screen.

The most important feature of viewdata, which makes it different from teletext, is that it is *interactive*. In other words, a viewdata customer can transmit information through the viewdata network as well as receive it.

In the UK the viewdata service provided by British Telecom is called *Prestel*. In the Prestel service most of the information is paid for by organisations that wish to provide the information. The Prestel service is provided over the telephone system, and so throughout the time he is connected to it, the user must pay for the telephone call, at normal call rates. In addition, the user must pay a fee for consulting most pages of information (but not index pages and some other pages). This fee is paid to British Telecom, which then passes it on, less commission, to the information provider.

The French viewdata system, Minitel, is far more widely used than Prestel. This is largely because telephone subscribers are provided with Minitel terminals free on request, and because services available on Minitel are widely advertised.

Viewdata systems, such as Prestel in the UK, have a much larger database than teletext systems such as Ceefax. The information is stored in a network of computers, with each computer serving a local area of customers but also capable of transmitting data to another computer in the network and so to customers in other areas.

Viewdata electronic mail (VEM)

Another facility of a viewdata system is a 'gateway' whereby data on a customer's own computer files can be transmitted to another viewdata customer via the viewdata network. The sender must key in the recipient's viewdata address number. The data is despatched and the recipient (if his terminal is switched on) receives a message on his screen asking him to prepare to receive the data. Alternatively, the data is stored locally until the recipient switches on his terminal and is ready to receive the data. A security measure can be introduced for confidential information: the recipient can only obtain the message by keying in a password.

BPP Publishing

Value Added Network Services (VANS)

VANS is a collective term for the range of computer services provided by external organisations, which are used in conjunction with the telephone network or another communications network. The term 'value added network services' derives from the idea that by combining a computer system with a communications network, the service is able to provide something extra (an added value) to the user, greater than the sum of the values of its components. Examples of VANS are:

(a) electronic mail (the added value here being the facility to hold messages in an electronic mailbox);

(b) services that provide financial information to subscribers, for example on share prices, foreign exchange rates and interest rates;

(c) bibliographic database systems (in libraries of computerised information);

(d) viewdata services such as Prestel;

(e) electronic data interchange.

Exercise 4

What commercial possibilities are opened up by the scope to send viewdata messages to specific recipients and obtain responses from them?

---

6   Document image processing (DIP)

Document image processing is an electronic form of filing. In a DIP system, a document is passed through a *scanner* and a *digitised image* is then stored on a storage device (perhaps an *optical disk*). This can then be retrieved at will and shown on a computer screen. The image of the document can include handwriting and diagrams. The process is the same as that employed in fax machine technology. That is, the image is recorded but the system does not identify the marks on the paper as letters or numbers. A scanner scans a whole page of input and records and stores a pattern of dots, according to whether areas of the paper original are black or white.

An example of a DIP system is Philips' Megadoc. As an indication of the power of DIP systems, one manufacturer has indicated that one optical disk could contain 60,000 pages of A4.

Some DIP systems not only store the electronic image of a document, but allow stored documents to be used in other office systems. It might be possible to display, on a VDU, both a scanned document and keyed-in text commentary.

The advantages are that:

(a) reduced storage space is needed;
(b) the same document can be viewed by different users simultaneously;
(c) documents cannot be lost as the image is on disk.

The main cost savings from using DIP are in storage and retrieval, as the time taken to hunt for a paper file is eliminated. In order for these savings to be achieved, documents must be scanned as soon as they are received by the mail room.

Applications of DIP include:

(a) handling written customer enquiries;

(b) desktop publishing by enabling photographs or other images to be stored;

(c) the management of accounting transactions. All the documentation relating to an accounting transaction can be referenced to the ledger record: an entry in the sales ledger for example could be accompanied by images of all the related paperwork.

A possible disadvantage of DIP is that a lot more information is stored than is strictly necessary. So, companies installing a DIP system should bear in mind the following.

(a) The *importance* of the documents, if their loss would be a major disaster.

(b) How often documents are *accessed*. If a document or file is greatly in demand, document imaging might be a useful technology.

(c) The *volume* of documents involved: small volumes of documents probably do not justify the expense of a DIP system. Large volumes, which would otherwise cost a lot in storage space and handling time, almost certainly do.

An example of a company which uses DIP is National Westminster Bank, which has three image scanners in its card services centre. Letters are read by scanner, processed overnight and are ready for use by the following morning. Typically 18,000 to 20,000 items might be processed every day. The introduction of credit card annual fees together with the marketing of financial products from the card services centre means that a lot of correspondence is received at the centre.

The customer's file can be on-screen within seconds. Previously any caller's letter would have to be retrieved from filing and the customer then called back. This incurred additional costs for the bank. Natwest's use of DIP is an example of the introduction of information technology making office procedures simpler, cheaper and quicker.

Exercise 5

Why could a DIP system not, on its own, read the address on a letter received and start a draft reply incorporating that address?

7 Office automation's effect on business

Office automation has an enormous effect on business, in a variety of ways.

(a) The processing of routine data can be done in greater volumes, at greater speed and with greater accuracy than with manual systems.

(b) There might be less paper in the office (but not necessarily so) with more data processing done by keyboard. Data transmission is likely to shift from moving paper to moving data electronically. Files are likely to be magnetic disk files or microform files rather than paper files.

(c) Office staff will be affected by computerisation.

   (i) Office staff will need to show a greater computer awareness, especially in areas of the office where computerisation is most likely to occur first, such as the accounts department.

   (ii) Staff will need to learn new habits, such as the care of floppy disks and VDU screens, how to use keyboards and remembering to make back-up copies of files for security purposes.

(d) The nature and quality of management information will change.

   (i) Managers are likely to have access to more information. Information is also likely to be more accurate, reliable and up to date. The range of management reports is likely to be wider and their content more comprehensive.

   (ii) Planning activities can be more thorough, with the use of models (such as spreadsheets for budgeting) and sensitivity analysis.

   (iii) Information for control should be more readily available. For example, a computerised sales ledger system should provide prompt reminder letters for late payers, and might incorporate other credit control routines. Stock systems, especially for companies with stocks distributed around several different warehouses, should provide better stock control.

   (iv) Decision making by managers can be helped by decision support systems.

(e) The organisation's structure might change.

   (i) Stand-alone PCs allow local office managers to set up good local management information systems, and localised data processing. Multi-user systems and distributed data processing systems also put more data processing power into local offices, giving local managers access to centrally-held databases and programs. Office automation can therefore encourage the decentralisation of authority within an organisation.

   (ii) On the other hand, multi-user systems and distributed data processing systems help head office to keep in touch with what is going on in local offices. Head office can therefore readily monitor and control the activities of individual departments, and retain a co-ordinating influence.

(f) Office automation commits an organisation to continual change. The pace of technological change is rapid, and computer systems, both hardware and software, are likely to be superseded after a few years by something even better. Computer maintenance engineers are often unwilling to enter into maintenance contracts for hardware which is more than a few years old, and so organisations are forced to consider a policy of regular replacement of computers.

(g) Office automation, in some organisations, results in better *customer service*. When an organisation receives many telephone enquiries from customers, the staff who take the calls should be able to provide a prompt and helpful service if they have on-line access to the organisation's data files.

Telecommuting

Consider the following facts.

(a) Office space is expensive.

(b) Many people feel that time spent commuting between their homes and their offices is time wasted.

(c) For practical purposes, information distributed electronically takes no longer to travel 100km than 100m.

Telecommuting is a solution to problems (a) and (b) by applying fact (c). It is now quite possible technically for employees of many descriptions to work from home. A PC at home enables a user to handle data just as if he were in the office, using spreadsheet and word processing packages. Links to the office provide a means of transmitting information and receiving new data. Links are provided by means of a modem at each end of the telephone line. A network allows communication with the office and with colleagues in their homes by e-mail.

Advantages of telecommuting include the saving of office space and the elimination of travelling time. A disadvantage is the loss of face-to-face contact, which can be very important in meetings and negotiations and is not fully compensated for by e-mail or by telephone calls. A means of overcoming this is videoconferencing.

Exercise 6

In what sort of organisation would office automation not be worth the expense?

Notes

Chapter roundup

(a) In the electronic office, PCs are linked in a network and communications with people and computers outside the office use electronic methods.

(b) Electronic mail can be a substitute for correspondence on paper.

(c) Telex is a way to send typed messages. Voice mail avoids the need to type messages, and videoconferencing allows discussions to be held between people in widely dispersed locations.

(d) Fax machines enable text and diagrams to be transmitted electronically. Electronic data interchange enables computers to communicate with each other directly.

(e) Electronic funds transfer is a means of transferring money between bank accounts.

(f) Teletext and viewdata systems make data publicly accessible.

(g) Document image processing avoids the need to pass incoming letters from the mail room to the addressees on paper.

(h) Office automation can bring greater management control, and can improve customer service. It also makes telecommuting feasible.

Quick quiz

1   What are the advantages of electronic mail over paper correspondence?

2   What is the main strength of the telex system?

3   What is videoconferencing?

4   What are the main difficulties in setting up an electronic data interchange system?

5   What systems are used to transfer funds between banks?

6   What is the key difference between teletext and viewdata?

7   What are the advantages of document image processing?

8   How might office automation affect an organisation's structure?

Solutions to exercises

1   The report could be prepared using a word processing package in Manchester, and then transmitted by electronic mail to Cardiff. The manager in Cardiff could amend the report on his PC, and then send it to the marketing director over the head office's local area network. The marketing director could use his PC to take extracts from the report and edit them for incorporation into the report on the north of England.

2   (a)   Voice mail
      (b)   Videoconferencing
      (c)   Telex

3   It is faster and safer (cheques could be lost in the post), and it reduces the amount of paperwork needed.

4   Advertisements can be sent to selected people, and they can then place orders through viewdata.

5   A DIP system records a picture of a piece of paper. It does not recognise the marks on it as letters and numbers, so it cannot use them in any sort of word processing.

6   In a very small business, where a certain number of full-time staff are needed anyway (perhaps to deal with customers) but those staff have enough free time to deal with administration using manual methods, there would be no point in investing money in office automation.

11 THE COMPUTERISATION OF BUSINESS FUNCTIONS

Your objectives

After completing this chapter you should:

(a) appreciate the need for a strategy for information technology;
(b) know the stages in the systems development life cycle;
(c) know the purposes of a feasibility study;
(d) be aware of the likely costs and benefits of a computer system;
(e) know the main techniques of systems investigation;
(f) appreciate the role of systems analysis;
(g) understand the use of dataflow diagrams;
(h) appreciate the concept of entity modelling.

---

1   The need for a strategy for information technology

Information technology (IT) has a major impact on businesses. It is therefore important for management to have a clear strategy for selecting, developing and implementing computer systems.

Michael J Earl (in *Management Strategies for Information Technology*) lists nine reasons justifying the case for a strategy for information technology.

Information systems and information technology:

(a) involve high costs;
(b) are critical to the success of many organisations;
(c) are now used as part of a commercial strategy in the battle for competitive advantage;
(d) are required by the economic context;
(e) affect all levels of management;
(f) may mean a revolution in the way information is created and presented to management;
(g) involve many stakeholders, not just management, and not just within   the organisation;
(h) make technical issues important;
(i) require effective management as this can make a real difference to successful IT use.

IT is a high cost activity

Many organisations invest large amounts of money in IT, but not always wisely. Much of the expenditure is on the leading technologies in end-user computing, and on high performance niche areas (such as expert systems and computer integrated manufacturing), rather than on

---

traditional data processing. Despite all the expenditure, there may be a delay before the new facilities are exploited to the full. The benefits of IT expenditure might be delayed until the skills of users have improved.

IT is critical to the success of many organisations

IT functions in an organisation:

(a) as a *support activity* (providing ad hoc responses to queries), which is useful but not critical to organisational success;

(b) as a *production activity*, ensuring the smooth running of current operations;

(c) as a *turnround activity*, in which IT is used to open up new opportunities (for example to enhance the flexibility of marketing and production of consumer goods);

(d) as a *strategic activity*, where without IT the firm could not function at all (for example many financial services companies *depend* on computers, telecommunications and databases, just as a manufacturing company depends on raw materials).

In developing a strategy a firm should assess how important IT actually is in the provision of products and services. In the financial sector, many products or services would be inconceivable without IT.

IT as a strategic weapon

IT can be used as a strategic weapon in the following ways.

(a) IT may give an organisation a competitive advantage.

(b) IT can be used to improve productivity and performance, although some studies have concluded that broader changes to the work environment are also needed. Computer aided design (CAD) and computer integrated manufacturing (CIM) are two examples.

(c) IT can be used to alter the management and organisational structure of the business (perhaps by using e-mail or telecommuting).

(d) IT can be used to develop new businesses. For example Reuters (the news and financial information agency) created an electronic market place where subscribers could trade in shares.

IT as required by the economic context

Earl argues that IT is an enabling technology, and can produce dramatic changes in individual businesses and whole industries, especially where there are other major forces for change. For example, when the US airline system was deregulated, it encouraged the growth of computerised seat reservation systems (such as SABRE as used by American Airlines, which always displayed American Airlines flights in preference to others). In short, IT can be both a cause of major changes in doing business and a response to them.

IT at all levels of management

IT can permeate all levels of management through management information systems. This trend is likely to continue, and so IT will become a routine feature of office life, a facility for everyone to use. IT is no longer a centralised technology.

IT and its effect on management information

Advanced executive information systems, decision support systems and expert systems can be used to enhance the flexibility and depth of MIS.

IT also has a longer term effect on the production processes about which information is collected. For example, having manufacturing controlled by computers changes the costs of many manufacturing processes. The era where manufacturing was a mass production exercise producing standardised products and employing a large labour force, so that wages were the predominant costs, is in some sectors over. A number of new costing systems have been developed to reflect this. In broad terms, the ingredients of product costs, and hence the techniques used to measure them, have been substantially altered by IT.

IT and stakeholders

A stakeholder is a person or organisation that has an interest in an enterprise. IT affects many stakeholders, as many parties both within and outside the organisation have an interest in IT. An organisation must take steps to manage these external stakeholders. Parties interested in an organisation's use of IT are as follows.

(a) Other business users (for example when they want common standards for electronic data interchange). These can form into lobbying groups.

(b) Governments (for example as telecommunications regulators, or as sponsors of research projects such as the Alvey program in the UK or the Esprit program for the European Community).

(c) IT manufacturers, who must often pioneer the development and use of new technology. Users need to make their voices heard so that they can influence what manufacturers do. The existence of competing standards is a problem.

(d) Consumers.

(e) Employees and internal users.

The importance of technology

Any strategic view of IT must take technical issues into account. Ignoring the technology-based choices in IT is rather like ignoring interest rates when you are borrowing money. An example from the financial services industry, which depends heavily on information systems, is provided by two UK building societies. Their merger was abandoned because of incompatibility between their computer systems.

The importance of management

It is argued that success or failure in implementing IT is a result not so much of the systems themselves as of the management effort behind them. For example, information systems will fail if:

(a) they are used to tackle the wrong problem (that is, the use of IT has not been thought through in the wider organisational context);

(b) senior management are not interested;

(c) users are ignored in design and development;

(d) no attention is given to behavioural factors in design and operation.

Exercise 1

Give an example of an industry where the introduction of information technology by one large company to improve customer service may force other companies to introduce similar technology.

---

2 The systems development life cycle

In the early days of computing, systems were developed in a fairly haphazard fashion. The consequence was poorly designed systems which cost too much and were not suited to users' needs.

The National Computing Centre in the 1960s developed a more disciplined approach to systems development, which could be applied almost anywhere. This was called the *systems development life cycle*. It contained the following stages.

(a) *Feasibility study.* Those conducting the study take a brief look at the present system and identify alternatives, one of which is recommended to management on the basis of its costs and benefits. A formal report is the result of the study which may include stages (b) and (c) below in some circumstances.

(b) *Systems investigation.* This is a thorough fact-finding exercise, using a number of methods to investigate current systems requirements and problems, volumes of data processed and so on. This may be largely conducted during the feasibility study.

(c) *Systems analysis.* Once facts about the present system have been established, the present system is analysed in terms of its problems, working methods, bottlenecks, inefficiencies and so on. Again, substantial analysis work may be conducted during the feasibility study.

(d) *Systems design.* The design is broadly based on that suggested during the feasibility study, but will go into considerable detail on inputs, outputs, files, security and so on. The main documentation produced here is the *system specification*.

(e) *Implementation*. This stage includes the writing of computer programs, testing and changeover to the new system.

(f) *Review and maintenance*. Maintenance involves keeping the system up to date, and the system should be subject to review to see that it conforms to the requirements identified in the feasibility study.

A final stage perhaps missing from this analysis is *identification of a new problem*, once the system is up and running which can lead to a new feasibility study to look at solutions to the problem. If we add this stage, we have a complete cycle of development.

In the remainder of this chapter, we will look at the first three stages in the systems development life cycle.

Exercise 2

Why would it be a mistake to write programs for a new system before the systems design stage has been completed?

---

3 The feasibility study

A feasibility study, as its name suggests, is a formal study to decide what type of system can be developed which meets the needs of the organisation. Practice will vary between different organisations.

Some of the reasons for having a feasibility study are that new systems:

(a) can cost a great deal to develop;

(b) can be very disruptive during implementation;

(c) can have far reaching consequences in a way an organisation conducts its business or is structured.

The feasibility study group

A feasibility study team should be appointed to carry out the study (although just one individual might be given the task for a small project). Membership of the feasibility study team will probably be limited to a few individuals, including both managers from the user departments and individuals with technical knowledge of computer systems, including a *systems analyst* (a specialist in the analysis and design of whole systems).

At least one person must have a detailed knowledge of computers and systems design. In a small concern it may be necessary to bring in a systems analyst from outside.

At least one person should have a detailed knowledge of the organisation and in particular of the workings and staff of the departments affected. Managers with direct knowledge of how the current system operates can contribute enormously to the study. They will know what the information needs of the system are, and whether any proposed new system will do everything that is wanted. They are also likely to be in a position to recognise improvements that can be made in the current system.

The terms of reference of a feasibility study

The terms of reference of a feasibility study might consist of the following items.

(a) To investigate and report on an existing system, its procedures and costs.
(b) To specify objectives for the system.
(c) To define the system requirements.
(d) To establish whether these requirements are being met by the existing system.
(e) To establish whether these requirements could be met by a new system.
(f) To recommend the most suitable system to achive the objectives.
(g) To prepare a detailed cost budget for the proposed system, within a set limit.
(h) To prepare a draft plan for implementation within a set timescale.
(i) To establish a detailed design, implementation and operating budget.

The costs and benefits of a proposed system

Cost-benefit analysis is an important part of a feasibility study. It means comparing all the costs and benefits of a proposal, to see whether the benefits are likely to outweigh the costs. However, it is complicated by the facts that many of the system cost elements are poorly defined and that benefits can often be highly subjective in nature.

In general the best cost estimates will be obtained for 'turnkey' systems bought as a whole from an outside vendor who provides a cost quotation against a specification. Less reliable cost estimates are generally made where the work is to be performed by the organisation's own employees.

The costs of a new system will include:

(a) *Equipment costs* (capital or leasing costs) of:

    (i)   computers and peripherals;
    (ii)   ancillary equipment;
    (iii) the initial system supplies (disks, tapes and stationery);

(b) *Installation costs:*

    (i)   a new building (if necessary);
    (ii)   the computer room (wiring, air-conditioning and so on);

(c) *Development costs* (or systems analysis, programming and changeover costs);

(d) *Personnel costs:*

    (i)   staff training;
    (ii)   staff recruitment or relocation;
    (iii) staff salaries and pensions;
    (iv) redundancy payments;
    (v)   overheads;

(e) *Operating costs:*

(i) consumable materials (tapes, disks and stationery);
(ii) maintenance;
(iii) accommodation costs;
(iv) heating, power, insurance and telephone costs;
(v) standby arrangements.

A distinction can be made between capital costs (incurred once) and revenue costs (incurred every year).

The benefits from a proposed new system must also be evaluated. These will include:

(a) savings because the old system will no longer be operated. The savings should include:

(i) savings in staff costs;
(ii) savings in other operating costs, such as consumable materials;

(b) extra savings or revenue benefits because of the improvements that the new system should bring, including:

(i) more sales revenue and so additional contribution;
(ii) better stock control and so fewer stock losses from obsolescence and deterioration;
(iii) further savings in staff time, resulting perhaps in reduced future staff growth;

(c) possibly, some one-off revenue benefits from the sale of equipment which the existing system uses, but which will no longer be required. Secondhand computer equipment does not have a high value, however. It is also possible that the new system will use less office space, and so there will be benefits from selling or renting out the spare accommodation.

There might be *intangible benefits*, which it is impossible to give a money value to. These might include:

(a) greater customer satisfaction, arising from a more prompt service;
(b) improved staff morale from working with a better system;
(c) better decision-making resulting from better MIS.

Exercise 3

Is it true that when a system is already computerised and a replacement computer system using improved technology is proposed, a feasibility study is pointless as it is already known to be feasible to computerise the system?

---

4   Systems investigation

Techniques used in gathering information to investigate the present system include:

(a)   interviews;
(b)   questionnaires;
(c)   observation and inspection of records.

The facts obtained from the investigation must be fully recorded.

Interviews

Interviews with members of staff can be the most effective method of fact finding. There are some guidelines for conducting a fact finding interview. The interviewer must be able to adapt his approach to suit the individual interviewee, rather than following a standard routine and should be fully prepared for the interview. He should:

(a)   inform employees *before* the interview that a systems investigation is taking place, and its purpose explained;

(b)   ask questions at a level appropriate to the employee's position within the organisation;

(c)   not be too formal, but should encourage the interviewee to offer opinions and suggestions;

(d)   not jump to conclusions or confuse opinions with facts;

(e)   not propound his own opinions in the interview;

(f)   refrain from making 'off the record' comments during the course of the interview, for example about what he is going to recommend;

(g)   conclude the interview by summarising the main points (so that the interviewee can confirm that the interviewer has understood what the interviewee has said).

Questionnaires

The use of questionnaires may be useful when a limited amount of information is required from a large number of individuals, or when the organisation is decentralised with many separate locations. Questionnaires may be used in advance of interviews to save the analyst's and employees' time.

It should be remembered that:

(a)   employees ought to be informed before receiving questionnaires that a systems investigation is to take place, and its purpose should be explained;

(b)   questions must be designed to obtain *exactly* the information necessary for the study;

(c) busy employees may consider it a waste of time to answer page after page of questions, and may be unwilling to do so, or may put questionnaires in a 'pending' tray.

If a questionnaire is necessary, for example to establish the function of all employees within the organisation, the systems analyst may design a form that enables the individual to list his duties under various headings. The form should be designed with the specific organisation in mind.

Whenever possible, questionnaires should:

(a) not contain too many questions;

(b) be organised in a logical sequence;

(c) include an occasional question the answer to which corroborates the answers to previous questions;

(d) allow each question to be answered by 'yes' or 'no' or a tick;

(e) be tested independently before being used. The test answers should enable the systems analyst to establish the effectiveness of his questions and help determine the level of subsequent interviews and observations;

(f) take into account the sensitivity of individuals in respect of their job security, change of job definition etc.

Observation

Once the systems analyst has some understanding of the methods and procedures used in the organisation, he or she should be able to verify findings and clarify any problems areas by an observation of operations. Observation is a useful way of cross-checking with the facts obtained by interview or questionnaire. Different methods of recording facts ought to produce the same information, but it is not inconceivable that staff do their work in one way, whilst management believe that they do something different.

Document investigation: document description forms

The systems analyst must investigate the *documents* that are used in the system for input and for output.

One way of recording facts about document usage is the *document description form*. This is simply a standard form which the systems analyst can use to describe a document. Here is an example.

```
                    DOCUMENT DESCRIPTION FORM
TITLE OF DOCUMENT ..........................................................................
DOCUMENT NUMBER ...........................................................................
ORIGINATING DEPT ........................... NO OF COPIES ...................
FILLED IN BY ....................................................................................
COPIES SENT TO ..............................................................................................
REMARKS
```

DATA ITEM DESCRIPTION	MAXIMUM ITEMS PER DOCUMENT	SIZE/ PICTURE	ENTERED BY	REMARKS

```
PREPARED BY                 DATE          PROJECT
(SYSTEMS ANALYST)
```

Notes

(a) *Data item description*. This column lists all the items on the document. For example, a sales order form will include the name of the customer, the invoice address and the delivery address for the customer, the date of the order, items ordered, the quantity of each item ordered, the signature of the customer and so on. The maximum number of times each item appears on the document is shown in the next column.

(b) *Size/picture*. The size of the data item (which might be fixed or variable) is given. In the case of variable length items, the maximum size might be indicated on the form. 'Picture' means the format of the item, in terms of alphabetic, numeric or other characters. For example:

A(15)	means 15 alphabetic characters (letters)
9999	means four numeric characters (digits)
A99	means a letter followed by two numeric characters
9(6)	means six numeric characters

(c) *Entered by*. This indicates the person or machine responsible for entering the data item on the document.

(d) *Remarks* leaves space for the systems analyst to make any further notes, such as where the data comes from, whether the size of the data item is the maximum size of a variable length item or a fixed length item and whether the completed document is checked and authorised by a supervisor.

Exercise 4

Criticise the following question addressed to a clerk in a department which might be computerised.

'Why do you think the present system is so inefficient and requires such gross overstaffing?'

5   Systems analysis

Systems analysis is a detailed look at a current system and what a new system will be required to do. It leads on to systems design, which is the development of a new system that will meet these requirements. Systems analysis is carried out by a systems analyst, who might be employed in the organisation's DP department or an external consultant.

The chief analyst, preferably the one who was also responsible for the feasibility study, will have individuals with differing backgrounds and experience (technical and business) working in his team.

Systems analysis might be done in two stages, depending on the size of the project.

(a)   The first stage is carried out during the feasibility study. The feasibility study team must go into some detail about the current system and the requirements for a new system, and this means having to do systems analysis work.

(b)   If the feasibility study report recommends a new system, and the recommendation is accepted, the second stage in the systems analysis work might be an even closer analysis of the current system, which will then lead straight into systems design work.

These two stages in systems analysis would only differ in the amount of detail they go into, and so the length of time they might take. The two stages could be combined into one, and all the systems analysis work could be done during the feasibility study.

Exercise 5

What might be the benefits of analysing an existing system in detail, rather than just listing in outline the tasks performed (such as 'record sales and produce invoices').

---

6.   Methodologies and techniques for systems analysis and design

Various methodologies (systems of methods for solving problems) are available to use in systems analysis and design. Most modern approaches to systems analysis and design:

(a)   focus on the information needs and requirements of users as a justification for processing methods and techniques;

(b)   work on a top-down philosophy from the general to the specific;

(c)   leave physical implementation until last.

Methodologies like SSADM (Structured Systems Analysis and Design Method) document the analysis and design process extensively. Each stage requires a number of documents to be provided, as a sign that it has been completed, and to ensure that the outputs from one stage are used as inputs to the next. Some methodologies may be too elaborate for some systems development, so users may adapt them to their own particular needs.

All methodologies use various techniques. Some techniques are helpful in creating the broad outline design of the system; others are used for the more detailed work of program or file analysis and design.

Data modelling

A data processing system is created to take input data, process it and produce output. The term 'data modelling' is sometimes used to describe the technique of looking at a system from a *data handling* perspective, and answering the following questions.

(a) What data is needed?
(b) Why is it needed?
(c) What is the data used for?
(d) Who uses the data?
(e) Where does the data originate and how?

The answers to these questions, once obtained, should then lead on to other, more detailed questions.

(a) When is the data needed, and how frequently?
(b) When does the source data originate?
(c) How should the data be processed?
(d) Where should the data be filed?
(e) How should the data be maintained and updated, and who should be responsible for this?
(f) Who should be allowed access to file data?

Data flow analysis

Data flow analysis is a broadly applicable design technique, which may be used for manual as well as computerised systems. The description of how data is handled does not in any way imply that a specific technology ought to be used, and so it is a method for understanding how a system works without forcing computerisation upon it.

When a systems analyst first looks at a system, to find out how the data is processed (or should be processed), all he or she wants to do is to sort out what data is used, who uses it, and where it is stored. One useful way of recording the ways in which data is processed, without bothering with the hardware used, is a *dataflow diagram* (DFD).

Dataflow diagrams

The symbols which might be used in a dataflow diagram are as follows.

(a) DATA SOURCE
     DATA DESTINATION

People or computers are data sources or data destinations, that is, they output or receive data.

(b) DATA STORES

Identifying number of data store → Name of data store

Data stores include transaction records, data files, reports and documents. A data store is a point which holds data, and receives a data flow.

(c) DATA FLOWS

A data flow represents the transfer of data from one point in the system to another. This may involve a document transfer or it may simply involve notification that some event has occurred without any detailed information being passed. When a data flow occurs a copy of the data transferred may also be retained at the transmitting point. A data flow could be in any physical form, for example a letter, a telephone call, a fax or an electronic exchange between computers.

(d) DATA PROCESSES

Identifying number of process

Data processes take data from a data store, process it and send the results to a data store. The processes could be manual or computerised.

A data process will use or alter the data in some way. An example of a process which simply uses the data would be an output operation, where the data held by the system is unchanged and it is merely made available in a different form, for example printed out. A process which alters the data would be a mathematical computation or a process such as sorting in which the arrangement of the data is altered. Systems vary widely in the amount of data processing which they perform. Some systems are dominated by the amount of data movement which they provide, whilst others are concerned much more with transforming the data into a more useful form.

Exercise 6

The production department of a company requests some materials from stores on a form. The stores department files this form, after sending a note back saying that the materials requested are currently out of stock. The reply is filed by the production manager. Identify the data sources, data destinations, data flows and data stores involved.

An example will show what a dataflow diagram records. The example used here is a sales and warehousing system.

Three dataflow diagrams are shown; each is prepared to record a certain level of detail.

A level-0 DFD shows the inputs and outputs of the system and makes the system boundary clear. In the organisation shown, customers send in orders on an order form. The organisation despatches the goods and completes a two-part delivery note. The top copy goes to the customer and the bottom copy is sent to the accounts department for invoicing and accounting purposes. When suppliers send goods in, their despatch notes are retained.

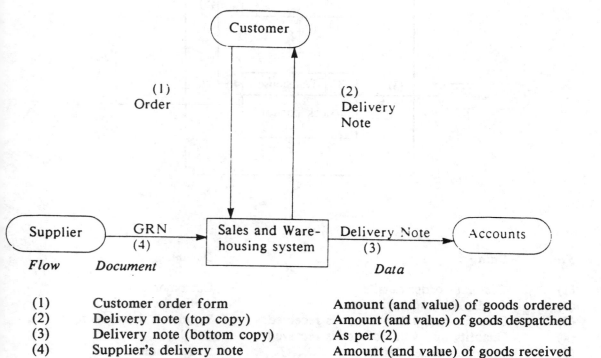

(1)	Customer order form	Amount (and value) of goods ordered
(2)	Delivery note (top copy)	Amount (and value) of goods despatched
(3)	Delivery note (bottom copy)	As per (2)
(4)	Supplier's delivery note	Amount (and value) of goods received

A more detailed level-1 DFD which details the data flows between the subsystems in the system might appear as follows. Here, the 'sales and warehousing system' process which was shown in a single box is analysed in more detail, and the data flows between the separate departments within this function are shown. Customer orders are received by the sales department. The sales department checks with accounts that the order is within the customer's credit limit. If so, goods are requisitioned from the warehouse, from where they are passed to despatch. Two despatch notes are made out: one is sent to the customer and the other to the accounts department. Goods are also received from suppliers; details of goods are shown on the supplier's delivery note, from which a GRN is made out and sent to the accounts department.

Notes

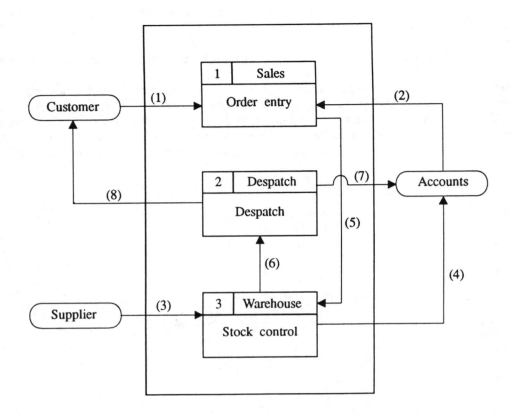

Flow	Data	Document
(1)	Customer order details	Customer order
(2)	Credit limit authorisation	Authorisation list
(3)	Quantity and value of goods received	Supplier's delivery note
(4)	Quantity and value of goods received	GRN
(5)	Customer order details	Requisition
(6)	Quantity and value of goods despatched	Instruction
(7)	Quantity and value of goods despatched	Despatch note
(8)	Quantity and value of goods despatched	Despatch note

A separate level-2 DFD would then be prepared for each of the sales, despatch and warehouse subsystems. The diagram below shows the data flows *within* the warehouse. Similar diagrams would be prepared for each of the other subsystems.

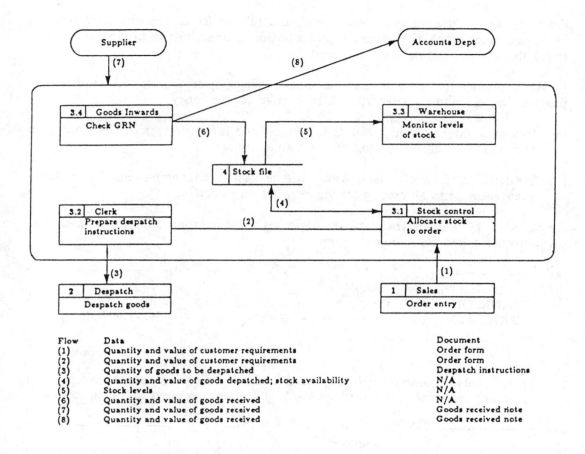

Flow	Data	Document
(1)	Quantity and value of customer requirements	Order form
(2)	Quantity and value of customer requirements	Order form
(3)	Quantity of goods to be despatched	Despatch instructions
(4)	Quantity and value of goods depatched; stock availability	N/A
(5)	Stock levels	N/A
(6)	Quantity and value of goods received	N/A
(7)	Quantity and value of goods received	Goods received note
(8)	Quantity and value of goods received	Goods received note

Exercise 7

A set of dataflow diagrams is to be prepared to show an organisation's entire system for paying its employees. Give some examples of sub-systems which would appear on a level-1 dataflow diagram and have their own level-2 dataflow diagrams.

Data analysis

Any set of data must be structured in such a way that users of the system can access and process data in the ways they want to. This is particularly true of databases, which require flexibility in the way in which information is handled.

The person creating the set of data must first carry out an analysis of all the data for processing and filing, because a full and accurate analysis of data in the system is crucial to the construction of complete and workable sets of data. Data analysis involves defining the items of data, not simply the flow of data.

BPP Publishing

Entity modelling

One approach to data analysis is *entity modelling* (also called *logical data analysis*). An *entity* is an item (such as a person, a job, a business, an activity, a product or a stores item) about which information is stored.

In single application systems (such as a sales ledger system, a payroll system or a purchase ledger system) a record will be created for an entity.

(a) In a sales ledger system, records will be created for customers. A customer is an entity, and all customers together are an *entity set*.

(b) Similarly, in a payroll system, records will be created about employees. An employee is an entity, and all employees together are an entity set.

We can identify *relationships* between attributes. Here are some simple examples. The diagrams are called *Bachmann diagrams*.

(a)

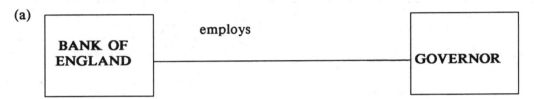

There is the relationship *employs* between the Bank of England and the governor. It is a *one-one* relationship because the Bank of England employs only one governor.

(b)

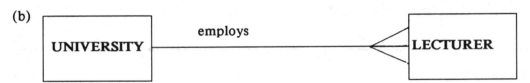

The university employs a large number of lecturers. The relationship is *one-many*.

(c)

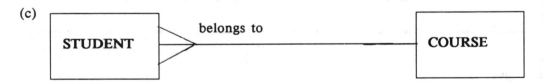

Many students belong to one course. The relationship is *many-one*.

(d)

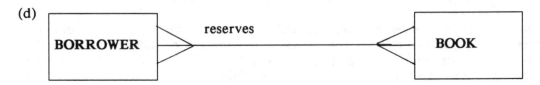

A large number of borrowers wish to reserve a large number of books. The relationship is *many-many*.

Exercise 8

Of what types are the following relationships?

(a) Lecturer works for Edinburgh University.
(b) People work for employers.
(c) Programs are produced by Microsoft.

A diagram for the relationships between some of the entities involved in running a business might be as follows.

Entity	Relationship	Entity
Customer	Receives many	Invoice
Customer	Places many	Order
Invoice	Is for one	Delivery
Order	Has many	Delivery
Product	Is ordered on many	Order
Supplier	Supplies many	Product
Product	Is supplied by many	Supplier

Chapter roundup

(a) An information technology strategy is important because of the high costs involved, because of the difference information technology can make to an organisation's competitiveness and because of the impact which information technology can have on all levels of management.

(b) The systems development life cycle covers the recognition of a problem, the feasibility study, the investigation and analysis of the existing system, the design and implementation of a new system, the review and maintenance of the new system and the recognition of any new problems.

(c) A feasibility study is intended to ensure that the development of a new system is only undertaken if the benefits are likely to outweigh the costs.

(d) Existing systems may be investigated using interviews, questionnaires and observation.

(e) Systems analysis involves obtaining a detailed understanding of the existing system, using techniques such as dataflow diagrams and entity modelling.

Quick quiz

1   In what ways can information technology be used as a strategic weapon?

2   Which parties are likely to be interested in the use of information technology by a major organisation?

3   What are typical terms of reference of a feasibility study?

4   What benefits of the use of information technology are likely to be intangible?

5   What are the features of a good questionnaire?

6   What does SSADM stand for?

7   What might be shown in different levels of dataflow diagrams?

8   What types of relationship between entities can there be?

Solutions to exercises

1   A car hire company might introduce a computerised system to allocate cars to customers and pre-print the paperwork for customers to sign, thus ensuring that cars are available when required and are easy to collect and return. Customers would tend to use such a company in preference to other companies without such technology.

2   Programs are written to perform particular tasks. Only after the systems design stage has been completed is it clear exactly what tasks need to be performed.

3   No. The point of a feasibility study is to assess whether it is possible to achieve improvements cost-effectively. Such an assessment is needed for a proposed change from one computer system to another, just as much as for a proposed change from a manual system to a computer system.

4   The question is an insult to the department and would probably make the clerk fear for his job. After it had been asked, the clerk would probably not co-operate with the interviewer, and might give him false information.

5   It might be found that some small stages are unnecessary, or that some stages which might appear to be unnecessary at in fact needed because they provide important controls or input to other stages.

6   The production department is a data source and the stores department is a data destination for the data flow which is the request for materials. The stores department's file is a data store for the form. The stores department is a data source and the production department is a data destination for the data flow which is the notification that the materials are out of stock. The production manager's file is a data store for the note.

7   Collection of information on hours worked
Collection of information on new employees and employees leaving
Computation of gross pay, deductions and net pay
Production of payslips
Sending information to a bank to pay wages
Paying tax and national insurance to the Inland Revenue

8   (a)   Many-one
(b)   Many-many
(c)   Many-one

12 SYSTEMS DESIGN

> *Your objectives*
>
> After completing this chapter you should:
>
> (a) be aware of the distinction between outline design and detailed design;
> (b) be aware of the main aspects of output design;
> (c) know the main considerations affecting input design;
> (d) know the main considerations affecting document design;
> (e) be able to state the qualities of a good source document;
> (f) be able to state the features of a good coding system;
> (g) know several different types of code;
> (h) be able to recognise well designed and badly designed keyboard/screen dialogues;
> (i) know the main considerations affecting file design.

1   Outline design and detailed design

The first stage in systems design is to prepare an outline design showing the data flows. The methods used (such as dataflow diagrams) are the same as in systems analysis. The difference is that instead of finding out what happens in an existing system, the designer sets out what should happen in order to achieve the objectives of the new system.

The techniques used to prepare a detailed design for a computer system, once the outline system design has been prepared, are likely to vary between systems.

(a) Where a system uses application-specific files, the design of the system will involve deciding what data will be held on each file.

(b) When a system uses a database, the design of the system will focus on how the database should be structured.

In both cases, the designer must consider the form and contents of both inputs and outputs. In this chapter, we shall consider these detailed design issues. The design sequence might be:

(a) outputs (results), including documents, codes, screens and dialogues;
(b) inputs (data), including documents, codes, screens and dialogues;
(c) files;
(d) procedures (programs).

The writing of programs is not considered here, as it requires specialist knowledge of programming languages.

2 Output design

The specification of what output the user wants from a system dictates the requirements for both input and files in the system, since the data input or held on file must be sufficient to provide the output.

Output design will cover three separately identifiable types of results.

(a) *External results* will be sent out to people outside the user's organisation. These include invoices and purchase orders.

(b) *Internal results* will be distributed within the organisation. These include management reports, error reports and audit listings.

(c) *Internal system results* give information relating to the operation of the system itself, such as system operating statistics and control totals and reports.

The design of output will cover the following aspects.

(a) *Identification of output.* All output report documents and VDU screen displays must be clearly specified and uniquely identified.

(b) *Content and format.*

(c) *Frequency of production.* The frequency with which the output will be produced must be specified, including whether there might be cases of special *urgency*. Response times for keyboard interrogations should be specified. Reports might be routinely produced (every week, month or year) or produced only on demand.

(d) Where appropriate, the *conditions giving rise to the production of output* should be specified. That is, what needs to happen for a particular report to be produced?

(e) The *volume* of expected output must also be specified. When output volumes are very large, and a mainframe computer is being used, the systems analyst will probably opt for high-speed printer output. When output volumes are low, the systems analyst might choose to use a low-speed printer, perhaps situated at a location remote from the mainframe computer.

(f) The *sequence* in which output is produced must be specified.

(g) The *output medium* must be specified (for example screen, paper or microform). Also the number of copies required must be considered. Output which will be used as input to another program will need a computer readable medium, such as a magnetic disk.

The choice of output medium will have regard to both whether a hard copy is required and the required quality.

The costs and benefits of output must be considered. The user might ask for information that would be too costly to produce in view of the benefits obtainable from it. Questions that the systems designer might consider in designing the output are as follows.

(a) Is the user asking for too much information?
(b) Can two or more required outputs be combined into a single multi-use output?
(c) Is the output required as frequently as specified, or can the frequency be reduced?
(d) Should output be produced automatically, or only on demand?

BPP Publishing

(e) Does the response time have to be short?
(f) Should the user be allowed some control over the format and sequence of output?

The answers to these questions cannot be decided by the systems analyst alone, but he or she should discuss these matters with the user.

Example: output design

In a department store, there are 50 cash desks where customers pay for their goods. The department store has a point of sale computer system, with each cash desk terminal linked to a central computer. A stock master file includes details of selling prices and quantities held in stock for each item.

List the possible contents of a printed output report:

(a) for each customer;
(b) for management (on a daily basis).

Solution

The customer's output report is his or her receipt. This will give:

(a) the name of the store;
(b) the store's VAT registration number;
(c) the date and time of the transaction;
(d) a list of items purchased, and their prices;
(e) the total price for all the customer's purchases;
(f) possibly, the method of payment;
(g) if payment is in cash, the amount of cash paid and the change given.

The output for a daily management report might include:

(a) a list of the total quantity and value of sales for each stock item;
(b) total sales for the day, possibly analysed by department or cash desk;
(c) a list of quantities of each item still held in stock;
(d) a list of stock items for re-ordering and quantities already on order.

Exercise 1

A factory includes 12 production lines, each making a different product. All materials, labour time, power used, good output and output rejected are recorded for each line on a computer system. Suggest contents for:

(a) a daily report for the production supervisor;
(b) a monthly report for the board of directors.

3   Input design

The design of input is important because in most computer systems, data is first of all collected in human-readable form and must be converted into computer input. People are thus very much involved in providing the data that the computer system will use, and in input design the systems analyst must balance the requirements of the system with the personal capabilities of its users.

Considerations in input design include the following.

(a)   Which input data will become 'standing' or 'static' master file data and which input will be regular transaction data? There should be no unnecessary re-input of data. For example, if master file data includes a customer's name, address and account number, it should only be necessary to input the account number with any transaction data. Transaction records should not contain the name and address.

(b)   What *volumes* of input are expected? Large volumes are likely to lend themselves to a batch processing system rather than a demand processing system.

(c)   What will the *frequency* of input be? Infrequent transaction data might suggest a demand processing system using keyboard terminals.

With batched input, we must consider:

(i)   how often transaction data must be input (daily, weekly or monthly);
(ii)   how often input data must be used to keep the master file up to date with standing data, that is how often *file maintenance* should be carried out.

(d)   In what *sequence* should batched data be input? For example, data for file maintenance ought to be input before transaction data, to ensure that the standing data on the master file is up to date before the transaction data is processed.

(e)   *Where* will data be collected or captured for input? Where will it be converted into machine-readable form? In general, it is preferable to capture data (in machine-readable form) as soon as possible and to keep to a minimum the transcription of data from one document to another before input.

(f)   What should the *input medium* be? Are inaccuracies costly or unacceptable, and so should there be *verification* of input? How extensive should checks be?

(g)   *What data* should be input? and in *what form?*

Data preparation control

In addition to input design, the systems analyst should give some consideration to data preparation control. Depending on the system, data preparation control may be applied by data preparation staff at a computer centre. Alternatively, data might be keyed in by staff in the user department. Data preparation design work must try to ensure that:

(a)   all the data that should be input is received and fed into the system;

(b)   all the data is processed through the system (apart from any erroneous data which is rejected, and which must also be accounted for).

Data preparation also includes any required *verification* of data.

Data preparation control in a batch processing system is achieved by means of batch control, that is collecting incoming documents into batches and attaching a batch control document (showing its serial number) to each batch. Batching offers several advantages.

(a) It helps in the allocation of work between data preparation staff: individual staff can be given specified batches of input to prepare, and their accuracy and speed can be monitored.

(b) Locating errors is simplified, because exception reports from the computer program notifying error conditions and rejected input can show which batch the incorrect entry belongs to.

(c) An incorrect batch can be removed individually, so that the remaining input can be processed without difficulty.

To help with batch control, the systems analyst should give some thought to:

(a) whether batches should be a constant size (all containing the same number of input records) or whether a batch control document record should identify the number (and perhaps the total value) of records in the batch;

(b) how data preparation management should be notified of what batches to expect. For example, can batches be received at regular intervals from the clerical staff preparing the original input forms, and can a list be provided of the batches sent?

Batch control assists with the control of input data. Control totals on batch control documents (for example the total value of all invoices in a batch) can be compared with control totals of records processed by the computer, so that a check can be carried out within a program that all the submitted data has been processed or can be accounted for by rejection reports.

Exercise 2

Transactions data is collected on forms which are filled in by hand. Not all of the handwritten data is to be keyed into the computer system, and some of the data which is keyed in is not processed immediately.

(a) Suggest features of the forms which would make it easy for staff keying in data to identify the data which should be keyed in.

(b) Should the data not required immediately be keyed in straightaway or should it be keyed in later, when it is required for processing?

---

4 Document design (form design)

In designing a system, an analyst may have to design a large number of different forms or documents for input data and for output. Although document design is largely a matter of common sense and experience, you should not forget the purpose of the document, nor the points discussed below.

The purpose served by a document is to ensure the effective transmission of necessary information. A good document will allow the required information to be obtained, transmitted, interpreted, filed and retrieved at minimum total cost. The total cost includes not only the printing and paper costs but also the handling costs. The latter may be significantly increased by bad design.

Before attempting to design a document the analyst must consider whether the document is really necessary, or whether there is another document, either existing or proposed, which serves or could be made to serve the same purpose. To help with analysing the documents, the analyst should prepare a document analysis form for each document in the existing system and for each document required in the new system.

The document analysis form for input documents is similar to a document description form (used to record facts about documents used in the existing system during systems investigation) and will include:

(a)   the *identification:* the document title and number;
(b)   the *purpose* of the document;
(c)   the *origination* of documents, both the place and the means of origination;
(d)   the *contents* of the document;
(e)   the *sequence* of the data;
(f)   the *volume* of use: maximum, minimum, average and seasonal fluctuations;
(g)   the *frequency* of preparation, at present and in the foreseeable future;
(h)   the *files* affected by the input, both transaction and master files.

The analyst must also consider the files used and should prepare a file analysis form to identify the purpose, content, layout and volume of records. The organisation and content of files may affect the format of the input document.

Exercise 3

The production department of a company uses a standard requisition form to obtain goods from stores. Set out possible entries on a document analysis form in respect of such a requisition form.

In designing a form there are a number of decisions to be made. These can be split into five areas: content, lay-out, make-up, printing and paper.

Computer graphics packages now make form design a relatively simple task. A number of alternative designs can be prepared and tested.

The content of forms

Generally, the content of a form will be determined by the system to which it belongs. There are, however, some items which appear on most forms, including:

(a) a title;
(b) a serial number;
(c) a date;
(d) some narrative, in the form of instructions and subsidiary headings;
(e) units such as hours, £'s or tonnes;
(f) a signature (perhaps with authorisation);
(g) the destinations of copies (for example copy 1 - accounts; 2 - production control).

The title of a form should be descriptive and easy to remember. The narrative, that is the headings or instructions relating to spaces where entries are required, must also be given careful consideration. The words used must be matched to the educational and technical level of both the originator and the interpreter.

The layout of forms

Points to consider include:

(a) the direction of the paper;
(b) the position of the title;
(c) the position of the identification code and the serial number (normally near a corner);
(d) the position of entry headings (near the spaces to which they relate);
(e) the entry sequence. Entries should always follow a logical sequence;
(f) the boxing of items, to make reading the form or filling it in easier.

The document may contain 'heading' information which is common to a number of repeated items ('variable' information). For example on a sales invoice the customer name, address, account number and invoice number is heading information whereas the product details such as quantity, description, code number and price is variable information, with several products likely to be listed on a single invoice.

Make-up, printing and paper

Considerations in this area will include:

(a) make-up:

    (i) the size of the form (for ease of handling and filing; and to allow enough space for all the information);
    (ii) the colour (*colour coding* may be used for ease of identification);

(b) printing:

    (i) the number of copies required (multi-part sets may be needed);
    (ii) the filing requirements (the position of the identification code and the serial number);
    (iii) the typeface (for easy reading and to stress important data);

(c)   the paper quality and thickness (how easily might a thin paper form be damaged, and how long will a form be kept?)

Qualities of a good form

A good form is one which is designed so that information can be easily:

(a)   *obtained:* the layout of the form and instructions on how to fill it in should be clear to the user. As much information as possible should be pre-printed to avoid error and reduce the workload. The form must be easy to use. Turnround documents might be a possibility;

(b)   *transmitted:* the form must allow for easy handling and transmission. For example it may need to be sent by post, and should therefore fit into a standard size envelope;

(c)   *interpreted:* the layout of information on the form must be in a clear, logical sequence so that it can be readily understood. A good title will help, and colour coding might also clarify its use. The use of different typefaces should be considered.

(d)   *filed:* the size of filing cabinets or trays should be considered;

(e)   *retrieved:* the problems of easy retrieval of a form from file should also be considered. In a hard copy file, the position of the serial number or some other key field of the record may be very important.

Exercise 4

Why might different considerations apply to the design of forms purely for internal use and forms to be sent to users outside an organisation?

Printing forms costs money and waste (for example by spending unnecessarily on form size, form quality or the number of copies in a set) should be avoided. Furthermore, data should only be gathered if the cost of doing so is justified by its value. Hidden costs may include the cost of writing the source documents, and the cost of data preparation and filing in a computer system.

In computer systems the entries on forms may have to be transcribed into a machine readable medium but the forms may have functions other than data collection for computer processing. For example, a sales invoice has to function as a sales invoice and so its contents may contain data which is not required for processing. The layout of the invoice must:

(a)   indicate clearly which data is to be transcribed into a machine readable medium, for example by shading parts of the document, by entering the data in a particular section of the document or by using chemically coated or carbon backed documents for selective duplication;

(b) show the data in keying-in sequence from left to right and from top to bottom of the sheet.

5 Code design

Linked with document and file design is the problem of code design. The purpose of a code is to identify items. Codes are often used because they can identify items more concisely and precisely than written descriptions. Coding can save data capture and preparation time, and it certainly facilitates computer processing. Coding saves internal storage space during processing and backing storage space. Codes can be re-converted into what they stand for by reference to standing data on a master file or reference file whenever uncoded output is required.

Classifications and codes

Classifications are groupings of items according to their characteristics. Individual items can be classified according to the groups to which they belong. *Coding* is a system for identifying in a shortened symbolic form the group that a particular item belongs to.

The following are the features of a good coding system.

(a) The codes are easy to use and to communicate.

(b) The system allows for expansion.

(c) If there is a conflict between the ease of use of a code by the people involved in a system and its manipulation by a computer, the human interest dominates.

(d) The system is flexible so that small changes in item classification can be incorporated without major changes to the system.

(e) The system provides unique reference codes for key items such as customer account numbers, supplier account numbers, stock code numbers or employee numbers.

(f) The system is comprehensive, so that every item can be suitably coded.

(g) Codes are brief, to save clerical time in writing out codes and to save storage space in computer memory and on computer files. At the same time codes are enough to allow for the suitable coding of all items.

(h) The likelihood of errors going undetected is minimised. *Check digits* are used. These are extra digits which are written as part of the code, but which can also be worked out from the rest of the code. A computer can work out what the check digits should be and compare them with the actual check digits. Any discrepancy shows that a mistake has been made.

(i) There is no duplication of the same code for different items.

(j) There is a readily available index of codes.

(k) Existing codes are reviewed regularly and out of date codes are removed.

(l)   All codes are of the same length. There are exceptions to this principle however, where different length codes are used for reasons of logical construction (as with hierarchical codes, see below) or to reflect operational requirements (as with telephone exchange codes).

(m) Code numbers are issued from a single, central point. Users are not allowed to add new codes to the existing list independently.

Exercise 5

Look at the ISBNs (International Standard Book Numbers) of some books (usually found on the back cover, or immediately after the title page in the front of the book). These numbers are issued by a single authority in each country. The first digit indicates the part of the world in which the book was published. The next group of digits indicates the publisher (for example, 14 for Penguin). The next group of digits is a number for the particular book, and the last digit is a check digit. Consider which of the above features of a good coding system the ISBN system displays.

Various coding systems (or combinations of them) may be used when designing codes. The systems include the following.

(a)   With *sequence codes*, no attempt is made to classify the items to be coded. Items are simply given the next available numbers in sequence. New items can only be inserted at the end of the list, so the codes for similar items may be very different. Here is an example.

    1   =   saucepans
    2   =   dusters
    3   =   kettles
    4   =   pianos

Sequence codes are rarely used when a large number of items are involved, except for document numbering (as with invoice numbers).

(b)   *Block codes* provide a different sequence for each different group of items. For example for a particular firm, customers may be divided up according to area.

    South East   Code numbers 10,000-19,999
    South West   Code numbers 20,000-29,999
    Wales   Code numbers 30,000-39,999

The coding of customer accounts is then sequential within each block.

(c)   *Significant digit codes* incorporate digits which are part of the description of the item being coded. Here is an example.

5000	Electric light bulbs
5025	25 watt
5040	40 watt
5060	60 watt
5100	100 watt

(d) *Hierarchical codes* are allocated on the basis of a tree structure where the inter-relationship between the items is important. Here is an example.

5	Computers
5 2	Hardware
5 2 1	Memory and storage
5 2 1.4	Storage devices
5 2 1.4 7	Magnetic media
5 2 1.4 7 3	Floppy disks

(e) With *faceted codes*, different features of the item are represented by the code. For example in a clothing store there might be a code based on the following facets.

Garment type	Customer type	Colour	SizeStyle

If SU stood for suit, M for man and B for blue, a garment could be given the code SU M B 40 17. Similarly ND F W 14 23 could stand for a woman's white nightdress size 14, style 23. The advantage of this system is that the type of item can be deduced from the code.

6 Screen design and dialogue design

Displays which contain a lot of data are often virtually useless since people cannot readily identify the important information. Whenever displays are being designed it is vital to consider their purpose and to present the information so that the users can quickly see and understand it.

Screen design

The VDU is used as both an input and an output device in many systems, and the systems designer has the job of designing the layout of the data on the screen. Relevant considerations are the same as those for the content and layout of forms.

Keyboard/screen dialogue

When the computer asks for information from the user, it should give a helpful prompt (such as 'please input sales total') rather than an uninformative '?'. When the user wants to ask for information from the computer, he or she should be able to do so in a natural way. This process can be helped by presenting the user with a menu of options, and inviting a choice between them. Thus a library catalogue system might offer a list such as:

1	-	Author search
2	-	Title search
3	-	Subject search

The user would then be invited to type 1, 2 or 3.

The dialogue should have a natural flow to it, clearly related to the user's understanding of the transactions being processed.

Exercise 6

A company sells several products over the telephone, customers paying by credit card. At the start of a call, the salesperson initiates a computer program to take the customer's personal details and order, and in the course of the conversation the salesperson types this information into the computer, requesting information from the customer in response to prompts on a VDU. Suggest an appropriate sequence for the prompts, so that the customer will feel that the order is being taken in a natural way by a human being.

---

7 File design

A systems analyst must also design the transaction files, reference files and master files or the database used in a system.

In designing master files, considerations will include the following.

(a) Is random access of the file by the system or the user needed?
(b) Is a quick response time needed?
(c) What data should the files contain?
(d) How will the files be used for processing transaction data?
(e) What facilities should be available for file interrogation?
(f) How will the files be maintained?
(g) How large will the files be, and what capacity for file growth should be built in?

If there is a choice of file medium (essentially, a choice between tape and disk or between types of disk), the factors governing the decision are:

(a) the required speed of movement of data between the storage devices and the computer's memory;

(b) the way in which records should be ordered for access (for example, is sequential ordering appropriate?);

(c) the need to allow enough room on the file for both the current volume and expected expansion;

(d) the expected 'hit rate', that is the ratio of the number of transaction records in a typical updating run to the number of master file records.

The systems analyst must provide facilities to insert new records onto the file and to amend or delete existing records. Adequate space must be allowed in the file for newly-inserted records. There might also be a requirement to *interrogate* the file, which might involve random access from a remote terminal.

Exercise 7

A company's accounting system is to be computerised. It is possible that eventually the number of products sold by the company will double, and the number of its customers will increase to three times the present number. All customers buy all products. The number of suppliers to the company is, however, expected to remain the same as at present. File sizes have already been calculated, based on the company's present level of activity but allowing for individual monetary and other amounts to have any reasonable number of digits. By how much would you multiply the calculated file sizes for each of the following files to determine the required computer file sizes, assuming that an extra 50% of the final anticipated level of activity is to be added as a safety margin?

(a) The sales (debtors) ledger, which requires an entry for each purchase of each product

(b) The purchases (creditors) ledger, which requires an entry for each order for each product

(c) The stock list

Chapter roundup

(a) The production of an outline systems design resembles the analysis of the existing system. In detailed systems design, outputs, inputs, files and programs must be designed.

(b) In the design of output, its content, format, frequency of production, volume, sequence of production and medium should all be considered.

(c) The designer of output should also consider whether all the output initially requested really ought to be produced.

(d) In the design of input, its volume, frequency, sequence and medium should all be considered, along with the method of data collection and conversion into machine-readable form, and what data actually needs to be input.

(e) Controls should be applied to the preparation of data.

(f) Proposed documents should be assessed for usefulness, and their contents and roles in the system should be analysed.

(g) There are certain standard contents which appear on most forms, and standard points to bear in mind in the layout of forms.

(h) A good form is one which makes it easy to record, file and retrieve information.

(i) Codes should be concise, yet easily intelligible. Coding systems include sequence, block, significant digit, hierarchical and faceted codes.

(j) A screen should be designed with the same care as a form. A keyboard/screen dialogue should use obvious English phrases, rather than codes which are hard to remember.

(k) In the design of files, the first thing to consider is how the files will be used. Requirements for methods of access, speed of access and space for expansion are all relevant.

BPP Publishing

Quick quiz

1   What are the three types of output to consider in output design?

2   What questions could be asked if it is suspected that the output asked for is excessive?

3   How should the data held on a master file be used to avoid unnecessary re-input of data?

4   What items appear on most forms?

5   What considerations of make-up, printing and paper are relevant to form design?

6   What are the qualities of a good coding system?

7   What is a hierarchical coding system?

8   List the factors which should be considered when designing master files.

Solutions to exercises

1   (a)   Good output from each line
Rejected output from each line
Materials used on each line
Labour time used on each line, analysed into normal time and overtime
Good output per labour hour

(b)   Monthly output of each product
Total materials, power and labour costs
Cost per unit of each product, analysed into materials, power and labour

2   (a)   Data to be keyed in should be surrounded by boxes, or data not to be keyed in should be written on shaded areas of the forms.

(b)   All data should be keyed in straightaway and stored in a storage device until required, so that each form need only be handled once by the keying in staff (so as to save time).

3   Title: Requisition form
Number: Req 1
Purpose: To obtain goods from stores for production
Origination: Production department, filled in by production supervisor
Contents and sequence: (i)   Date
(ii)   Item required
(iii)   Quantity required
(iv)   Date required
(v)   Location to be delivered to
(vi)   Special notes

Volume of use: Maximum 15 a day
Minimum 4 a day
Average 10 a day
Seasonal fluctuations - none
Frequency of preparation: As volume of use; no changes foreseen
Transaction files affected: Materials transfers
Materials orders
Master files affected: Production costs
Purchases ledger

4   Forms for internal use need not look very smart, and they may use abbreviations which will be understood by all staff affected. Forms to be sent to users outside the organisation will probably need to be printed to a higher standard on higher quality paper, and they must not use abbreviations which are not generally used outside the organisation.

5   The ISBN system:

allows for expansion;
provides unique reference codes;
is comprehensive;
minimises the likelihood of errors;
does not use the same code for different items;
makes all codes the same length;
ensures central control over the issue of codes.

6   Name
Address
Products required (including quantities)
Credit card number
Credit card expiry date

7   (a) $2 \times 3 \times 1.5 = 9$
(b) $2 \times 1 \times 1.5 = 3$
(c) $2 \times 1.5 = 3$

13 IMPLEMENTATION

Your objectives

After completing this chapter, you should:

(a) know the main stages in installing and implementing a computer system;
(b) know how to install a PC system;
(c) know what special arrangements are necessary to install a mainframe computer;
(d) understand the importance of tests and the role of test data;
(e) be aware of the steps in file conversion and of the problems which can arise;
(f) know four methods of changeover, and the factors affecting the choice between them;
(g) be aware of the scope of a performance review;
(h) be aware of how to assess a system by considering its outputs;
(i) understand the role of system maintenance.

1 System installation and implementation

The responsibility for successful system installation should rest with a team headed by a suitably senior manager, probably from the department which will use the new system. Membership of the team will vary from organisation to organisation, and according to the size and importance of the new system.

(a) In an organisation with its own data processing department, the team will include a systems analyst, or the data processing manager.

(b) In an organisation without a data processing department, the team should ideally include a person who already has some knowledge of data processing systems from his or her own experience.

(c) For a small office PC system using an off-the-shelf software package, the office manager will probably be given the job without other staff.

The tasks of this team are to co-ordinate the activities leading up to the installation and testing of the system and to make sure that these activities are carried out satisfactorily and on time.

The main stages in the installation and implementation of a computer system once it has been designed are:

(a) installing the hardware and software;
(b) testing;
(c) file conversion;
(d) changeover;

(e)   post-implementation review;
(f)   system maintenance.

Items (a) to (d) in this list do not necessarily happen in a set chronological order, and some of them can be done at the same time; for example system testing and master file creation can be part of the same operation.

Installing the hardware and software: PCs

With a PC system, the dealer may agree to install the system for the customer, but he may not, and the customer may have to install the hardware. This should not be difficult, provided that the manufacturer's instruction manuals are read carefully.

The office accommodation for PCs and peripheral equipment will need some planning.

(a)   PCs can be used in any office environment, but they generate some heat when they operate (just like any other machine) and so it is inadvisable to put them in small, hot rooms.

(b)   Large desks may be advisable, to accommodate a screen and keyboard and leave some free desk space for the user.

(c)   There should be plenty of power sockets: enough to meet future needs as the system grows, not just immediate needs.

(d)   If noisy printers (such as daisy wheel printers) are to be used, it may be advisable to locate these in a separate room, or at least fit them with printer hoods (covers), to cut down the noise for office workers.

(e)   There should be a telephone close to the PC, for communicating with the dealer or other organisation which provides system support and advice when the user runs into difficulties.

The software may also need installing. To install the software, the computer user must follow the instructions in the user's manual.

There will be an initial software installation to load the operating system, such as MS-DOS. Thereafter, whenever the PC is switched on at the start of the day, the bootstrap program will automatically load the operating system.

Software packages can be loaded onto the hard disk. There is an initial registration process to register the package with the PC. When this has been done, the user is only licensed to use the package on that machine.

Once the PC is working, the user should learn how to make *back-up copies* of disks and should make working copies of the software disks supplied (keeping the originals as back-up copies). This will not be possible if disks are copy-protected (and the user's manual will say which disks are copy-protected and which are not) but it will protect at least some of the software from accidental erasure. Back-up copies of data files held on hard disk can be made on floppy disks. Back-up copies of an entire hard disk might be made on a tape streamer.

Insurance should be arranged against losses from fire or theft. It is also possible to obtain insurance against the accidental loss of data. If all the data on a hard disk were lost, for example, it could be a long job to re-enter all the lost data, but with insurance cover, the cost of the re-inputting would be paid by the insurance company.

Exercise 1

What additional planning would be needed if a network of PCs, rather than a single PC, is to be installed?

The installation of a mainframe computer

A mainframe computer installation is a major operation which must be carefully planned. Issues in planning the installation include the following.

(a)   *Site selection*, whether in an existing or a new building. Factors in the choice of a site include the need for:

   (i)   adequate space for the computer and its peripherals, including room to allow servicing;
   (ii)   room for expansion;
   (iii) easy access for computer equipment and supplies (it should be unnecessary to knock holes in outside walls, as has happened, in order to bring equipment in);
   (iv)   nearness to principal user departments;
   (v)   strong flooring (so that the equipment does not fall to the floor below);
   (vi)   space for a library, a stationery store, the data preparation department and programmers' offices.

(b)   *Site preparation*, including the need for:

   (i)   air conditioning (temperature, humidity and dust);
   (ii)   special electricity supplies;
   (iii) raised floors (or false ceilings) to cover cables;
   (iv)   fire protection devices;
   (v)   furniture.

(c)   *Arrangements for standby equipment* to ensure continuity of processing in the event of power or computer failure. Such equipment may include rechargeable storage batteries, standby generators and standby computers.

(d)   *Planning for delivery*. Delivery can cause considerable disruption and it is often desirable for it to take place over a weekend.

Once all the required rooms have been completed, decorated and furnished, the equipment can be installed. This is the manufacturer's responsibility and his engineers will install it and carry out tests. Any further maintenance or repair of the equipment will normally be carried out by the manufacturer under a maintenance agreement.

In addition to the computer equipment, all the ancillary equipment (such as desks and trolleys) and the consumable stores (stationery, magnetic tapes, disks and so on) must be delivered and allocated to the appropriate work areas and stores.

2 Testing

A system must be thoroughly tested before implementation, otherwise there is a danger that the new system will be implemented with faults that might prove costly. The scope of tests will vary with the size of the system.

(a) When a system is designed in-house there should be *program tests* for each individual program in the system. There will then be tests of the interfaces between individual programs, in overall *system tests*.

(b) The user department will want to carry out tests on the system, whether it is designed in-house or bought from a software house. The initial tests ought to be carried out by management personnel, who know the current operational system well and who also ideally know something about computers. The tests would be intended to sort out any major problems, using dummy (invented) data.

Various personnel will be involved in system tests.

(a) The project manager will have overall responsibility for the project, and must ensure that the tests are planned and executed properly, and that the system is fully documented.

(b) Systems analysts must check that the system achieves the objectives set for it, and does not contain any errors.

(c) Programmers must be on hand to cure any faults which program tests had not spotted.

(d) The computer operations manager will be in charge of data preparation work and operations in the computer room and will report any faults or weaknesses to the data processing manager and the chief systems analyst.

Test data should be constructed to test all conditions. Data including all the possible errors which the system ought to detect (such as wage payments to a non-existent employee) should be included. Unusual, but feasible, transactions should also be included so as to see how the system handles them. Examples could include several sales orders from the same customer in the same batch input, or two wage packets in the same week for the same employee.

The data used in tests will not be wanted when the system is implemented, and so it does not matter whether data for the tests comes from current transactions or from historical data. Many managers prefer to use historical data, because it is then possible to check the output of the new system against the output that the current system actually produced.

Acceptance testing

Acceptance testing is the testing of a system by the user department, after the system has passed its system test. Tests are conducted by the user department's managers in order to:

(a) find software errors which exist but have not yet been detected;

(b) find out exactly what the demands of the new system are;

(c) find out whether any major changes in operating procedures will be necessary;

(d) test the system with large volumes of data;

(e) train staff in the new system and the new procedures.

These bulk tests on the system involve checks on:

(a) error correction procedures;

(b) the relationships between clerical and computer procedures;

(c) the timing of computer runs;

(d) the capacity of files;

(e) file handling, updating and amendment procedures;

(f) systems controls, including auditing requirements;

(g) procedures for data capture, preparation and input and the distribution of output.

Exercise 2

What unusual or erroneous transactions might be included in the test data for a stock control system?

---

3 File conversion

File conversion means converting existing master file records and reference file records to a form suitable for the new system. A system cannot become operational until master files for the new system have been created.

File conversion is a major part of systems implementation. It can be expensive because it often means the conversion of existing manual file records into a medium usable by the computer. This may involve the transcription of records, or parts of them, onto specially designed forms before they are keyed in.

File conversion can be tedious and time consuming. Because of the volume of data that must be copied onto the new files, the problem of *errors* getting onto the master files is a serious one, in spite of data validation checks in the file conversion program. Once the file has been created extensive checking for accuracy is essential, otherwise considerable problems may arise when the new system becomes operational.

Where the file conversion is from manual records the manager or systems analyst in charge of planning the conversion must establish:

(a) the location of the data (is all the data for each record on one form or on several forms?);

(b) whether the existing forms are suitable for data capture;

(c) whether the data format and sequence are suitable for the computer system;

(d) whether the existing records are maintained centrally or not;

(e) whether each form is easily accessible;

(f) the volumes involved;

(g) whether the existing files are to be converted directly or amalgamated in some way.

Before starting to load data about actual customers, suppliers or employees, management should check whether the system must be registered under the Data Protection Act 1984.

The stages in file conversion from manual files to computer files are normally as follows.

(a) Ensure that the original record files are accurate and up to date.

(b) Record the old file data on specially designed input documents. This will usually be done by the user department personnel (with additional temporary staff if required) following detailed instructions laid down by the systems analyst. These instructions will include the procedures for allocating new code numbers and for checking the accuracy and completeness of the data entered on the input documents (usually verification by another person and the calculation of control totals are used).

(c) Transcribe the completed input documents onto the computer media. This may be done by user department staff keying in the data from terminals, or in large systems, by data preparation staff at the computer centre.

(d) Use special programs to read the transcribed data and produce the required files in the appropriate form. These programs would include checks on the input data. The contents of the file must then be printed out and checked back in full to the data input forms (or to the original files if possible).

(e) Correct any errors that this checking reveals.

If there is an existing computer system, the difficulties of file conversion will usually be reduced. Existing computer files can be converted to new computer files by using a special *conversion program*.

Other problems of file conversion which must be considered and planned for by the systems analyst include the following.

(a) The possible need for additional staff, or the use of a computer bureau, to cope with the file conversion and prevent bottlenecks.

(b) The establishment of cut-off dates where files are being converted. Processing after a cut-off date is done on the new file.

(c) The decision as to whether files should be converted all at once, or whether the conversion should be file by file or record group by record group, with subsequent amalgamation.

Exercise 3

What checks might be appropriate when existing computer files are converted using a specially written conversion program?

---

4 Changeover options

Once the new system has been fully and satisfactorily tested the changeover can be made. This may be by direct changeover, parallel running, pilot operation or phased implementation.

Direct changeover

In this method, the old system is completely replaced by the new system in one move. This may be unavoidable where the two systems are substantially different, where the new system is a real-time system or where extra staff to oversee parallel running are unobtainable. While this method is comparatively cheap, it is risky (system or program corrections are difficult while the system has to remain operational) and management must have complete confidence in the new system. The new system should be introduced during slack periods and in large systems it may be introduced application by application, allowing several months between each stage to ensure that all problems are cleared up before the next stage becomes operational.

Parallel running

In this method the old and new systems are run in parallel for a period of time, both processing current data. Cross checks can then be made.

This method is fairly safe if there may be problems with the new system. However, if there are differences between the two systems cross-checking may be difficult or impossible. Furthermore, there is a delay in the actual implementation of the new system, a possible indication of lack of confidence in the new system and a need for more staff to cope with both systems running in parallel. This cautious approach, if adopted, should be properly planned, and the plan should include:

(a) a firm time limit on parallel running;
(b) details of how much data should be cross-checked;
(c) instructions on how errors are to be dealt with;
(d) instructions on how to cope with major problems in the new system.

Pilot operation

This is cheaper and easier to control than parallel running, and provides a greater degree of safety than does direct changeover. Only part of the data (say the sales in one region) is handled by the new system until it has been shown to work satisfactorily. If there is real concern about the new system, part of the data could be pilot-run on the new system while still being processed on the old system - a combination of parallel running and pilot operation.

Phased implementation

In *phased implementation*, a complete logical part of the old system (for example, the invoice issuing system) is chosen and run as a unit on the new system. If this works well the remaining parts are then transferred. Gradually the whole system can be transferred in this piecemeal fashion. Again, planning should involve setting strict time limits for each phase and instructions on how problems are to be dealt with. It must be remembered that two systems have to be controlled and additional staff may be required.

When deciding upon which method, or combination of methods, should be used for the changeover, management should consider:

(a) how co-ordination of the changeover is to be achieved;

(b) how to ensure complete and accurate communication throughout the system during the changeover period;

(c) the method of controlling errors and the amount of system change or program modification that can be permitted;

(d) the people who are involved, how the change affects them and how they can be trained and get used to working the new system;

(e) the maintenance and operation methods of the new system;

(f) the method of monitoring and evaluating the results of the changeover.

The *duration* of any parallel running or pilot operation can vary quite substantially between systems, from days to months. However, with tailor-made software purchased from a software house, it may be important to complete the changeover quickly, because the software house's debugging warranty (an agreement to correct program errors, called *bugs*) will normally expire three months after the date of purchase.

Timing is important. The new system should be installed and become operational at a time that is convenient to the user, preferably when the workload is fairly light, and certainly not at a time of peak workload. An accounting system might be installed to coincide with the beginning of a new accounts year.

On the satisfactory conclusion of parallel running or pilot operation, the system will go fully operational, benefiting from the lessons learned during tests and the changeover period.

Exercise 4

A company is computerising its sales system, using phased implementation. The system for debt collection is to be implemented first, followed by the system for issuing invoices. The debt collection system will automatically issue reminder letters based on the invoices issued but unpaid. Could there be problems if the invoice issuing system is amended during its implementation?

---

5 Post-implementation review

The system should be reviewed periodically so that any unforeseen problems may be solved and to confirm that it is achieving and will continue to achieve the desired results. Indeed in most systems there is a constant need to maintain and improve applications and to keep up to date with technological advances and changing user requirements.

The system should have been designed with clear, specified objectives, and justification in terms of a cost-benefit analysis or other performance criteria. Post-implementation review should establish whether the objectives have been met, and if not, why not, and what should be done.

In appraising the operation of the new system immediately after the changeover, a comparison should be made between actual and predicted performance. This will include (amongst other items) consideration of throughput speed (the time between input and output), the use of computer storage, the numbers and types of errors and queries, and the cost of processing.

The scope of reviews

Reviews will vary in content from organisation to organisation, but the matters which will probably be looked at are as follows.

(a) The rate of growth of file sizes and the number of transactions processed by the system. Trends should be analysed and projected to assess whether there are likely to be problems with long processing times or inefficient file structures due to the volume of processing.

(b) The staffing needs of the system, and whether they are more or less than estimated.

(c) Any delays in processing and the consequences of any such delays.

(d) The efficiency of security procedures.

(e) The error rates for input data. High error rates may indicate inefficient preparation of input documents, an inappropriate method of data capture or poor design of input media.

(f) Whether any amendments to the system are needed.

(g) External factors. Unforeseen circumstances might have affected system performance.

(h) Whether output from the computer is being used to good purpose: how is it used? is it timely? does it go to the right people?

(i) The adequacy of the system documentation.

(j) The costs and benefits of the system.

    (i) Have expected benefits been achieved or not?
    (ii) Are any unplanned benefits apparent?
    (iii) Are the costs of the system comparable with estimates?

(k) Users' comments on the system.

(l) Operational running costs, examined to discover any inefficient programs or processes. This examination may reveal excessive costs for certain items, even if costs in total may be acceptable.

A report on the review, making appropriate recommendations, should be prepared for submission to senior management.

The efficiency of a system can be assessed by looking at its outputs and inputs.

Outputs from a computer system

With regard to outputs, the efficiency of a computer system might be enhanced in any of the following ways.

(a) More outputs of some value could be produced with the same input, for example:

(i)   if the system could produce more management information;
(ii) if the system could make information available to more people who might need it.

(b) Outputs which have little or no value could be eliminated from the system. For example:

(i)   if reports are produced too frequently, they could be produced less often;
(ii) if reports are distributed too widely, the distribution list could be shortened;
(iii) if reports are too bulky, they could be reduced in size.

(c) The timing and frequency of outputs might be improved. Information should be available in good time for the information-user to be able to make good use of it. Reports that are issued late might lose their value. Computer systems could give managers immediate access to the information they require, using special software such as databases.

It might be found that outputs are not as satisfactory as they should be, perhaps because:

(a) *access* to information from the system is limited, and could be improved by the use of a database and/or a multi-user or network system;

(b) *output volume* is restricted because of the method of data processing used (for example, stand-alone PC systems might be slower and less efficient than multi-user systems) or the type of equipment used. A system's capabilities might be limited by:

(i)   the software's capabilities;
(ii) the size of the computer's main store;
(iii) the capacity of the computer's backing storage;
(iv) the number of printers linked to the computer;
(v)   the number of terminals.

A frequent complaint with many PC systems is that the operator may have to wait for certain outputs. For example, if an operator wants to call up a particular file, he or she might have to wait before the file becomes available. File enquiries can involve a lengthy wait too. Computer systems with better storage devices facilities can reduce this operator waiting time, and so be more efficient.

Inputs to a computer system

The efficiency of a computer system could be improved if the same volume and frequency of output could be achieved with fewer inputs or by inputting data more efficiently. For example, multi-user systems might be more efficient than stand-alone systems. Multi-user systems allow several operators to access the same files at the same time, so that if one person has a heavy workload and another is currently short of work, the person who has some free time can help his or her busy colleague.

Management might also wish to consider whether the checks on input data are too extensive, or could be achieved at less cost.

(a) In traditional batch processing systems, it might be unnecessary to verify all input data.

(b) An alternative method of input might be chosen. For example, if an accounts system is switched to an integrated system (instead of separate systems for the sales ledger, purchase ledger and nominal ledger) a single transaction need be input only once, thus saving input time and effort and improving the accuracy and reliability of processing.

Exercise 5

Why might a restructuring of a company's middle management, which does not affect the data processing department directly, make a review of the computer system appropriate?

---

6 System maintenance

System maintenance involves:

(a) updating the system, to adapt it to developments in the user's methods of operation or to environmental changes as and when they occur (for example new legislation). New processing requirements, changing volumes of processing and new methods of organisation and operation all make changes necessary. Systems must be amended to keep them functional;

(b) correcting errors as and when they are found;

(c) documenting the system updates and corrections.

With large computer systems which are designed in-house a systems analyst and a programmer in the data processing department might be given the responsibility for system maintenance.

With purchased software packages, the software supplier might agree with a customer to provide details of any new versions of the software package as they are produced, and might agree terms for providing new versions to replace old ones.

There is also likely to be an agreement between the supplier of software and the customer for the provision of a software support service. Software support involves providing experts in a system to give advice and help when a customer runs into difficulties. The help will initially be given by telephone. If a telephone call does not resolve the problem, the software expert will visit the customer's premises within a period of time agreed in the contract between the software supplier and the customer.

The key features of system maintenance ought to be *flexibility* and *adaptability*, so that:

(a)   the system, perhaps with minor modifications, can cope with changes in the computer user's procedures or volume of business;

(b)   the computer user can benefit from advances in computer hardware technology without having to switch to another system altogether.

If applications exceed the capabilities of computing resources all is not lost because it is possible to cope with increasing volumes and communication needs by enhancing the existing computer system, by:

(a)   increasing its memory by adding memory modules;
(b)   installing disks of greater capacity and higher speed;
(c)   installing a more powerful processor;
(d)   changing to faster printers;
(e)   installing additional terminals or network facilities.

Types of maintenance

Maintenance may be classified into three types.

(a)   *Corrective maintenance* means correcting errors as they arise.

(b)   *Perfective maintenance* means making improvements, usually in response to user requests. Users may ask for more facilities, or for software to be made easier to use (more *user-friendly*).

(c)   *Adaptive maintenance* means making changes to take account of changes in the environment. For example, changes in tax law might require changes in payroll programs.

Hardware maintenance

Computer hardware needs to be maintained. Maintenance services are provided:

(a)   by the computer manufacturers themselves; or
(b)   by third-party maintenance companies.

Maintenance of hardware can be obtained:

(a) on a contract basis. PC maintenance contracts are usually negotiated annually;

(b) on an ad hoc basis, calling in a maintenance company whenever a fault occurs.

Exercise 6

Give examples of how changes in a computer system for the benefit of some users might adversely affect other users within the same organisation.

Chapter roundup

(a) When a new system is to be implemented, more needs to be done than physically installing the new hardware. The new system must be tested, files must be converted, the changeover must be carefully managed and the new system must be reviewed and maintained.

(b) Installing a PC system is fairly straightforward, but the instructions of the hardware manufacturer and the software suppliers must be followed carefully.

(c) Installing a mainframe computer requires careful planning and site preparation.

(d) Both individual programs and the whole system must be tested, using test data designed to reproduce all conditions which may arise in practice.

(e) File conversion is time consuming and prone to errors. Careful planning and thorough checking are therefore required.

(f) A new system may be implemented by direct changeover, by parallel running, by pilot operation or by phased implementation.

(g) A post-implementation review should be wide-ranging, but should have clearly defined terms of reference.

(h) Inputs and outputs together define what a system actually does for its users, and should therefore be looked at closely in a review.

(i) System maintenance is needed so that the system can continue to meet the changing needs of its users.

Quick quiz

1   Which stages in the installation and implementation of a computer system could be carried out simultaneously?

2   In what ways should the layout of an office be considered when planning the installation of a PC system?

3   How do program tests differ from system tests?

4   What are acceptance tests?

5   What facts about manual files should be established before their conversion to computer files?

6   What are the normal stages in the conversion of manual files to computer files?

7   Distinguish pilot operation from phased implementation.

8   What matters might be considered in a post-implementation review?

9   What arrangements are normally available with software suppliers for system maintenance?

Solutions to exercises

1   The locations of all the PCs, the server and any shared peripherals (such as printers) must be planned. Cable runs between PCs must also be planned.

   A decision is needed on which software is to be available on which machines. Special licences are needed to share software between all machines in a network.

2   Re-ordering an item which is already on order.
   Ordering items not previously held.
   Requesting non-existent items from stores.
   Returning 20 units of an item to stores when only 15 were issued.

3   A sample of records on the new file should be compared with the corresponding records on the old file, to ensure that conversion was accurate. A sample of records on the old file should be compared with those on the new file, to ensure that all the old records did get converted.

4   Yes. The debt collection system will take data from files produced by the invocie issuing system. Any changes to the format of those files (for example putting the date before the amount in the record for each invoice, when they had been the other way round), might make it impossible for the debt collection system to obtain the data it needs.

                                                          BPP Publishing

5 Managers need information in order to do their jobs. The information must be relevant to their areas of responsibility. If those areas change, the information which should be supplied will also change, and this may require some changes to the computer system.

6 Sales data might be presented by region to suit one manager, whereas another might prefer it to be presented by product.

Detailed production records might be required to help the purchasing manager to check on the amounts of materials issued, creating extra work for the production supervisor.

14 TRAINING

> *Your objectives*
>
> After completing this chapter you should:
>
> (a) understand the need for training at all levels in an organisation;
> (b) be aware of the main methods of training available;
> (c) understand the role of documentation in training;
> (d) be aware of how people may react to the introduction of new systems;
> (e) know some appropriate responses to adverse reactions to change.

1   Methods of training

Staff training in the use of information technology is as important as the technology itself. Without effective operation at all levels computer systems can be an expensive waste of resources.

It is a major exercise to train possibly tens of thousands of employees. Here are some of the ways to meet these requirements.

(a) Traditional lectures given at training centres
(b) Computer-based training (CBT) involves on-screen practice on the system itself
(c) In-house video production, involving interactive videos
(d) Clear and comprehensive documentation and manuals for the system

Staff training policies should cover both *technological* skills needed and, if the job is to become more people-orientated, *interpersonal* skills.

Training is not simply an issue for clerical staff. As microcomputers are used more and more as management tools, training in information technology affects all levels in an organisation, from senior managers learning how to use an executive information system to accounts clerks learning how to record transactions.

Why train senior managers?

Managers who are knowledgeable about computers and related technologies make wiser decisions than less knowledgeable managers in the following areas.

(a) The allocation of resources to information systems
(b) Planning for information systems
(c) Establishing an appropriate corporate culture for technological development
(d) Appraising advice from information technology professionals

Senior management can be trained in a number of ways of varying degrees of formality:

(a) completely informal, such as:

(i)   newspapers (most of the quality press run articles on computing);
(ii)   subordinates (getting subordinates to demonstrate a system);
(iii) individual demonstrations of computer systems for senior executives;

(b) semiformal, such as:

(i)   executive briefings;
(ii)   video demonstrations;
(iii) short seminars, designed around an issue that is narrowly defined;

(c) formal sessions such as day courses, probably necessary if managers are to learn how to use a particular system.

Training middle management

The type of training middle management receives is likely to be more structured and more tailored to the particular applications within their remit.

Middle management are responsible for the correct use of systems in an age of distributed processing and end-user computing. They are also responsible for implementing in detail the organisation's computer security policy. They therefore need to have some basic understanding of the actual systems they are responsible for.

Managers do not need to know in detail how computers work. They need to know how to define information requirements, how to integrate systems and what computing can do for them.

Exercise 1

Senior and middle management need not learn programming languages such as COBOL. What computer skills should they acquire so that they can make good use of management information systems?

Training users

Users need a number of different types of computer and systems training.

(a) *Basic literacy in data processing* such as the concept of a file, updating, maintenance and so forth, is needed. This might help users to relate the workings of a manual system to its computer replacement. Also, some basic ideas on how to use a computer efficiently can be usefully taught.

(b) Users also need to learn how to use a *particular application* quickly, even if they do not go into the finer points of it. Such training may also give users an overall view of the system, its commands and procedures.

(c) Users might sometimes need a *refresher course*, especially if they do not use a particular application regularly.

(d) Users need training while operating the application (learning by doing).

(e) Users might need to be trained in the use of fourth generation languages.

Some of these facilities are provided by the computer system itself. For example, many software packages have a help facility which enables users to get information about the system while they are using it. The use of such facilities has the advantage of encouraging users to become acquainted with the technology they will be using, and to develop their skills at their own pace.

Training can also be provided by:

(a) reading the user manuals;

(b) *disk-based tutorials* provided by a software house;

(c) attending courses that the dealer or employer provides;

(d) attending courses on a leading software package (such as Lotus 123) or an operating system (such as MS-DOS) provided by a third party training establishment.

With large computer systems, extensive training of large numbers of staff will probably be necessary. Additional training measures may include:

(a) lectures on general or specific aspects of the system;

(b) discussion meetings, possibly following on from lectures, which allow the staff to ask questions and sort out problems;

(c) internal company magazines, to explain the new system in outline;

(d) handbooks, detailing the new documentation and procedures. Handbooks for different purposes will often be prepared by different persons, for example:

    (i) systems specifications, prepared by systems analysts;
    (ii) software manuals, prepared by manufacturers or by software houses;
    (iii) program specifications, prepared by senior programmers;
    (iv) computer operating instructions, prepared by programmers or by the software supplier;
    (v) data preparation instructions, prepared by the operations department;
    (vi) data control and library procedures, prepared by the operations department;
    (vii) clerical procedure manuals, prepared by analysts and user departments.

(e) using tests on the new system to give staff direct experience before the system goes live.

Training will be the ultimate responsibility of the information director or of the personnel department in cooperation with users and computer professionals.

User documentation

At some stage before staff training takes place, the system must be fully documented for users. User documentation must tell users what they need to know in order to run programs.

User documentation is used to explain the system and to help to train staff. Additionally, it provides a point of reference should users have problems with the system in the future.

Explaining the system involves:

(a) specifying the inputs needed to the system, the format of input records, the content of each record field, the coding systems used and so on. If the system uses keyboard input, the user documentation should also set out the VDU screen designs for input, the nature of any menus or other screen prompts, the nature of any interactive processing and so on;

(b) explaining the nature of the processing methods, for example on-line input and file enquiry;

(c) specifying the nature of the system's files and what they contain;

(d) explaining the system's outputs, for example reports and documents, including the meaning of any exception reports where input data has been rejected as invalid or queried;

(e) giving instructions about what to do in the event of a system failure;

(f) establishing the clerical procedures or other ancillary procedures needed.

Exercise 2

Some computer systems incorporate documentation which the user can access during processing, by entering a 'help' command. However, only one screenful of information can be displayed at once, and different users may need different kinds of advice. How might menus be used so that users can quickly access the information they need?

---

2 The human factors in systems development and implementation

Technological change and the working environment

Technological changes have extensive effects on the world of work.

(a) Semi-skilled jobs will be taken over by robots and computers. There will be fewer jobs or more part-time jobs, and so less need for supervision.

(b) There may be degrading of old skills, or an end to the need for old skills. New skills will be needed, and:

(i)   there will be more pressure on managers to provide training or re-training for staff;

(ii) management development will be more important, to keep managers up to date, and to motivate them as advancement gets harder.

(c)   As equipment becomes simpler to use, there could be opportunities for greater flexibility in manning, with one worker able to carry out more varied tasks. In manufacturing, there may be more continuous shift work working (24 hours a day), to keep expensive assets in constant use.

(d)   Since more jobs will be part-time, there will be less need for full-time employees. More work will be contracted out, and full-time jobs will be lost. Managers will have to deal with external contractors instead of issuing directions to their own staff.

(e)   Better communications systems, portable computers and so on reduce the need for people to work together in an office. There will be more working at home. Several managers can then share the same small office, and come into work only occasionally.

(f)   Working at home is likely to speed up moves towards contracting out, and some managers might become self-employed consultants with a main client (the former employer) and a number of smaller clients who are picked up as the individual gradually markets his or her services more widely.

(g)   Improved information systems should help managers to plan and control work more effectively.

(h)   Better information systems open up opportunities for:

(i)   more *centralisation* of decision making by top management;
(ii) reducing the number of middle managers.

Areas of concern

Job security and status. Employees might think that a new system will put them out of a job, because the computer will perform routines that are currently done manually.

Even when there is no threat of losing jobs, a new system might make some staff, experienced in the existing system, feel that all their experience will be worthless when the new system goes live, so that they will lose status within the office.

Resistance to a new system might stem from a fear that it will result in a loss of status for the *department* concerned. For example, the management of the department concerned might believe that a computer system will give control over information gathering and dissemination to another group in the organisation. Dysfunctional behaviour might include:

(a)   interdepartmental squabbling about access to information;

(b)   a tendency to disregard the new sources of information, and to stick to old methods of collecting information instead.

Career prospects. Managers and staff might think that a new system will damage their career prospects by reducing the opportunities for promotion. When the effect of a system is to reduce the requirement for staff in middle management and supervisory grades, this could well be true. On the other hand, today's successful manager should be able to adapt to information technology, and developing a career means being flexible, accepting change rather than resisting it.

Social change in the office. New systems might disrupt established social systems in offices. Individuals who are used to working together might be separated into different groups, and individuals used to working on their own might be expected to join groups. Office staff used to moving around and mixing with other people in the course of their work might be faced with the prospect of having to work in isolation at keyboards, unable to move around the office as much. Where possible, new systems should be designed so as to leave the social fabric of the workplace undamaged. Group attitudes to change should then be positive rather than negative.

Bewilderment. It is easy for individuals to be bewildered by change. The systems analyst must explain the new system fully, clearing up doubts and inviting and answering questions, from a very early stage in systems investigation onwards through the design stages to eventual implementation.

Fear of depersonalisation. Staff may be afraid that the computer will take over and they will be reduced to being operators chained to the machine, losing the ability to introduce the human touch to the work they do. This is not wholly unrealistic.

Dysfunctional behaviour might follow from antagonism of operating staff towards data processing specialists who are employed to design and introduce a computer system. It might include:

(a) an unwillingness to explain the details of the current system, or to suggest weaknesses in it that the new system might eradicate. Since data processing staff need information from and participation by the operating staff to develop an efficient system, any such antagonism would impair the system design;

(b) a reluctance to be taught the new system;

(c) a reluctance to help in introducing the new system.

A new system will reveal weaknesses in the previous system, and so another fear of computerisation is that it will show up exactly how inefficient previous methods of information gathering and information use had been. If individuals feel that they are put under pressure by the revelation of any such deficiencies, they might try to find fault with the new system too. When fault-finding is not constructive, that is not aimed at improving the system, it will be dysfunctional in its consequences.

In extreme cases, dysfunctional behaviour might take a more drastic form. Individuals might show a marked reluctance to learn how to handle the new equipment, they might be deliberately slow keying in data, or they might even damage the equipment in minor acts of vandalism.

Exercise 3

How might staff working on PCs at home linked to a central computer be monitored to ensure that their productivity does not fall?

Overcoming the human problems

To overcome the human problems with systems design and implementation, management and systems analysts must recognise them, and do what they can to resolve them.

(a) Employees should be kept fully informed about plans to install new systems, how matters are progressing and how new systems will affect what people do.

(b) It should be explained to staff why change is for the better.

(c) User department employees should be encouraged to participate fully in the design of a new system, when the system is a tailor-made one. Participation should be genuine.

   (i) Their suggestions about problems with the existing system should be fully discussed.
   (ii) The systems analyst's ideas for a new system should be discussed with them.
   (iii) Their suggestions for features in the new system should be welcomed.

(d) Staff should be informed that they will be spared boring, mundane work because of the possibility of automating such work and so will be able to take on more interesting, demanding and challenging work.

(e) Employees should be told that they will be able to learn new skills which will make them more attractive candidates either for internal promotion or on the external labour market. For example, experience with databases or spreadsheet models could greatly enhance an office worker's experience.

(f) A training programme for staff should be planned in advance of the new systems being introduced. If there are to be job losses, or a redeployment of staff, these should be arranged in full consultation with the people concerned.

(g) Careful attention should be given to:

   (i) the design of work organisation;
   (ii) the development or preservation of 'social work groups';
   (iii) the relationship between jobs and responsibilities in a new system.

(h) Change should be planned and managed. Reductions in jobs should be foreseen, and redundancies should be avoidable if plans are made well in advance (for example staff could be moved to other jobs in the organisation). Training (and retraining) of staff should be organised.

(i) A member of staff should be appointed as the office expert on the system, to whom other members of staff can go to ask for help or advice. When the software is bought as an off-the-shelf package, this office expert should be the person who contacts the software supplier about any problems with the system.

(j) *Management and a new system.* When a system is designed in-house, the systems analyst should:

   (i) produce changes gradually, giving time for personnel to accept the changes;
   (ii) build up a good personal relationship with the people he or she has to work with;
   (iii) persuade management to give sound guarantees for the future;
   (iv) work towards getting employees to accept change as a matter of course;

(v)   be willing to listen to and act on criticisms of the system under design.

(k)   The system should not be introduced in a rush. Users of the system should be given time to become familiar with it. Implementation by means of parallel running might be advisable.

(l)   Confidence between the systems analyst and operational staff should be built up over time.

(m)   The systems analyst should have the full and clearly expressed support of senior management.

This checklist has concentrated on staff. However, in the long term it is also likely that middle management will be affected by computerisation.

Exercise 4

What concerns might middle management have about the effects of computerisation?

> **Chapter roundup**
>
> (a)   Staff training, in both technological skills and interpersonal skills, is essential to the success of new computerised systems.
>
> (b)   Managers who will not be engaged in the daily operation of the system still need to be trained, so that they may make wise planning, resource allocation and control decisions.
>
> (c)   Users need detailed training in the operation of a system. They also need to be provided with good quality user documentation, so that they can find out what to do in any situation which might arise.
>
> (d)   Staff may well react adversely to the introduction of a new system, because methods of working and the social structure of the organisation may change, and because staff may be concerned about job security.
>
> (e)   To overcome such problems, staff should be kept fully informed and consideration of the human factor should be built into the development and implementation process.

Quick quiz

1   What methods are available to train senior managers?

2   What types of training are needed by users?

3   What methods are available to train users?

4   How is the working environment likely to be changed by the introduction of new technology?

5   What are the main fears which office workers might have when new technology is introduced?

6   What steps can be taken to overcome resistance to technological change?

Solutions to exercises

1   How to extract data from files
    How to formulate queries to get data from databases
    How to use spreadsheets and financial modelling packages
    How to combine text, figures and graphs to produce reports

2   When the 'help' command is used, an initial screen relevant to the type of processing being carried out at the time could be given. This would give some basic information, and would end with a menu including options such as:

    (a)   exit from help and resume processing;
    (b)   details of commands which can be used at the current stage of processing;
    (c)   how to obtain printed output of the results of processing so far;
    (d)   information on other topics (to be specified by the user).

3   The central computer could record the times when a PC is switched on and the number of transactions processed (or number of words typed) each day. However, companies considering such monitoring should be aware that it may lead to low staff morale and even to legal action for repetitive strain injury brought on by pressure of work.

4   They might be concerned that top management might no longer need middle management as gatherers and processors of information, because a computerised MIS could do that job just as well. The number of staff might fall, reducing the requirement for middle management.

BPP Publishing

15 SECURITY AND CONTROLS

Your objectives

After completing this chapter you should:

(a) understand the need for security and controls;
(b) be aware of the main risks to data;
(c) know the main personnel controls;
(d) know the main physical security and access controls;
(e) understand the need for protection against hacking and viruses;
(f) know the elements of good office practice in relation to computer systems;
(g) be aware of the main back-up procedures and the need for standby facilities;
(h) know how costs, progress and amendments can be controlled when a new system is being designed;
(i) be aware of criteria governing the level of operational control to be built into the system;
(j) understand the need for controls over implementation, file conversion and system amendments;
(k) understand the purposes of data processing standards;
(l) know the uses and contents of system documentation;
(m) understand the need for application controls;
(n) know how data capture, data transcription and data transmission may be controlled;
(o) know what validation checks may be applied;
(p) know what output, file and database controls may be applied;
(q) be aware of some hardware controls.

1 The need for security and controls

Data, software and hardware are valuable resources and must be kept secure from being wrongly changed or being destroyed accidentally or deliberately. Data must also be secured against wrongful disclosure.

(a) Organisations which lose computerised data, perhaps because of a hardware fault or a telecommunications fault, can suffer financial loss. They might, for example, lose records of amounts of money owing to them for purchases.

   Computer users should do all they can to prevent the loss or corruption of data. The cost of repairing a hardware fault may be just a fraction of what it might cost to reinstate data that is lost because of a hardware fault.

(b) Data about a company's operations which might be of interest to the company's competitors should not be allowed to fall into their hands. Confidential data which is being word processed might be vulnerable to unauthorised access.

(c) The Data Protection Act 1984 incorporates a principle that computerised personal data be kept secure against wrongful disclosure.

(d) If computerised data is not protected properly, there will be scope for computer fraud.

Data controls

There is also a need for controls to ensure that data is:

(a) collected in full and with accuracy;
(b) generated at the appropriate times;
(c) kept up to date and accurate on file;
(d) processed properly and accurately, to provide meaningful and useful output.

If these requirements are not met, management may make wrong decisions based on inaccurate data, and routine processing of transactions will be subject to errors.

The three general aims of controls are:

(a) error detection: ensuring that any errors are found;
(b) error correction: ensuring that errors are put right;
(c) error reduction: making it less likely that errors will arise in the first place.

What can go wrong?

Data processing by computer creates extra problems for control because of its special characteristics, which are that:

(a) large volumes of data are concentrated into files that are physically very small;

(b) large quantities of data are processed without human intervention, and so without humans knowing what is going on. This places great reliance on the accuracy of programs and of data on file;

(c) it is easy to lose data on file. Equipment can malfunction, data files can become corrupt and store meaningless data, data can get lost when files are copied, and data files are susceptible to loss through theft, flood or fire;

(d) unauthorised people can gain access to data on files, and read confidential data or tamper with the data. This is a particular problem with on-line systems because access to a computer program and master file can be from any remote terminal. It is even possible for 'hackers' to use their home computers to gain access to the files and programs of other systems;

(e) information on a computer file can be changed without leaving any physical trace of the change.

It does not help matters that computers lack judgement, and errors in data processing by computer can go undetected when this would not be the case with manual data processing. For example, a payroll system might produce a salary cheque for an employee of £0.00 or for £1 million, and would not know that it had done something wrong. This sort of problem can be overcome by building range checks and reasonableness checks into a program as a data validation routine.

A further problem is that programmers are experts, and with careful planning, a dishonest programmer can tamper with a program to his own benefit. A case has been recorded, for example, of a programmer who arranged for all fractions of a penny in salaries to be paid into a bank account which the programmer opened and from which he took the money. Several thousand payments mounted up over time into substantial sums of money.

Accidental error can cause problems too. What is to stop a computer operator from using a disk containing master file data to take output from a different program? If this were done, the data on the master file could be wiped out. This is such an important source of potential error that controls to prevent this from happening should be built into any computer system.

Computer systems controls must be maintained regardless of the size of application or method of processing (batch or real time). If certain controls are difficult to establish in a microcomputer system (for example division of responsibilities), more emphasis must be placed on other controls.

Exercise 1

To what extent is a sole trader with no employees, keeping accounting records on her own PC, at risk from the dangers to data and systems mentioned above?

The risks to data

The dangers associated with information storage on a magnetic medium include the following.

(a) *Physical security*
Tapes or disks can be stolen, mislaid or damaged or destroyed by fire, flood or vandalism.

(b) *Environmental security*
Tapes and disks are susceptible to magnetic fields, dust and extremes of temperature and humidity. Although in modern PCs the problems of environmental control have been reduced, they are still quite important.

(c) *Loss of confidentiality*
Information stored in magnetic files may be accessed by unauthorised persons. This is a particular problem in larger systems with remote terminals, or in time sharing or computer bureau applications.

(d) *Processing the wrong file*
Since data is in magnetic form, and not visible, the wrong file could be read, or a file could be overwritten when its data is still needed.

(e) *Hardware or program corruption*
Hardware or software faults may damage or destroy the data on files.

Controls which can be implemented to counter the risks described above fall into two categories.

(a) *General controls* ensure that the computer environment is secure. They fall into two groups:

    (i) administrative controls, which are designed to support the smooth continuing operation of systems;

    (ii) system development controls, which are designed to ensure that any new system does not present new risks to the environment.

(b) *Application controls* are built into operations, and ensure that processed data is accurate and complete.

2 Administrative controls

Some controls can be applied at relatively small cost, simply by introducing sensible administrative and organisational measures.

Administrative controls are controls over data and data security that are achieved by administrative measures. They should be applied:

(a) in the data processing department, where an organisation is large enough to have one; and

(b) in other offices. With PC systems, administrative controls will include controls over handling the computer hardware, software and files.

Administrative controls should include:

(a) controls over personnel;
(b) the segregation of duties;
(c) physical security;
(d) access controls;
(e) protection against hacking and viruses;
(f) good office practice;
(g) back-up and standby facilities.

Personnel

Controls related to personnel, which were developed before the advent of computers, include:

(a) job rotation, so that employees change jobs at random intervals, thus making it uncertain that an individual will be able to set up a breach of security in the time available;

(b) enforced vacations;

(c) access to information granted not on the basis of rank in the management hierarchy or precedent, but on a need to know basis.

Some employees, such as the systems analyst and the computer security officer, are always in a position of trust. However, a well-designed security system puts as few people as possible in this powerful position.

Exercise 2

Why is it a useful control to force staff to take their holiday entitlements?

The segregation of duties

Work should be divided between systems analysts, programmers and operating staff, and operations jobs themselves should be divided between data control, data preparation and computer room operations. The functions of an organisation structure, as far as control is concerned, are:

(a) to assign responsibility for certain tasks to specific jobs and individuals. A person in a given job is responsible for ensuring that certain controls are applied. Some jobs are specifically control jobs. These are the jobs of the data control clerks and, to a large extent, of the file librarian (see below);

(b) to prevent fraud. It is easier for a person to commit fraud if he can input data, write programs and operate the computer all by himself. By dividing up the work, it is made harder to commit fraud or tamper with data, except in collusion with others.

Duties may be segregated by ensuring that no member of staff works on more than one of:

(a) data capture and entry;
(b) computer operations;
(c) systems analysis and programming.

In addition, within the computer operations section, the computer operators should ideally not be responsible for data control, nor should they be responsible for looking after the computer file library.

An organisation chart and procedure manuals which set out clearly who does what, and what practices are forbidden, should be prepared.

In the case of PC systems these organisational controls often do not apply. The person who operates the computer also inputs data, and may even write his or her own programs for it. In these cases, however, it is essential that the data being processed is not such as to have a bearing on the assets of the business. For example, if a PC were to be used for a sales ledger system or a payroll system, the person responsible for data input and operating the PC should neither design the system nor write its programs, and there must also be suitable internal and external audit checks of the system.

Data processing staff should be properly trained in security and control measures and the need for them.

The file librarian and data control clerks

The functions of the *file librarian* and *data control clerks* should strengthen administrative controls in mainframe installations.

(a) The *librarian* has the task of looking after the computer files, and making sure that:

    (i) the files are kept physically secure, protected from damage, theft and unauthorised access;

    (ii) the files do not get lost, and are always traceable;

    (iii) external file labels are maintained and a log is kept of what data is on each physical file;

    (iv) files are not purged until it is safe to remove the data and reuse the disk or tape;

    (v) the correct version of a file is used for processing;

    (vi) back-up copies of files are made whenever required;

    (vii) files are issued only to authorised personnel.

(b) *Data control clerks* have the task, as their job title suggests, of helping to control the data that is input to and output from processing. The control section might:

    (i) receive batched input documents from a user department. It would then check that the number and identity of the batches received tallied with the batch control document submitted by the user department. Lost batches of data would be immediately identified;

    (ii) schedule the input data for processing, and the files and programs needed to do the processing;

    (iii) monitor rejected or dubious data items (as shown on *exception reports* generated by the computer) and where necessary, see to the immediate correction and re-submission of these items;

    (iv) receive output from the computer, and check that it appears to be correct, for example making sure that every batch has been processed;

    (v) distribute the output to the user department, and liaise with it on all problems.

Exercise 3

Give an example of a fraud which might be committed by a dishonest employee responsible both for entering data and for dealing with exception reports, but which would be prevented if the exception reports went directly to a manager for review.

Physical security

Physical security comprises two sorts of controls:

(a) protection against disasters such as fire and flood;
(b) protection against intruders gaining physical access to the system.

The physical environment has a major effect on information system security, and so planning it properly is an important part of an adequate security plan.

Fire is the most serious hazard to computer systems. The destruction of data can be even more costly than the destruction of hardware. A proper fire safety plan is an essential feature of security procedures, in order to prevent fires, detect fires and put out fires. Fire safety includes:

(a) site preparation (appropriate building materials and fire doors);
(b) detection (smoke detectors);
(c) extinguishers (such as sprinklers);
(d) training for staff in observing fire safety procedures.

Methods of controlling human access include:

(a) personnel (security guards);

(b) mechanical devices (such as keys, whose issue is recorded);

(c) electronic identification devices (such as card-swipe systems, where cards are passed through readers).

It may not be cost effective or convenient to have the same type of access controls in the whole building all of the time. Instead, the various security requirements of different departments should be estimated, and appropriate boundaries drawn. Some areas will be very restricted, whereas others will be relatively open.

Physical installation security

Measures to ensure physical security in the computer room are as follows.

(a) Computer rooms should be kept locked when not in use. Only authorised personnel should have keys. Locks to computer rooms should be secure.

(b) Computer files should be kept locked in a safe place, such as a fireproof safe.

(c) The physical conditions in which the hardware and files are kept should be suitable, that is not too hot, damp or dusty. Unscreened electric motors should not be used in or near the file library, because they might corrupt data on magnetic file media.

(d) Measures should be taken to minimise the risks of fire. Waste paper should not be allowed to pile up. Computer rooms should have smoke alarms and be fully equipped with fire extinguishers.

Exercise 4

What are the relative advantages and disadvantages of security guards and electronic identification devices?

Access controls

Access controls are controls designed to prevent unauthorised access to data files or programs. Access controls which can be built into a system's software are:

(a) passwords;
(b) encryption and authentication.

Passwords

Passwords can be applied to data files, program files and parts of a program. The computer does not allow a user access to the relevant facilities until he or she has typed in the appropriate password.

(a) One password may be required to read a file and another to write new data.

(b) The terminal user can be restricted to the use of certain files and programs. For example in a banking system, low grades of staff are only allowed access to certain routine programs.

Virtually all mainframe or distributed processing systems use passwords. In order to access a system the user needs first to enter a string of characters as a password. If the entered password matches one issued to an authorised user the system permits access, otherwise the system excludes the user and may record the attempted unauthorised access. Keeping track of these attempts can alert managers to repeated efforts to break into the system, and so the culprits might be caught.

Many password systems come with standard pre-set passwords. It is essential that these be changed if the system is to be at all secure, since such common passwords may become widely known to people in the industry.

Passwords ought to be effective in keeping out unauthorised users, but they are by no means foolproof. Experience has shown that unauthorised access can be obtained.

(a) By experimenting with possible passwords, an unauthorised person can gain access to a program or file by guessing the correct password. This is not as difficult as it may seem when too many computer users specify obvious passwords (such as their spouses' names).

(b) Someone who is authorised to access a data or program file may tell an unauthorised person what the password is, perhaps through carelessness.

BPP Publishing

Data communications controls: encryption and authentication

When data is transmitted over a communications link or within a network, there are three security dangers:

(a)   a hardware fault;

(b)   unauthorised access by an eavesdropper;

(c)   direct intervention by someone who sends false messages down a line, claiming to be someone else, so that the recipient of the message will think that it has come from an authorised source.

Encryption is the only secure way to prevent eavesdropping (since eavesdroppers can get round password controls, by tapping the line or by experimenting with various likely passwords). Encryption involves scrambling the data at one end of the line, transmitting the scrambled data and unscrambling it at the receiver's end of the line.

Authentication is a technique to make sure that a message has come from an authorised sender. Authentication involves adding an extra field to a record, with the contents of this field derived from the remainder of the record by applying a formula that has previously been agreed between the senders and recipients of data.

Exercise 5

If passwords are issued to operators by a manager, there will probably be a list of passwords on paper, which could fall into the wrong hands. How could a system be arranged so that each operator has a password which has never been written down?

Protection against hacking and viruses

As it becomes common for computers to communicate over long distances, the risks of corruption or theft of data or even whole programs becomes much greater. Two interconnected security issues are hacking and viruses.

Hacking

A hacker is a person who attempts to invade the privacy of a system. Hackers are normally skilled programmers, and have been known to find out passwords with ease. The fact that billions of bits of information can be transmitted in bulk over the public telephone network has made it hard to trace individual hackers, who can therefore make repeated attempts to invade systems. Hackers have in the past mainly been concerned to copy information, but a recent trend has been their desire to corrupt it.

Viruses

Computer viruses are currently the cause of much concern. A *virus* is a piece of software which infects programs and data and which replicates itself. There are a number of types of virus.

A *trojan* is a program that while visibly performing one function secretly carries out another. For example, a program could be running a computer game, while simultaneously destroying a data file or another program.

A *logic bomb* is a piece of code triggered by certain events. A program will behave normally until a certain event occurs, for example disk utilisation reaches a certain percentage. A logic bomb, by responding to such conditions, maximises damage. For example it will be triggered when a disk is nearly full, or when a large number of users are using the system.

A *time bomb* is similar to a logic bomb, except that it is triggered at a certain date. Companies have experienced virus attacks on April Fool's Day and on Friday 13th. These were released by time bombs.

A *trap door* is not itself a virus, but it is an undocumented entry point into a computer system. It is not to be found in design specifications but may be put in by software developers to enable them to bypass access controls while working on a new piece of software. Because it is not documented, it may be forgotten and used at a later date to insert a virus.

Viruses can spread via data disks, but have been known to copy themselves over whole networks. The most serious type of virus is one which infects an operating system as this governs the whole running of a computer system.

How can organisations protect themselves against viruses?

(a) *Vaccine* programs exist which can deal with some viruses, but if the virus lives in the bootstrap program, the virus can work before the vaccine is loaded.

(b) Organisations must guard against the introduction of unauthorised software to their systems. Many viruses have been spread on pirated versions of popular computer games.

(c) Organisations should as a matter of routine ensure that any disk received from outside with data on it is virus-free before the disk is used.

(d) Any flaws in a widely used program should be rectified as soon as they come to light.

(e) There should be a clear demarcation between the storage of *data files* and *program files* on disk.

(f) Overall, organisations need to establish procedures and reviews to minimise the chance of infection. Virus protection controls should become part of the internal control system of an organisation, as with controls to prevent fraud.

BPP Publishing

Exercise 6

Viruses may be planted by disgruntled employees. What implications does this have for procedures when an employee is subject to disciplinary procedures, is dismissed or is made redundant?

Good office practice

There are several points of good practice which may seem minor, but which can together make a major contribution to the integrity of a system.

Data is often shared between users. There should be a designated data owner for each file, responsible for:

(a) keeping the data accurate and up to date;
(b) deciding who should have access to the data;
(c) developing security procedures in conjunction with the data security manager.

If computer printout is likely to include confidential data, it should be shredded before being thrown away.

Disks should not be left lying around an office. They can get lost or stolen. More likely, they can get damaged by spilling tea or coffee over them, or by allowing the disks to gather dust which can make them unreadable.

The computer's environment (humidity, temperature and dust) should be properly controlled. This is not so important for PCs as for mainframes, and hard disks are protected from dust. Even so, the computer's environment and the environment of the files should not be excessively hot. Temperature changes can cause disk failure, even with PCs.

Files should be backed up regularly. Procedures should not be allowed to slacken, with office staff not bothering to create back-up files because it takes them too much time.

Maintenance and support

All computers are covered by some kind of warranty from the manufacturer when they are bought new. Warranty periods range in length, typically up to one year. But what should the computer user do after the warranty period has expired?

(a) The user can decide to do nothing until the computer has a breakdown or other fault, and can then ask a third party computer repair company to come in and do the repair work. The drawbacks to this approach are that:

   (i) repair companies give priority treatment to contract customers. The waiting time for a non-contract customer might be very long;
   (ii) one-off repair charges will be very high.

(b) Instead, the user can arrange a maintenance contract with the manufacturer or a third party repair company. The cost of these contracts will be quite high (perhaps 10% to 20% of the hardware cost each year).

(c) A third option is breakdown insurance, which provides cover for breakdowns and certain consequential losses. Insurance provides cover against expense, but the computer user is left with the operational problem of how to get the repair work done within a reasonable time.

Computers are supplied with a diagnostic disk, which can be used to check for certain hardware faults such as a faulty microchip or a faulty disk drive. These faults can then be detected before any data is corrupted or lost.

Not all the data handling problems of a computer user are attributable to hardware or program faults. Quite often, the computer user comes across a problem that he or she does not know how to deal with. A telephone support service might be provided by the software or hardware supplier to help in these circumstances. The computer user can call for advice from an expert. Telephone support might also be provided to user departments by an *information centre* within the organisation.

Another important control measure, with PC systems in particular, is the appointment of a system expert in the office. This is a person who should be made responsible for learning as much technical detail about the office computer system as he or she can, so that the problems of other users of the system can first of all be referred to the office expert.

Exercise 7

What problems could arise if it is not clear who is the data owner for a file?

Back-up and standby facilities

A major aspect of system security is to ensure provision of the required services continuously without deterioration in performance. For many applications this will require that some duplication in the system be tolerated or even encouraged. For example, data may be made more secure by using back-up files to archive data. It would then be fairly easy to recover from data loss or system faults.

Administrative controls should be introduced:

(a) to enable file data to be recreated when a file is lost or corrupted;
(b) to provide stand-by hardware facilities whenever a hardware item breaks down.

Recreating file data when a file is lost or corrupted

One of the worst things that could happen in data processing by computer is the loss of all the data on a master file or the loss of a program. Files might be physically lost, for example the librarian might misplace a file, or a file might be stolen, but it is also possible for a file to become corrupted when it is amended and so come to include false data. A file might also be physically damaged and become unreadable.

Controls are therefore needed to enable a data or program file to be recreated if the original is lost or corrupted.

To recreate a master file, it is possible to go back to earlier generations of the master file and transactions files, do the data processing all over again and create a new version of the up to date master file.

The grandfather, father, son technique

The reconstruction of files may be achieved by use of the grandfather, father, son technique of keeping as many generations of master files, transaction files and reference files as is considered necessary. It is common to keep three generations (grandfather, father and son) of master files, and sufficient transaction files to recreate the father from the grandfather. If the most recent ('son') file out of a run is found to contain corrupted data, a corrected master file can be recreated by going back to the previous master file (the 'father') and the associated transaction file, and repeating the run. However, this technique cannot be used if the only copy of a file is overwritten during processing.

Dumping disk files

Disk files are often overwritten during updating, and so the grandfather, father, son technique cannot be applied. Instead, a copy of the disk file is periodically 'dumped' onto a back up file, usually a tape.

A typical procedure in a PC system is to make a copy, on to floppy disks, of each file on the hard disk every time the file is amended. Alternatively, the *entire* contents of the hard disk can be dumped onto a tape streamer as a matter of routine at the end of each day.

It might not be necessary to back up every disk which holds transaction data, or even some standing data. For example, word processing data is not necessarily of such importance as to warrant back-up copies. However:

(a) all program disks should have back-up copies. Some program disks which are bought from software manufacturers are copy-protected and cannot be backed up, but in these cases, the manufacturer is normally willing to provide a back-up copy to the customer as part of the package;

(b) all master files should be backed up after each updating run.

Backing up data on floppy disks can be done on a PC with two floppy disk drives by inserting the disk to be copied into one disk drive and a blank disk into the other, and using a DISKCOPY or COPY command to copy the data onto the blank disk.

Backing up a hard disk on to floppy disks can be more tedious, because a hard disk holds much more data than a floppy disk. Backing up a hard disk on to a tape streamer is quicker.

Back-up copies should be stored in a different place from the original files.

Stand-by hardware facilities

Hardware duplication will permit a system to function despite a hardware breakdown. The provision of back-up computers is costly, particularly where these systems have no other function. Many organisations will use several smaller computer systems and find that a significant level of protection against system faults can be provided by shifting operations to one of the systems still functioning. Where an organisation has only a single system to rely upon this ready recourse to a back-up facility is unavailable. In these instances one response would be to negotiate a maintenance contract which provides for back-up facilities. Alternatively, many computer bureaux will also provide access to back-up facilities though this will usually be rather expensive.

Exercise 8

Give some examples of businesses or activities where delays caused by the non-availability of computer facilities could be disastrous.

---

3 System development controls

When a computer system is developed from scratch, either in-house or by a software house, there should be controls over the system design, development and testing. Because of the time spent on systems development, the cost of it and the complexity and volume of work involved, it is essential to lay down high standards of control.

The main objectives of system development controls are:

(a) to ensure that new computer systems are developed only if they appear to be beneficial. System justification should be on the grounds of favourable cost-benefit analyses or other performance criteria;

(b) to ensure that each system under development has clear, specified objectives;

(c) to control the scheduling of development work;

(d) to ensure that suitable operational and administrative controls are built into the system design when it is being developed;

(e) to ensure that users acquire an understanding of the new system;

(f) to ensure that the system is properly tested, provides a suitable degree of control and also achieves its objectives;

BPP Publishing

(g) to establish a basis for management review of the system;

(h) to ensure that systems and programs are maintained when the system becomes operational;

(i) to ensure that proper and complete documentation of the system is created and maintained.

Many of these controls will be provided by the systems development methodology adopted.

The control of costs, progress and system design amendments

The *control of costs* can be achieved in three ways.

(a) Budgets and budgetary control variance reporting can be used. If actual development costs exceed the budget, the manager responsible for the over-spending will be required to take control action, or to justify the higher spending.

(b) Changes in the expected future costs and benefits of the system can be monitored. Costs already incurred in development work to date should be ignored, and the future development costs, expected system running costs and expected benefits should be the factors which determine whether it is worthwhile to continue with the system development.

(c) The post-implementation review of a project should study the actual development costs, system running costs and system benefits, to determine:

(i) whether the system is currently justifiable, or should be abandoned even at this late stage;

(ii) whether the original decision to develop the system was a good one;

(iii) by how much actual costs and benefits differed from expectations, the reasons for these differences and whether there are any lessons to be learned for the future.

Control over progress can be achieved through techniques such as critical path analysis.

Control over amendments to the system design are needed. Once development has started, it is all too easy for the systems analysts or user department managers to think of new features to add to the system, or improvements that can be made, with the result that amendments get written into the system as the design work progresses. Some amendments might be desirable; others might not be worthwhile.

Controls should be exercised over amendments, so that if any amendments are proposed which were not included in the system specification, they must be authorised at a suitable managerial level. The authorisation and details of the amendment should be included in the amendments section of the system specification.

Exercise 9

A sales system is being developed. The original specification makes no reference to discounts. An amendment to allow discounts for quantity, based on purchases in the previous six months, is proposed. What implications for the system as a whole would need to be considered before the amendment was approved?

Designing the system: the systems analyst and system controls

The adequacy of operational controls in the system will depend on the ability of the systems analyst to write suitable controls into the system when he or she is designing it. The systems analyst should build in controls based on the following guidelines.

(a) All data for processing should in fact be processed. There ought to be both administrative controls and program controls to monitor the completeness of data.

(b) Circumstances which may give rise to errors should be avoided.

(c) Errors which do occur should be detected, located and corrected as soon as possible.

(d) Controls must be simple and, whenever possible, should not interrupt the flow of data through the system. The ideal control fits smoothly into the system and becomes an integral part of it.

(e) Controls must not be excessively costly to apply. A reasonable level of control must be set as any attempt to ensure 100% accuracy would be uneconomical.

(f) The controls should be part of a general strategy, over the whole area of data processing activity, to prevent and detect fraud. A systems analyst should consult with the company's auditors when the system is being designed, not after all the work has been done.

(g) Systems analysts and designers should be aware of common security procedures.

(h) When the software is designed in detail, each interface between personnel and the computer system should be constructed so as to eliminate specific risks.

(i) Testing the system should involve simulating a fraud.

Testing

Program testing, system testing and the user department's acceptance tests are all important ingredients in development controls, to ensure that the programs are free of bugs (errors) and that the system works and meets its objectives.

Controls over file conversion

The conversion of master files is one of the big problems of systems implementation and proper procedures and controls must be laid down to ensure that there are no unauthorised conversions and that the correct records are accurately and completely transferred onto magnetic files. The procedures may include:

(a) full planning of the file conversion, including staff to be used, records to be converted (possibly via data preparation forms), controls to be set up and the date of conversion;

(b) the establishment of a control group to follow up errors which may occur during the conversion;

(c) printing out master files after conversion and manually checking them back to the original records (or data preparation forms);

(d) the reconciliation of accounting records to those kept under the old system;

(e) division of responsibilities among the conversion staff (additional staff may have to be brought in to help with the conversion);

(f) testing of the new master files using the test data and the control and documentation of any changes necessary.

System handover: the training of users

The handover of the computer system from the software and hardware experts to non-technical staff must be done in such a way that the computer users are able to learn as much about their system as they need to know. Training of staff will be necessary, but there should also be full, clear and non-technical documentation of the system - for off-the-shelf packages as well as for tailor-made software - in a *user's manual*.

Procedures for amending programs: modifications and enhancements after implementation

Procedures for controlling changes to programs are important because modifications or enhancements to programs that are already operational create opportunities for new errors in the program, or even for fraud.

(a) Program changes must be authorised by the user department, in writing and at the appropriate management level.

(b) The extent of the changes required should be assessed by a systems analyst, and the amendment should be specified in sufficient detail to enable a programmer to make the change.

(c) The amendment should be written by a programmer, who ought to refer to the existing documentation on the program and the original source program. Having amended the program, he or she should the test the new version. The amendments should be documented.

(d)   The systems analyst should carry out any further tests that seem necessary before authorising implementation of the new version of the program. The new program authorisation must be documented and sent to the file librarian, who will be responsible for ensuring that in future, the new version of the program is used for processing work.

(e)   The new version of the program should be monitored carefully when it is first used, in case any new errors appear.

Exercise 10

A company is converting from one computer system to another, and has some very large files to convert. It would be impractical to check full printouts of the old and new files against each other. In what other ways might the conversion process be checked for accuracy?

Data processing standards

Data processing standards are standards for the development, procedures and documentation of computer systems.

The purpose of standards is to minimise the likelihood of errors and misunderstandings in both the development and the operation of computer systems. More specifically, standards are helpful in the following ways.

The documentation of a computer system

Documentation is needed for systems and program specifications, and also for operator instructions. The existence of standards for documentation:

(a)   establishes the need to document a system;

(b)   provides a standard format for documenting the system, which helps to ensure that nothing is left out of the specification;

(c)   gives the people operating a system somewhere to look up and learn the system's operating requirements.

Management control

Standards should provide guidelines for managers to plan and control system development and then system operations.

(a)   Standards should suggest how management meetings should be scheduled during systems development, and how projects should be costed.

(b) There should be performance standards, so that actual performance can be measured against what should be expected.

(c) There should be standard job specifications, indicating who is responsible for each part of the system.

Communication of information about the system

Standard documentation provides a means whereby information about a system can be communicated, for example between programmers and systems analysts, and between system developers and the users and operators of the system.

Continuity after staff changes and an aid to training

People leave their jobs from time to time, or are absent for one reason or another. Unless a system is well-documented in a standard way, or has been designed according to standard procedures, it may be difficult for a person's stand-in or replacement to pick up the job where his predecessor left off.

Standards help people to learn a system. They are particularly helpful for staff moving from one job to another because they will have some familiarity with the format of documentation standards. For example, if a computer operator moves from his job in A Ltd to a new job in the computer centre of B Ltd, he will be able to learn his new job partly by referring to B Ltd's standards for computer operations. These standards will be similar in format to the ones used in A Ltd, and so the operator will know how and where to look up information that he needs to know.

An aid to system analysis and systems design work

Having standards helps the systems analyst in design work, in the following ways.

(a) Standards help to ensure that no aspect of system design is overlooked.

(b) Standards can help to steer a systems analyst's mind in the best direction. For example they can suggest controls to be built into the system.

(c) Standard documentation provides evidence that systems development controls have been carried out and that the system incorporates sufficient procedural and processing controls.

Exercise 11

What are the relative advantages and disadvantages of an organisation's writing its own data processing standards and its using externally published standards?

Documentation

Documentation for a system includes user manuals, hardware and operating software manuals, system specifications and program documentation.

Standardising the documentation, rather than allowing a systems analyst to provide the information in whatever way he or she chooses, acts as:

(a) an *aid to analysis*. By recording the information in a standard way that he or she has become used to, the systems analyst should be able to absorb the facts about a system more quickly. It will also facilitate analysis of a system by two or more systems analysts working together;

(b) an *aid to communication*. A standardised presentation of information reduces the likelihood of ambiguity and misunderstanding, and so helps systems analysts to communicate clearly with each other, with programmers and with computer operations staff. A programmer, for example, must be in no doubt about what a systems analyst wants, and familiarity with standard specifications will help in this respect;

(c) an *aid to design*. Because the systems analyst is working to a standard specification, he or she should be less likely to lose track of his or her thoughts over time;

(d) an *aid to completeness*. A standard provides a checklist of items to cover in the design. It ensures that the design is completed in full;

(e) an *aid to control*. Preparing standards is a stage in the design process, and so they help with management control of a project to design a new system (or even self-control of progress by the analyst). A target date can be set for the production of documentation standards for the planned system;

(f) an *aid to training and learning*. New data processing staff can learn a system more quickly if it has been specified and documented in a standard way. This facilitates *continuity*, given the inevitability of staff turnover over time.

Documentation is a feature of most systems analysis and design methodologies.

Data processing standards should ensure that all staff involved in the use of a computer system have proper instructions and that these have been fully documented. This means that there must be:

(a) operating instructions for each computer installation;

(b) operating instructions for each program;

(c) file library instructions, specifying how files should be labelled, safeguarded, issued and if necessary reconstructed;

(d) data conversion instructions for the data preparation staff;

(e) data control instructions for the control section;

(f) user department instructions.

The system specification

The system specification is a complete description of the whole system and must be kept up to date as parts of the system are changed or added to. Many of the problems in computer installations arise because of inadequate documentation and controls must be set up to ensure that updating procedures are always carried out.

The list below outlines the principal contents of a standard system specification.

(a) Introductory information
(b) System objectives
(c) System description
(d) Changeover procedure
(e) Equipment
(f) Output specification for each item of output
(g) Input specification for each item of input
(h) File specifications
(i) Test data
(j) Program specification for each program in the system
(k) System operating details
(l) Controls
(m) System costs and benefits

Program specifications

Program specifications or program documentation describe programs, using charts, full listings of the programs and details of test data and results.

Program specifications (excluding listings of the programs themselves) are drawn up by the systems analyst. A copy of a program specification is given to the programmer responsible for writing the program, and the programmer then uses the specification as the basis for writing and testing the required program. When the program has been written and tested, one copy of the final specification will form part of the overall systems specification, and a second copy will be retained by the programmer to form part of the programmer's own documentation for the program.

There should be a program specification for each program in the system. Each specification should include:

(a) an introduction, giving the program's name and purpose;

(b) a program description. The items in the description should be:

  (i)   detailed charts or narrative showing how the program works;
  (ii) a complete listing of the program;
  (iii) details of processing requirements;
  (iv) descriptions of file data;

(c) details of end of run procedures such as:

  (i)   output of control totals;
  (ii) dumping the results onto back-up files;
  (iii) operator messages;

Notes

(d) a schedule for program testing, including procedures for the preparation of test data and the evaluation of test results.

Exercise 12

Why might an organisation restrict access to detailed program specifications, rather than make them available to all staff?

Computer operations manuals

A computer operations manual provides full documentation of the procedures necessary to run the system. Amongst the matters to be covered by this documentation are:

(a) systems set-up procedures, including details for each application of the necessary file handling and stationery requirements;

(b) security procedures. Particular stress should be placed on the need to check that proper authorisation has been given for processing operations and the need to restrict use of the system to authorised operators;

(c) reconstruction procedures. Precise instructions should be given for matters such as file dumping and also the recovery procedures to be adopted in the event of a systems failure;

(d) system messages. A listing of all messages likely to appear on operators' consoles should be given together with an indication of the responses which they should evoke;

(e) operating system manuals. These are manuals that describe an operating system.

User manuals

User manuals or user documentation explain to users how to run a system, but do not give unnecessary technical details such as program listings. Matters to be dealt with include:

(a) acceptance testing: responsibilities for the preparation of test data and subsequently checking the test results;

(b) input: responsibilities and procedures for the preparation of input including requirements for the establishment of batch control totals and for authorisation;

(c) error reports: full explanations of the nature and form of error reports (such as reports of items rejected by computer checks) and instructions as to the necessary action to be taken;

(d) master file amendment procedures: full explanations of the authorisation and documentation required for master file amendments;

(e) output: what is produced, what form it takes and what should be done with it.

BPP Publishing

System changes manuals

Amendments to the original systems specification will almost inevitably occur, in addition to the computerisation of additional activities. The objective of a system changes manual is to ensure that such changes are just as strictly controlled as the original systems development and introduction. Four matters to be covered are:

(a) recording of requests and reasons for changes;
(b) procedures for authorising changes;
(c) procedures for documenting changes;
(d) procedures for testing changes.

Exercise 13

A computer operator using a batch processing system sees the message 'Batch control total discrepancy' on his screen, but does not know what to do about it. In which manual should he look for advice?

---

4 Application controls

Errors in data processing can easily occur. Application controls are intended to detect errors and ensure that they are corrected before processing proceeds further.

Input data can get lost, or it might contain errors. Human error is the greatest weakness in computer systems. The extensiveness of the input controls will depend on:

(a) the method of processing input data (for example keyboard input or OCR document input); and

(b) the cost of making an input error. If the consequences of input errors would be costly, the system should include more extensive input controls than if the cost of input errors were insignificant.

Errors may occur at various stages of data processing.

(a) *Errors in recording data.* Mistakes include:

    (i) writing an incorrect figure, such as £1243 instead of £1234; swapping figures around by mistake is referred to as a transposition error;

    (ii) spelling mistakes, such as getting a customer's name wrong;

    (iii) measuring mistakes, such as a timekeeper writing down an incorrect time for a job because he read his watch incorrectly;

(iv) classifying mistakes, such as a cost accountant recording a direct labour cost as an overhead item, or an expenditure in administration as a production cost.

(b) *Errors in transcribing data* or preparing data for further processing

   (i) *Transcription errors* occur when data is copied from one form to another. For example, a person might jot down some data on a piece of scrap paper, and then copy it incorrectly onto a formal document later on.

   (ii) *Data preparation errors* occur when the original captured data has to be transcribed into a form that the computer can read, such as a magnetic tape or magnetic disk. Errors arise because the original data can be copied wrongly into the machine- readable form. These errors are sometimes referred to as *data conversion errors*.

(c) *Errors in transmitting data.* These involve the loss or corruption of data which is sent to the computer, by post, courier or telecommunications link from a remote terminal.

(d) *Errors during processing.* Errors might occur or come to light during data processing, for three broad reasons.

   (i) It may become apparent during processing, when it would not necessarily have been apparent at the data capture stage, that there is something wrong with the transaction data. An attempt should be made to locate these errors as soon as possible, to prevent the computer from acting on invalid data. A *data validation* (or *data vet*) program is used to check the input data for errors that can be spotted by computer logic.

   (ii) It may become apparent during processing that there is something wrong with the master file data, or that it is impossible to match a transaction record properly with a master file record. Examples would be:

      (1) trying to record an invoice sent to customer number 234, when no such customer account has been opened;

      (2) trying to delete employee number 678 from the payroll, when there is no such employee in the payroll records;

      (3) trying to open a new account for supplier number 372 when there is already an account for that supplier.

   These are referred to as updating errors because they come to light when the master file is updated.

   (iii) There may be a programming error, that is a flaw in the logic of the computer program.

It is preferable to identify errors as they occur, rather than to leave dealing with them until later on in processing, because processing incorrect data would be time-consuming and wasteful, and it might also result in further errors caused by the original error.

Since errors should be identified as soon as they *do* occur, there should be checks for errors at each stage where errors *can* occur.

BPP Publishing

Exercise 14

Why is a programming error likely to be more serious than an updating error?

Controls over data capture

Errors in data capture are difficult to spot once they have been made, because they are often errors on the source document. They can be reduced by checking. One person's work might provide a check on the accuracy of another's. For example, the recording of suppliers' invoices could be checked by getting another person to add up the total amount of invoices received that day, from the invoices themselves. This total could then be checked against the total for invoices recorded.

Another way of dealing with errors in data capture is to reduce the likelihood of errors arising in the first place, by including as much pre-printed information on the data recording documents as possible, and by giving clear instructions about how the documents should be filled in.

The use of *turnround documents* and OCR, MICR, bar coding or, in some applications, plastic cards with magnetic stripes containing some of the input data reduces the need for manually-prepared input data, and so reduces data capture errors.

Controls over transcribing and converting data

If input data must be prepared manually, controls can be applied to minimise the number of errors.

(a) Staff who prepare data for input should be well trained and properly supervised.

(b) Data input documents should be in a format which helps the person preparing the data to fill them in properly.

(c) When data is input by keyboard, the screen should be formatted so as to help the keyboard operator to input the correct data. User-friendly software packages might provide on-screen prompts and formatted screens for input data.

If data must be converted from one form to another for input, for example from a paper document onto disk, the data could be keyed in twice to check for copying errors. However, this is expensive.

The staff who prepare the data should be encouraged to look for errors.

(a) If input is done by keyboard, the input data will be shown on the VDU screen and a visual check on the data can be made.

The input record will often have a key field identification code. For example a sales ledger file will consist of customer records, with each customer having a code number for identification. When a transaction record is keyed in, the customer code would be part of the input data and the program might search for the customer record on the sales ledger file, and display it on the VDU screen. The input operator could then check visually that the correct customer record is being processed.

(b) If input is done in batches, the program might produce a listing of the input data which could be checked for accuracy. Printed listings of input data also provide an *audit trail* in computerised accounting systems, so that internal and external auditors can follow transactions through the system later.

Controls over the transmission of data

When data is input from a terminal, the terminal user should be able to check that the data has been input fully and accurately by obtaining a printout back from the computer of all accepted data.

When input data is batched and physically despatched to a computer centre for processing, batch control checks can be applied to ensure that all the data that has been despatched is safely received at the computer centre. These checks involve:

(a) the user department giving each batch a unique identification number;

(b) the identification numbers of all batches being written on to a batch control document, by the user department supervisor. This document will be sent to the computer centre, with a copy being retained by the user;

(c) the data control clerks in the computer centre checking that the batches that are received tally with the batch numbers on the batch control document.

Exercise 15

Invoices received from a company's suppliers are batched, and are then given to the company's computer staff together with batch control slips showing control totals. What mistake could the batching staff make, which would definitely not be detected by the system of control totals?

Validation checks

Some checks on the validity of input data can be written into the system's programs. These *data validation* checks (or *data vet* checks) might be performed by a separate data validation program in a batch processing system. Alternatively, any program can incorporate validation checks on input data, for example on data keyed in from a terminal into an on-line system.

Data validation

The data validation program, or a program which incorporates data validation routines, will be the first program in each batch processing application. The program attempts to find errors in the input record or batch, to prevent them being processed any further.

The checks which can be made are logical checks which prevent some of the worst types of error from getting through to be processed. Data validation does not provide a comprehensive error check, however, and some errors on source documents are likely to go undetected. This emphasises the need for control over source document creation.

The main types of data validation check are outlined below. Note that the same type of check can be made on different fields of a record, and that not all types of check need appear in a data validation program. However, a single program might carry out dozens of validation checks on different records and fields.

(a) *Range checks* are designed to ensure that the data in a certain field lies within predetermined limits. For example in a wages application, the program may contain instructions to reject any clock card with 'hours worked' outside the range from 20 to 80 hours, and to print out a special report (for checking) on any clock card with hours worked outside the range from 35 to 60 hours.

(b) *Limit checks*, sometimes called credibility or reasonableness checks, are very similar to range checks, but check that data is not *below* a certain value, or *above* a certain value. In the previous example, the check on 'hours worked' might be that the value in the record field does not exceed 80. With a range check, there is an upper bound and a lower bound, whereas with a limit check, there is either an upper bound or a lower bound, but not both.

(c) *Existence checks* are checks on record fields to ensure that the data is valid for that field. For example:

   (i) check that the record type is 1, 2 or 3;

   (ii) check that the stock code exists by looking up the stock code number of the record in a reference file.

(d) *Format checks* (picture checks) check that the record has the required data fields and that each data field has data in the correct format. For example:

   (i)   check that the format is all numeric   9999   (here, four figures);
   (ii) check that the format is all alphabetic AAAAA (here, five letters);
   (iii) check that the format is alphanumeric   A999   (here, one letter followed by three figures).

(e) *Consistency checks* check that data in one field is consistent with data in another field. For example, in a payroll system, there might be a check that if the employee is a Grade C worker, he or she belongs to Department 5, 6 or 9.

(f) *Sequence checks* check that records and batches are processed in the correct sequence.

(g) *Completeness checks*

   (i) A check can be made to ensure that all records have been processed. For example, if a weekly processing run must include one record for each of the five working days of the week, a completeness check can ensure that there are five input records.

(ii) Completeness checks on individual fields would check that an item of data has not been omitted from an input record.

(h) *Check digits* are numbers (or perhaps letters) added to a code to give it some special mathematical property, which can be checked by the computer.

(i) *Batch total checks*. In a batch processing system, the number and/or the total value of the records processed by the computer from each batch, including rejected records, should reconcile with the control total(s) in the batch control slip, which will also have been input to the program.

When a validation check identifies an error, there are a number of possible outcomes.

(a) The record concerned will probably be rejected and processed no further with perhaps a message on screen. *Rejection reports* may be printed out at some stage during processing.

(b) The record concerned may not be rejected, but an *exception report* might still be output or the operator advised in some way on screen. This may happen, for example, where a range or limit check is not satisfied. Just because a record is not within pre-set limits does not automatically mean that it is incorrect. If it is valid, then not processing it would be a waste of time. However, administrative controls must ensure that all exception reports are followed up.

(c) If an error is revealed by batch controls, the whole batch must be rejected and checked.

Exercise 16

A computer program processes the monthly expenses claims of travelling sales staff. Give three examples of validation checks which might be carried out on the claims.

Output controls

There should be controls over output from computer processing.

(a) In a batch processing system, where data is batched and sent off to a computer centre, there should be a check to make sure that the batches that were sent off have been processed and returned.

(b) All input records that have been rejected by data validation checks and master file update checks must be looked at to find out the reasons. Corrected data should then be prepared for re-input. Some errors might need immediate correction, such as those on input records which have been rejected by data validation checks in a payroll program for preparing salary payments to staff.

BPP Publishing

(c) Output should be correctly distributed, and a log should be kept of the distributions that have been made. In a computer centre, this is the responsibility of the data control staff. In an office, someone has to be responsible for dealing with output from the printer.

(d) Output onto magnetic files should be properly labelled and stored.

File controls

Controls can be applied to ensure that:

(a) the correct files are used for processing;
(b) data is not lost or corrupted;
(c) if data is lost or corrupted, then it can be recreated;
(d) unauthorised access to data is prevented.

In a large computer centre, the administrative responsibility for the physical security of files belongs to the file librarian. With smaller computer systems, such as office PCs, responsibility for the correct labelling of disks and their physical security should be assigned to a member of staff.

Software controls over files

A number of controls can be written into program software. These include:

(a) file identification checks;
(b) checkpoints and recovery procedures;
(c) control totals.

File identification checks

The computer will check that the correct file has been loaded for processing before it will begin its processing operations. It can do this by checking the file header data written on the file in magnetic form, and comparing this data with data about the file that it has been instructed to process. If the computer has been instructed to process master file A, it will first of all check that master file A has indeed been loaded for processing, and that the correct generation of the file has been loaded.

A computer file has two labels.

(a) A label recorded in magnetic form identifies the data on the file. For example C2100 may identify the data as a stock master file (file 100) in the stock control system (C2).

(b) An external label, with an entirely different numbering system, is physically written on the file so that it can be identified by humans.

The file librarian may, for example, arrange that a file with external label 123456 should be used as a master file in the stock control system, created in run number 234. The magnetic data might record the file as C2100 from run 234 with a retention period until run 238. On run 235, the computer will check that file C2100 from run 234 has been loaded for processing. If it has not been loaded, the computer will report the error and will not process the file loaded.

Eventually, after run 238 has been completed some time later, the librarian will decide that the old master file from run 234 can be released and the file 123456 can now be used for other processing (for example as a transactions file in the payroll system). The magnetic data label of the file will change to identify the new data contained on the file, but the external label will be unchanged as 123456.

Checkpoints and recovery procedures

A *checkpoint* or *restart program* is a utility that intervenes at certain points (checkpoints) during the running of a program, and dumps the entire contents of memory onto a storage device.

Should anything turn out to be wrong with the running of the application program, the application program can be taken back to the checkpoint before the error occurred, and restarted with conditions exactly as they were before.

Control totals

A control total could be:

(a)   the number of records on a file;

(b)   the total of the values of a particular field in all the records on a file, for example the total of debts outstanding in all the customer records on a sales ledger file;

(c)   the number of records in a batch (a batch control total);

(d)   a hash total. This is a total that has no meaning, except as a control check; for example, the total of customer account numbers.

Control total checks are written into programs to ensure that:

(a)   no records have been lost;
(b)   no records have been duplicated;
(c)   input files have been read fully;
(d)   all output records have been written to output files.

Control totals are established in two different ways, for example by adding up the account numbers after the most recent run, and by taking the total after the previous run and adjusting it for new accounts and for accounts closed. Any difference between the totals can then be investigated.

BPP Publishing

Exercise 17

Why is it often worth having checkpoints part way through a processing run, rather than simply restarting a run from the beginning whenever something goes wrong?

Database controls

Databases present a particular problem for computer security. Databases can often be accessed by large numbers of people, and so there is a high risk of alteration, unauthorised disclosure or fraud.

It is possible to construct complicated password systems, and the DBMS can be programmed to give limited views of its contents to particular users.

However, there are problems in ensuring that individuals do not circumvent the controls by means of inference. For example, an employee database might forbid you to ask whether John is an employee in category A. However, if you know there are only three employee categories, A, B, and C, and there is no prohibition on asking about categories B and C, you can work out the members of category A by elimination. Inference controls may make this difficult by limiting the number of queries, or by controlling the overlap between questions.

Hardware controls over data and files

Computer hardware can break down or malfunction, or it may be used incorrectly. Controls can be established to identify such problems when they occur and to ensure the continuity of data processing when there is a hardware fault.

Examples of hardware controls to prevent or detect errors are as follows.

(a)   *Parity checks* are checks on the transfer of data from one hardware device to another, or from one storage location to another. Each byte of data has a parity bit added to it, set at 0 or 1 so that the number of 1 bits in the byte is an even number (or an odd number, depending on the machine). Whenever data is transferred every byte is automatically checked for even (or odd) parity, so that hardware faults in transmitting data incorrectly are likely to be identified.

(b)   *Write permit rings*, used with magnetic tape files, are plastic rings which must be physically attached to a tape reel before its contents can be altered. When tapes are stored in the computer file library, all write permit rings should be removed.

(c)   A *file mask* for direct access storage devices can be set to prevent either:

   (i)   all seek instructions preventing unwanted head movement when a file is being written sequentially; or

   (ii)   all write instructions, preventing alteration of the data.

(d) *Device interlocks* prevent input or output of data, once begun, from being interrupted or terminated. This helps to prevent the corruption of data by either a hardware fault or an operator error.

(e) *Overflow checks* are checks on overflow areas on direct access files.

There should be regular maintenance checks on hardware by qualified computer engineers, to prevent hardware faults.

Exercise 18

If a write permit ring is routinely inserted in every tape as it is taken out of the file library, there is no effective control. How might the insertion of write permit rings be controlled?

BPP Publishing

Chapter roundup

(a) Data needs to be protected from processing errors, system failures, unauthorised access and physical damage to the storage media.

(b) Administrative controls apply to the data processing environment. They include controls over personnel (such as segregation of duties), physical security measures, access controls (such as passwords), measures against hacking and viruses, rules for office practice and the provision of back-up and standby facilities.

(c) System development controls apply to the development of new systems or the amendment of existing systems. They are intended to ensure that systems are developed which meet the needs of the organisation and which do not cost more than they are worth.

(d) As part of the design process for a new system, controls will be built into the system. This addition of controls itself needs to be controlled, so that the controls built in are appropriate to the uses to be made of the system.

(e) Programs must be tested, and the conversion of files must be carefully controlled.

(f) Formal procedures are needed to control amendments to an existing system.

(g) Data processing standards are intended to ensure adequate documentation and management control, to ensure continuity after staff changes and to facilitate the design of systems.

(h) Good documentation should facilitate analysis, design, communication, control and training. The documentation for a system should include a system specification, program specifications, a computer operations manual, a user manual and a system changes manual.

(i) Application controls are incorporated within applications, in order to ensure complete and accurate processing of data. Controls are first applied to data capture, transcription, conversion and transmission. Data validation checks can then be applied, to ensure that the data input is reasonable both on the basis of inherently likely values and in the light of data already held on master files.

(j) The distribution of output, including error and exception reports, needs to be controlled, to ensure that all output is correctly acted upon. File controls are needed to ensure that the correct files are used for processing, and that files are retained for appropriate periods.

(k) Databases need to be controlled, to prevent unauthorised access or alteration.

(l) Some controls can be implemented in computer hardware.

Quick quiz

1   What are the objectives of data controls?

2   What are the two main classes of controls, and the two sub-classes of the first class?

3   What are the main personnel controls apart from the segregation of duties?

4   What are the functions of a file librarian and of data control clerks?

5   What are the main physical security measures which can be taken?

6   What access controls can be applied to data transmission?

7   Give some examples of types of computer virus.

8   What arrangements for maintenance of an office computer system can be made after the warranty period has expired?

9   Why is it important to create back-up copies of files?

10   How can the cost of developing new systems be controlled?

11   What criteria should be applied to the incorporation of controls in a new system?

12   How may data processing standards help continuity after staff changes?

13   What are the contents of a program specification?

14   What should be dealt with in a user manual?

15   Give some examples of errors which may occur or come to light during data processing.

16   How may the transcription and conversion of data be controlled?

17   Give one example of each of a limit check, a format check and a completeness check.

18   How does a computer check that it has been supplied with the correct files for processing?

19   What is a control total?

20   What is the purpose of a file mask?

Solutions to exercises

1   Fraud and unauthorised access are unlikely to be serious risks, but the accidental loss or corruption of data are significant risks, especially because it is easy to forget about precautions if there is no-one else to insist that they are taken.

2   If a member of staff is perpetrating a fraud, this is more likely to come to light if he is not there all the time to cover up the evidence as it arises.

3   An employee in the purchasing department might arrange for payments to a supplier to exceed the amounts owing, and in fact divert the excess to his own bank account. Such payments would show up on exception reports, which if they went to the employee himself could then be destroyed.

4   Security guards can get to know the staff and can act on their own initiative if intruders are spotted. On the other hand, they are expensive and they may become lax about security procedures.

   Electronic identification devices are cheap to run and always apply controls to the same standard. On the other hand, they cannot show initiative, and a device which reads a card cannot tell if a card has been stolen and is being used by an intruder.

5   Initial passwords could be issued on paper, but operators would be required to change them immediately to passwords of their own choosing. Each new password would be known only to the operator and the computer, and would never have been written down.

6   Employees who might have grievances should not have any access to computer systems. It may be necessary to make them serve out any period of notice at home.

7   Different people could update the file in an unplanned way, and could undo each others' work.

   The file might not get updated at all, because each user would assume that updating was someone else's responsibility.

8   Share and currency dealing businesses
   Computer-controlled manufacturing involving dangerous processes
   Air traffic control

9   The need to keep six-month running totals of purchases by each customer; these would often span the company's accounting year-end, so detailed data would have to be preserved after the year-end.

The need to create a system for fixing discount rates and the quantities which will trigger discounts. Are these to be standard, or may they vary between customers? If the latter, who is to approve the rates and who is to input them? How is fraud to be prevented? (An operator might give a discount to a customer improperly, in return for a bribe.)

10   Samples from the old and new files could be printed out and checked against each other. The old and new files could be copied onto disks and the copies checked against each other by a separate computer program.

11   An organisation's own standards will be tailored to its own needs, and will be well-understood by its employees. However, good standards take a lot of time and resources to write.

Externally produced standards are cheaper to obtain, but they may not fit the organisation's needs so well. However, they may raise important quality control issues which would simply not have occurred to people within the organisation. Similarly, the use of externally produced standards prevents members of the organisation from building existing slackness into the standards.

12   Someone who knows exactly how a program works might be tempted to amend it without authorisation, either because they think they know how to improve it or so as to perpetrate a fraud.

13   The user manual

14   A programming error may affect every transaction processed by the program, whereas an updating error may only affect one master file record.

15   An invoice could be lost before the batches were prepared.

16   Range check: is each claim between £100 and £900 in total?
Existence check: does each person making a claim exist?
Completeness check: have all the sales staff submitted claims?

17   A run might take up a lot of computer time, and it may therefore be worth saving the results of processing up to the last checkpoint before things go wrong. Also, working forwards slowly from that checkpoint may make it easier to find out what the problem is.

18   Rings might only be inserted when the person taking the tape produces an appropriate form signed by a supervisor.

16 COMPUTERS AND THE LAW

Your objectives

After completing this chapter you should:

(a) understand the background to the Data Protection Act 1984;
(b) understand the terms 'personal data', 'data user', 'computer bureau' and 'data subject';
(c) know the main provisions of the Act;
(d) know the Data Protection Principles;
(e) know the main exemptions from the Act;
(f) be aware of the offences which may be committed under the Act;
(g) know how an organisation should act to ensure compliance with the Act;
(h) be aware of how copyright law applies to computer software;
(i) know the main provisions of the Computer Misuse Act 1990;
(j) be aware of some other legal matters which arise in the context of computer systems.

---

1   The Data Protection Act 1984

The Data Protection Act 1984 was passed to address two particular concerns in the area of data processing.

(a) There was a growing popular fear that information about individuals which was stored on computer files and processed by computer could be misused. In particular, it was felt that an individual could easily be harmed by the existence of computerised data about him or her which was inaccurate or misleading and which could be transferred to unauthorised third parties at high speed and little cost.

(b) Unless the UK passed legislation adopting the principles of the Council of Europe Convention for the Protection of Individuals with regard to Automatic Processing of Personal Data, access to information about individuals which is stored on overseas computers might be denied to UK firms. This would have put the UK at a trading disadvantage against firms in other countries where such legislation had been passed already.

The Act is an attempt to afford some measure of protection *to individuals*. The terms of the Act cover data about individuals, *not corporate bodies*, and data which is processed mechanically, that is 'equipment operated automatically in response to the instructions given for that purpose', *not* data processed manually.

The Data Protection Registrar has suggested where the dividing line comes between equipment covered by the Act and equipment not affected by the Act. Modern telephones, which store some telephone numbers for automatic redialling, do *not* come under the Act, nor does telex or facsimile equipment which transmits data but does not process it. However, equipment other than computers is covered if it processes data automatically.

---

2   Definitions of terms in the Data Protection Act

In order to understand the Act it is necessary to know some of the technical terms used in it.

Personal data

Personal data is information about a living individual, including expressions of opinion about him or her. Data about other organisations is *not* personal data, unless it contains data about individuals who belong to those other organisations.

(a)   Personal data includes facts or opinions about a living individual, but does not include data about the data user's intentions towards the individual.

(b)   The individual must be identifiable from the data. If the data does not contain a name, but contains a code number (for example an employment number or an account number) from which the data user can identify the individual, it is personal data.

Data users

Data users are organisations or individuals who control the contents of files of personal data and the use of personal data which is processed automatically. Since the Act was passed the definition of 'data user' has been subject to much uncertainty and discussion, and so some guidance has been given by the office of the Data Protection Registrar. For example:

(a)   do subsidiary companies in a group have to register as data users, as well as the holding company? Usually they do;

(b)   are employees of an organisation data users? No, because they are only exercising control on behalf of their employers;

(c)   educational institutions will usually be regarded as the data users of any personal data held on their computer files but there may be special circumstances, for example, teachers or students using the computer for extra-curricular activities, when the institution is acting as a bureau and the individual teacher or student becomes the data user.

Computer bureaux

These are organisations (or individuals) which process personal data for data users, or allow data users to process personal data on their equipment. An organisation or an individual may be classified as a computer bureau under the Act even though not actually in business as a computer bureau.

Data subjects

These are individuals who are the subjects of personal data.

Exercise 1

Which of the following statements would be personal data?

(a) John Smith will probably earn £25,000 next year.
(b) X Ltd is insolvent.
(c) I intend to sell my car to John Smith.

---

3 The main provisions of the Data Protection Act

The Act can be summarised as follows.

(a) With certain exceptions, all data users and all computer bureaux must register with the Data Protection Registrar. To hold personal data without being registered as a data user, or to operate as a computer bureau without being registered as such, is an offence under the Act.

(b) Data subjects have certain legal rights.

(c) Data users and computer bureaux must adhere to the Data Protection Principles.

(d) The Act establishes certain civil legal proceedings and a number of offences.

(e) The Data Protection Registrar:

   (i) maintains a register of data users and computer bureaux;

   (ii) disseminates information on the Act and its operation;

   (iii) promotes the observance of the Data Protection Principles;

   (iv) considers complaints about contraventions of the Principles or of the Act's provisions.

Registration under the Act

The Data Protection Registrar keeps a register of all data users and computer bureaux.

Each entry in the register contains the following information.

(a) The name and address of the data user or the computer bureau
(b) A description of the personal data held by the data user and the uses made of the data
(c) The source or sources of the data
(d) Details of any other person or persons to whom the data might be disclosed

Unless a data user has an entry in the Register he may not hold personal data. Even if the data user is registered, he must only hold data and use data for the purposes which are registered.

A data user must apply to be registered. The Registrar may refuse an application for the following reasons.

(a) The Registrar thinks that the data user has not given sufficient information in his application.

(b) The Registrar believes that the data user might not adhere to the Data Protection Principles.

The Act requires a data user both to limit the use of personal data to the uses which are registered and also to abide by the Data Protection Principles. If the Registrar thinks that the Principles are being breached by a registered data user, he may issue an enforcement notice which orders the data user to take steps to remedy the breach. It is an offence to ignore an enforcement notice. In extreme cases, the Registrar might have the data user struck off the Register.

There is a right of appeal to a Data Protection Tribunal if a data user believes that he has been unfairly and unreasonably refused registration, or has been unfairly served with an enforcement notice or unfairly struck off the register.

The rights of data subjects

The Act establishes the following rights for data subjects.

(a) A data subject may seek compensation through the courts for damage and any associated distress caused by:

    (i) the loss, destruction or unauthorised disclosure of data about himself or herself;

    (ii) inaccurate data about himself or herself.

(b) A data subject may apply to the courts for inaccurate data to be put right or even removed from the data user's files altogether. Such applications may also be made to the Registrar.

(c) A data subject may obtain access to personal data of which he is the subject. (This is known as the *subject access provision*.)

(d) A data subject can sue a data user (or a bureau) for any damage or distress caused to him by personal data about him which is incorrect or misleading as to matter of *fact* (rather than opinion).

Exercise 2

What sorts of damage might a data subject suffer from incorrect or misleading data?

The Data Protection Principles

There are certain Data Protection Principles which registered data users must comply with. These are as follows.

Personal data held by data users

(1) The information to be contained in personal data shall be obtained, and personal data shall be processed, fairly and lawfully. Processing means amending, adding to, deleting or re-arranging the data, or extracting the information that forms the data.

(2) Personal data shall be held only for one or more specified (registered) and lawful purposes.

(3) Personal data held for any purpose or purposes shall not be used or disclosed in any manner incompatible with that purpose or those purposes.

(4) Personal data held for any purpose or purposes shall be adequate, relevant and not excessive in relation to that purpose or those purposes.

(5) Personal data shall be accurate and, where necessary, kept up to date.'Accurate' means correct and not misleading as to any matter of *fact*. An *opinion* cannot be challenged on the grounds of inaccuracy.

(6) Personal data held for any purpose or purposes shall not be kept for longer than is necessary for that purpose or those purposes.

(7) An individual shall be entitled:

(a) at reasonable intervals, and without undue delay or expense:

(i) to be informed by any data user whether he holds personal data of which that individual is the subject; and

(ii) to access to any such data held by a data user; and

(b) where appropriate, to have such data corrected or erased.

Personal data held by data users or in respect of which services are provided by persons carrying on computer bureaux

(8) Appropriate security measures shall be taken against unauthorised access to, or alteration, disclosure or destruction of, personal data and against accidental loss or destruction of personal data. The prime responsibility for creating and putting into practice a security policy rests with the data user.

The disclosure of personal data

The Act does not prevent a data user from disclosing personal information about an individual, if the user wishes to do so, and if:

(a) the person to whom the disclosure is made is described in the disclosures section of the data user's entry on the Register; or

Notes

(b) disclosure is required or permitted by one of the exemptions to the non-disclosure provisions.

This means that a data subject does not have an unrestricted right to object to the disclosure of personal data about himself or herself.

Exemptions

There are some exemptions from the Act or parts of it.

Unconditional exemptions from the Act as a whole cover:

(a) personal data which must be exempt so as to safeguard national security;

(b) personal data which the data user is required to make public by law;

(c) personal data held by an individual and concerned only with the management of his personal, family or household affairs or held by him for recreational purposes.

Conditional exemptions from the Act as a whole cover:

(a) personal data held as payroll and pensions data or for keeping the accounts of the data user. The exemption is conditional because if payroll details or accounts details are used for any purpose in addition to paying wages or pensions and keeping simple books of account, no exemption is available; the data user must register the fact that he uses payroll or accounts details both for a purpose that would normally be exempt and for the purpose or purposes which cause the exemption to be lost. For example, if a sales ledger file is used to assess the creditworthiness of customers, the exemption is lost;

(b) data held by unincorporated members' clubs and relating only to club members. The condition is that data subjects have been asked whether they object to these uses of data and they have not objected. Disclosure of such data may only be made with the data subjects' consent.

(c) data held only for the distribution of articles or information to the data subjects (for example for mailshot advertising) and consisting only of their names and addresses, or other particulars necessary for the distribution. The condition is as for (b), with the same requirement of consent for disclosure.

Exemption from subjects' right of access to data on them is available for:

(a) personal data held for the prevention or detection of crime, the apprehension or prosecution of offenders or the assessment or collection of any tax or duty;

(b) data for which legal professional privilege could be claimed. This would apply to a solicitor and his client;

(c) data held solely for statistical or research purposes.

Exemptions from the non-disclosure provisions cover:

(a) disclosures to safeguard national security;

BPP Publishing

(b) personal data which is disclosed for the prevention or detection of crime, the apprehension or prosecution of offenders or the assessment or collection of any tax or duty, where not to disclose the data would prejudice one of those purposes;

(c) disclosures to, at the request of or with the consent of the data subject;

(d) disclosures to the employees or agents of a data user or a computer bureau so that they can perform their functions as such;

(e) disclosures which are urgently needed to prevent injury or damage to the health of anyone;

(f) disclosures required by law or by a court order;

(g) disclosures for the purpose of obtaining legal advice or in the course of legal proceedings.

Apart from the main exemptions detailed above, there is also a word processing exemption. Operations performed only for the purpose of preparing the text of documents are not covered by the Act.

Exercise 3

A car dealer keeps data on potential customers for marketing purposes. The data includes details of each potential customer's current car. Which data protection principles might be breached if:

(a) the data is updated only once every two years?

(b) the dealer makes the data available to a journalist investigating customer dissatisfaction with a particular make of car?

Some implications of the Act

It is important to be aware of some of the implications of the Act.

(a) It is an offence for a company to transfer personal data to an overseas branch office, unless that office is in a country which has been named in the data user's register entry. Even then, the Registrar can issue a transfer prohibition notice to prevent any such overseas data transfers being made, for example if the recipient branch might not apply the Data Protection Principles. Such notices will usually be issued where it is believed that the data will be directly or indirectly transferred to a country which is not a signatory to the European Convention.

(b) When personal data is *printed out* from a computer file, the data on paper is not 'data' within the meaning of the Act, but it is 'information extracted from the data'. As such, it remains subject to the non-disclosure provisions of the Act. Appropriate security measures should therefore be taken to protect such printouts.

But if a data user receives a subject access request, the data user need only supply a copy of the data currently on file. Any information on a printout, which is no longer held on file as data, does not have to be disclosed.

Offences under the Act

The following offences are created by the Act.

(a) A data user is liable to prosecution if:

    (i)   he holds personal data without being registered, or without having applied for registration;

    (ii)   he knowingly or recklessly uses, obtains, discloses, transfers or holds data otherwise than as described in his registered entry;

    (iii)   he knowingly or recklessly supplies the Registrar with false or misleading information on an application for registration or a change of particulars;

    (iv)   he fails to comply with an enforcement notice;

    (v)   he fails to comply with a transfer prohibition notice.

(b) A computer bureau is liable for prosecution if:

    (i)   it knowingly or recklessly operates as a computer bureau in respect of personal data without being registered as such;

    (ii)   it knowingly or recklessly supplies the Registrar with false or misleading information for registration or a change of particulars;

    (iii)   it fails to comply with an enforcement notice.

Exercise 4

The managing director of a data user obtains a printout of personal data. He then leaves the printout unattended in the company's public reception area, for the sales director to collect. Before she does so, a member of the public comes in and reads the printout. No members of the public had appointments to visit the company on that day. Has an offence been committed under the Data Protection Act?

---

4   The practical implications of the Data Protection Act 1984

To ensure compliance with the Act, the following steps are recommended.

(a) The organisation should appoint a data protection co-ordinator. The co-ordinator's job is to arrange the organisation's registration and to ensure continued compliance with the Act's provisions after registration.

(b) In order to ensure complete and accurate registration and also continued compliance with the Act after registration, all relevant staff must be made fully aware of the implications of the Act.

(c) The registered entry should be amended whenever there is a change to the personal data that is being held and used.

(d) The co-ordinator should set up systems which will allow him:

   (i)   to monitor compliance with the Principles;

   (ii)   to meet subject access requests;

   (iii) to be made aware of any changes in the organisation which may require amendment to the registered entry.

(e) Whenever a new computer system is planned, or a new software package purchased, consideration should be given to whether a registration of the system under the Act is necessary. This should be a *formal* step in system design and development, so that it is never overlooked.

5 Copyright

Copyright in the UK is governed by the Copyright, Designs and Patents Act 1988. For the purposes of the Act, a computer program is a literary work, and copyright is infringed if it is 'stored or adapted' (this does *not* include storage in *memory*) without permission.

The problem for companies which produce software is that computer users can copy software from a program disk to a blank disk, much like recording music from a purchased cassette to a blank cassette. The Act gives the protection of copyright law to software writers, and to all software written before the Act as well as to software written subsequently.

(a) It is illegal to copy a program, for example from one floppy disk onto another disk, without permission from the copyright owner.

(b) This means that it is illegal for a firm to buy a program, copy it, and then sell the copy to another user. (However, *enforcing* legislation against piracy might be difficult, especially in those parts of the world where software piracy is common.)

(c) The legislation also affects computer users who want to use the same software themselves, but on several different computers. Generally speaking, each copy of the program must be authorised, unless there is some prior agreement. Software suppliers advise customers to make back-up copies of their programs, for security reasons, and if making a copy is authorised in this way, the law will not be infringed. Often, use of a program is limited to specified computers, or to all computers on a specified site, by the software supplier.

Users of software should institute appropriate procedures to prevent breaches of the law. These procedures should include the following.

(a) Draw up a set of rules for copying software, so that the organisation is not in breach of copyright through the ignorance of management and staff. For example, the organisation could require that every copy of a software package be authorised by the organisation's legal department. They would ensure that the copying did not breach the contract with the supplier.

(b) Ensure that employees are made aware of the organisation's rules in this regard.

(c) Make illegal copying a disciplinary offence.

(d) Maintain a record of copies made of software packages, identifying the computer hard disks where they are stored. The organisation can do an audit of its computers to ensure that there has been no copying in breach of the law or the agreement.

Software suppliers in the UK have formed the UK *Federation Against Software Theft* (FAST), which is prepared to bring legal action against organisations breaking copyright law. Moreover, if a breach is found, not only does the organisation have to pay damages and legal costs, but also the licensor might terminate the agreement to use the software. Imagine the chaos caused in many finance departments if the right to use Lotus 123 suddenly disappeared. It might also be hard to obtain licences from other software suppliers if the legal action results in a bad reputation. An alternative to the embarrassment of legal action is to submit to an audit conducted by FAST.

Reverse engineering

One of the greatest sources of competition in the PC market has been the growth of clones, or cheap imitations of products currently available. To a large extent, this has been achieved by a process of so-called *reverse engineering*. This means dismantling a product to see how it is made, and so learning how to make a similar product.

The European Community has considered legislation which would greatly restrict the scope of reverse engineering.

(a) A user lobbying organisation, Computer Users in Europe, is against restrictions on reverse engineering, on the grounds that it will limit the number of add-on programs.

(b) The manufacturers stand to benefit as their control over software development will be maintained.

Such legislation would affect users if the competitive nature of the computer market is not maintained.

Exercise 5

What sort of illegal copying of software within an organisation would not be detected by an audit of the organisation's computers and disks?

6   The Computer Misuse Act 1990

The Computer Misuse Act 1990 was enacted to respond to the growing threat of hacking to computer systems and data. There was some dispute as to whether hacking was a crime. For example, if you had illegally read data, this was not theft, as the original data was not stolen.

The Act has created three new offences.

(a)   *Unauthorised access.* An offence is committed by a hacker, who, knowing that he or she is unauthorised, tries to gain access to another computer system. It is the attempt which is the crime: the hacker's success or failure is irrelevant.

(b)   *Unauthorised access with intent to commit another offence* results in harsher penalties than (a) above. It might be a suitable charge if a hacker had been caught in the early stages of a fraud.

(c)   *Unauthorised modification of data or programs.* Amongst other acts, the deliberate introduction of computer viruses into a system is an offence. However, the simple addition of data is not an offence, just its corruption or destruction. Guilt is based on the *intention* to impair the operation of a computer or program, or to prevent or hinder access to data.

The maximum penalty for each offence is as follows.

(a)   Unauthorised access: imprisonment for up to six months and/or a fine of up to £2,000

(b)   Unauthorised access with intent to commit another offence: imprisonment for up to five years and/or an unlimited fine

(c)   Unauthorised modification: imprisonment for up to five years and/or an unlimited fine

Individuals or companies may take out private criminal prosecutions. Prosecuting someone for a breach of the Computer Misuse Act need not be left to the Crown Prosecution Service.

7   Other legal matters

So far this chapter has dealt with data protection, copyright and computer misuse. There are other areas of an organisation's use of computers where the law can intervene, or where attention to the legal aspects of a decision can be beneficial to the organisation.

If an organisation is buying a computer system, or having one designed and installed by an outside supplier or consultancy, then the contract should specify performance targets and penalties for breaching them.

A faulty computer program which produces incorrect VAT or tax returns may result in legal action by HM Customs & Excise or the Inland Revenue. The faulty program may not be sufficient excuse to avoid penalties. An organisation might ask the software supplier to indemnify it against any penalties caused by errors in the software.

Employers can be prosecuted under the Health and Safety at Work Act 1974. Also, sufferers from repetitive strain injury or other illnesses related to the use of computer terminals, might be able to sue their employers for negligence. The design and use of VDUs is the subject of a European Community directive, which came into force (for new equipment) at the end of 1992. Equipment purchased before that date must be brought up to standard by the end of 1996.

Exercise 6

How might an organisation's computer operations be adversely affected by the unauthorised addition of data, without any corruption of existing data?

Chapter roundup

(a) The Data Protection Act 1984 was passed to safeguard the privacy of living individuals (data subjects).

(b) Personal data comprises both facts and opinions about data subjects. The Act applies to both data users and computer bureaux.

(c) Data users and computer bureaux must register under the Act, and must notify any changes to their registrations.

(d) Data subjects may see the data held about them, and may challenge factual inaccuracies.

(e) Data users should comply with the eight data protection principles.

(f) There are some exemptions to the Act as a whole (both unconditional and conditional exemptions), to subjects' right of access to data and to the non-disclosure provisions.

(g) There are several offences under the Act.

(h) Organisations should institute procedures to ensure compliance with the Act.

(i) Computer software is covered by copyright legislation. A buyer of software is normally authorised to make only specified use of the software, which may be restricted to certain computers or to all computers on a certain site.

(j) Under the Computer Misuse Act 1990, unauthorised access to a computer system and the unauthorised modification of data are offences.

(k) A contract for the supply of a computer system should clearly specify what is to be supplied, and any liability of the supplier for consequential losses should the system not perform as it is meant to.

(l) The health and safety risks to employees from computer systems should be borne in mind.

Quick quiz

1 Give some examples of electronic equipment not covered by the Data Protection Act 1984

2 Are employees of a company which is a data user themselves data users?

3 What information is included in a data user's registration?

4 What rights do data subjects have?

5 State the data protection principles.

6 What unconditional exemptions to the Data Protection Act 1984 as a whole are available?

7 What offences are created by the Data Protection Act 1984?

8 What procedures should be established by an organisation to avoid breaches of copyright in software bought and used by it?

9 What are the three offences under the Computer Misuse Act 1990?

10 Give an example of consequential loss which may be suffered by a user of a computer system which does not perform as it should do.

Solutions to exercises

1 (a) Personal data: an expression of opinion about a living individual.
   (b) Not personal data: about a company.
   (c) Not personal data: an expression of intention.

2 He might be pursued for a debt he does not owe.

He might be falsely recorded as having previously defaulted on debts, and therefore be unable to obtain credit.

He might be falsely recorded as having been convicted of a crime, and therefore be unable to get a job.

3 (a) Principle (5), because the data is not kept up to date.

   (b) Principle (3), because the disclosure may be nothing to do with the data user's registered purposes.

4 Yes: the data was disclosed through the managing director's recklessness, because there is always a risk that someone will come into a company's public reception area.

  BPP Publishing

5   Copying onto disks which employees then take home.

6   Files could be filled up, and processing slowed down, by the addition of, for example, fictitious customers to the sales ledger (even if they all had nil account balances so that no monetary amounts were affected).

BPP Publishing

BPP Publishing

BPP Publishing

BPP Publishing

REVIEW FORM

Name:

College:

We would be grateful to receive any comments you may have on this book. You may like to use the headings below as guidelines. Tear out this page and send it to our Freepost address:
BPP Publishing Ltd, FREEPOST, London W12 8BR

Topic coverage

Objectives, exercises, chapter roundups and quizzes

Student-friendliness

Errors (please specify and give a page number)

Other

BPP Publishing